FORD INLINE SIX

HOW TO REBUILD & MODIFY

Matt Cox and Barton Maurer

S-A DESIGN

CarTech®

CarTech®

CarTech®, Inc.
6118 Main Street
North Branch, MN 55056
Phone: 651-277-1200 or 800-551-4754
Fax: 651-277-1203
www.cartechbooks.com

Edit by Wes Eisenschenk
Layout by Monica Seiberlich

ISBN 978-1-61325-517-9
Item No. SA472

Library of Congress Cataloging-in-Publication Data

Written, edited, and designed in the U.S.A.
Printed in China
10 9 8 7 6 5 4 3

DISTRIBUTION BY:

Europe
PGUK
63 Hatton Garden
London EC1N 8LE, England
Phone: 020 7061 1980 • Fax: 020 7242 3725
www.pguk.co.uk

Australia
Renniks Publications Ltd.
3/37-39 Green Street
Banksmeadow, NSW 2109, Australia
Phone: 2 9695 7055 • Fax: 2 9695 7355
www.renniks.com

Canada
Login Canada
300 Saulteaux Crescent
Winnipeg, MB, R3J 3T2 Canada
Phone: 800 665 1148 • Fax: 800 665 0103
www.lb.ca

CONTENTS

Introduction 4
About the Authors 4

Chapter 1: History and Planning 5
Engine Variants 5
Expectations 8

Chapter 2: Engine Removal 12
Safety 12
Vacuum Lines and Fittings 14
Steel Lines 14
Electrical Connections 15
Coolant Hoses 15
Engine Removal 16

Chapter 3: Disassembly 18
Organization 18
Preparation for Disassembly and Inspection 19
External Parts Removal (Left Side of Engine) 23
External Parts Removal (Right Side of Engine) 26
External Parts Removal (Front of Engine) 29
Cylinder Head Removal 32
Harmonic Balancer, Oil Pan, and Front Cover Removal 36
Piston, Rod, and Crankshaft Removal 40
Head Disassembly 47

Chapter 4: Machine Work 50
Clean and Inspect Block 51
Clean and Inspect Crankshaft 53
Clean and Inspect Connecting Rods 54
Clean and Inspect Cylinder Head 54
Machining 55
Crankshaft Machining 56
Balancing the Engine 60
Camshaft Bearings and Core Plugs 63
Cylinder Head Machining and Assembly 65

Chapter 5: Assembly 73
Engine Stand 74
Short-Block 74
Crankshaft Installation 75
Piston and Connecting Rod Installation 78
Front Cover Installation 85
Oil Pump and Oil Pan Installation 86
Front Engine Accessory Installation 87
Left Side of Engine Installation 88
Cylinder Head and External Parts 92
Cylinder Head Placement 92
Pushrod Installation 94
Valve Cover Installation 95
Exhaust Manifold Installation 96
Distributor Installation 98
Prepare to Reinstall Engine 101

Chapter 6: Reinstallation and Break-In 102
Engine Installation 102
Fuel Line and Carburetor Installation 105
Coolant Hose Installation 106
Exhaust System 108
Filling the Cooling System 108
Engine and Transmission Oil 109
Electrical 110
Engine Starting 111
Break-In Procedure 112

Chapter 7: Performance Upgrades 114
Air Intake 118
Carburetor/Fuel Injection 119
Carburetor Upgrades 122
Fuel Injection 124
Distributor 124
Exhaust and Header 128
Performance Single- and Dual-Exhaust Options 133
Camshaft and Valvetrain 133
Staged Performance Upgrades 136

Chapter 8: Performance Modifications to Original Parts 141
Cylinder Block 141
Cylinder Head 144
Carburetor Swaps and Adapters 147
Cylinder Head Porting 149
Valves and Combustion Chamber 153
Valvetrain 154
Get out There and Drive! 160

INTRODUCTION

Most people who rebuild an inline 6-cylinder engine do it for one of just a handful of reasons. The first reason is to keep the car original. This can be from a sense of obligation to the car. The person who is restoring the car may feel like the car deserves to remain in the configuration in which it was originally built. On the other hand, it may be a financial decision. If the original engine is rebuilt, a lot of other upgrades are not necessary, as opposed to if a V-8 was transplanted. Owners who rebuild an inline 6-cylinder engine typically want a fun car that they can enjoy driving whenever they want, maybe even every day (weather permitting).

Another reason (and let's be honest here) is that most owners of classic cars want to stand out in a crowd. In the car-show world of expensive, ultra-high-horsepower V-8 engines, almost nothing stands out more than an inline 6-cylinder engine! This is true whether it is in a Mustang or Falcon, or under the hood at an all-Ford show. Owners who put their 6-cylinder cars in shows will confirm that when they are in a row of beautifully restored or highly modified V-8 cars, there are always spectators who see the inline six and comment, "Oh look, a little six!" This is usually followed by a story about the person's brother, cousin, aunt, or best friend in high school who had a car with an inline six. They are great conversation starters.

The last common reason to rebuild the six is because it is a challenge. Many owners have owned multiple cars in their lifetimes, and most of them were V-8s. V-8s, obviously, are more popular. There comes a time for some builders, though, when they just want a new challenge to build something they have never built before.

Whether it is to be different or to take on a new challenge, if they keep their performance expectations reasonable, they will not be disappointed. In stock form, the inline six is a sturdy, solid engine that should give years of faithful service. With some typical hot rod upgrades, it can provide performance equivalent to a small-block V-8 and be different at the same time!

So, whatever your reason is for rebuilding your inline 6-cylinder, settle in, read this book, and plan to build an engine that will meet your needs and allow you to stand out when you pop the hood.

ABOUT THE AUTHORS

Matt Cox

Matt Cox has been an avid Ford 6-cylinder fan since he got his first car in 1979. It was, of course, a 6-cylinder 1966 Mustang. While working as a technician, Matt finished his college degree in management from Park University and went on to get a Master of Business Administration degree from Kansas University. With degrees in hand, Matt went to work for one of the Big Three in Detroit, where he works to this day.

Longtime fans of the Ford small six probably remember a company called Classic Inlines that was run by Mike Winterboer. When Mike passed away unexpectedly, the products that he had developed seemed to be at risk of vanishing forever. After much agonizing, Matt decided to step up and buy the remaining inventory from a friend of Mike's with the intention of starting a business patterned after Classic Inlines. That business stumbled along until Matt was able to reintroduce the aluminum cylinder head that Mike had commissioned. Now, Vintage Inlines is a going concern dedicated to keeping interest in these engines alive.

Matt considers it an honor to write this book and share what he has learned from all of the knowledgeable 6-cylinder owners that he has met through the years.

Bart Maurer

You could say that Barton Maurer was born into the automotive field. It all started when Bart's grandfather, a Seabee during World War II, opened a full-service garage on the eastside of Detroit on his return home after serving his county. When he was old enough, Bart's father went to work with his dad. About 20 years later came Bart's turn to go to work with his dad and grandfather. Too young to really do any work, his job was mainly to be spoiled by his grandparents and bug his dad. In the late 1970s, the business was sold, and Bart's grandparents retired.

Bart's father purchased an auto parts store. This is where Bart really started working—coming there after school to sweep, clean, and stock the shelves. Bart's dad taught him how to turn brake drums, rotors, and flywheels and to press bearings and U-joints and perform other services. He also taught Bart how to fix the business's delivery vehicles; he wasn't even old enough to drive yet!

After Bart graduated from high school, he and his father opened an automotive machine shop. The first employee, an older machinist named Al, took Bart under his wing and taught him the ins and outs of cylinder head and block machining. Everything that Bart has learned has been on the job through trial and error. Bart has a natural knack for the business; you could say that he took to engine machining, general machining, and engine performance like a duck to water. If you ask Bart, the keys to success are learning from your mistakes, thinking with an open mind (sometimes out of the box), and listening to others because you never know what you will learn.

CHAPTER 1

History and Planning

The version of the Ford inline 6-cylinder engine that we are rebuilding for this book is considered the third generation. The first generation was a series of flatheads that included the 226- and 254-ci engines in production from 1941–1953. The second generation was a series of engines built between 1952 and 1964 and included 215-, 223-, and 262-ci versions. Both the first and second generations found use in passenger cars and pickup trucks, as did the fourth generation. The fourth generation started with the 240 in cars and trucks, and then only the very popular 300 was used in trucks.

None of these engines should be confused with third-generation engines that were nicknamed the *Thriftpower Six*, the *Special Six*, and sometimes the *Falcon Six* (depending on the year). The third generation is also called the *small six* by many enthusiasts. The small six was used in small- to medium-size passenger cars of the 1960s and 1970s and saw service in the E-Series vans of the mid-1960s and the early Broncos.

After a shortage of Cologne V-6s in the late 1970s, which had been chosen as the base engine for the new Fox-Body Mustang, the small six was brought back and produced in a slightly different version, known to enthusiasts as the *low-mount starter* version. There were no performance improvements to this last version of the engine.

Engine Variants

Since this is a rebuild book and not a history book, the amount of detail is just enough to inform you. More details are available from various online and print resources for the avid enthusiast.

This history is intended to give the builder a general idea of how the passenger-car Ford inline 6-cylinder engine of the 1960s and 1970s came about and how it evolved over the years. It is not intended to be an exhaustive account with every specification change over the years. To that end, here are some of the highlights of the evolution of an engine that many people have come to love over the years.

Early versions of the third-generation Ford inline six (1960–1964) can be quickly identified by the three core plugs on the passenger's side of the block. These engines have the less desirable four main bearings supporting the crankshaft. The fact that the earliest 200-ci engines had four main bearings is sometimes overlooked.

144 Cubic Inch

Ford introduced the 144-ci inline 6-cylinder engine in September 1959 as the base engine in the new-for-1960 Falcon compact car. Under the financial management of Robert McNamara, Ford engineers designed what is considered Ford's third-generation inline 6-cylinder engine. The engine was economical to build and had an appropriate amount of power for the time and reasonable fuel economy.

Originally known as the Thriftpower Six, the engine was built at Ford's Lima, Ohio, engine assembly plant. Production for all US variants remained at Lima through the end of production in 1984.

The engine received its 144 ci from a 3.5-inch bore and a 2.5-inch stroke. Along with an 8.7:1 compression ratio, it yielded 84 hp measured at the crankshaft. Originally designed with just four main bearings, the 144 and its successor (the 170-ci version) were not considered robust. The four main bearings simply did not provide enough support, so vibrations and premature wear were more prevalent than they were in later versions of the engine.

170 Cubic Inch

By 1961, Ford started building a 170-ci version of the engine. The extra cubic inches were courtesy of increasing the stroke to 2.94 inches. This size increase resulted in a power gain of more than 20 hp and brought the advertised rating to 105. Both the 144 and the 170 versions, along with the earliest 200-ci engines, can be distinguished from later engines by the three (versus five) core plugs on the right side of the engine block.

200 Cubic Inch

In 1965, Ford addressed the vibration and durability issues by upgrading the block to have seven main bearings. This improvement is what earned the engine a reputation for durability. The bore and stroke were increased to 3.685 and 3.126 inches, respectively, and brought the engine to 200 ci and 120 hp. Another major improvement was the introduction of hydraulic lifters. This upgrade required the addition of oil passages to the lifter bores to facilitate the hydraulic lifters. Improvements were noticed in quieter operation and how the need for routine valve adjustments was eliminated.

This engine was the base engine for the Mustang from September 1965 through the 1970 model year. Beginning with the first seven-main-bearing engines, the number of core plugs visible on the right side of the engine increased to five. This is the easiest visible indication that an engine has the desirable seven main bearings.

250 Cubic Inch

The next improvements to the base engine did not come until the 1969 model year, when the size was increased to a whopping 250 ci. The old adage, "There's no substitute for cubic inches," certainly applies to this upgrade. Unlike previous engineering changes, this resulted in an obviously larger block to accommodate the increased stroke. The deck height

Starting with the 200-ci engines in 1965, the blocks were cast with seven main bearings. This improvement corrected some vibration and durability issues experienced on the earlier 144 and 170 engines. It was also the beginning of a very good reputation for durability.

From the outside of the engine, it is easy to identify the seven-main-bearing engines. Rather than three core plugs like the early engines, seven-main-bearing engines have five core plugs. Even when the engine is in the car and the exhaust manifold is attached, the core plugs will be visible.

(the distance from the crank centerline to the top of the block) increased by almost 2 inches. The block is also slightly wider to make room for the larger counterweights needed to increase the stroke to 3.910 inches.

Other changes were made as well, including changing the bellhousing bolt pattern to that of the small-block V-8, which is one that is popular with builders today. While most likely a financial decision at the time, it allows builders to use any V-8 transmission, including the popular T-5 manual 5-speed, which was made popular in the 1980s in 5.0-liter Mustangs and other performance vehicles. Unfortunately, this is not true for the previous engines, which needed an adapter (if the T-5 can be used at all).

The bottom end of a seven-main-bearing engine has received high praise for strength and durability. The same cannot be said for the cylinder head. Known as an integral intake manifold, the intake is cast as part of the head. The length of the runners and the numerous 90-degree angles result in uneven fuel flow, which leads to rough idle and uneven cylinder wear.

Integral Intake Manifold

The elephant in the room that has not yet been addressed is the cylinder head. The year 1969 was also the year that the first significant improvements were made to the cylinder head in the US. Almost anyone who has tried to upgrade the performance of any of these US small-six engines has come up against the brick wall known as the integral intake manifold, which is often referred to as the *intake log*. In this instance, integral refers to the fact the intake manifold was cast as part of the cast-iron head, thus the term *integral*.

The 1963 Falcon of Kelly and Will McLearran is capable of quarter-mile times in the mid-10-second range. A 250-ci engine with an aluminum cylinder head and a large turbocharger send the power through an automatic transmission to the Ford 9-inch rear end. Will is the mechanic, and Kelly is the driver.

It is generally acknowledged that the integral intake was designed as a money-saving feature as a concession to McNamara. It certainly did nothing to help performance due to the numerous 90-degree angles that the air/fuel mixture had to deal with on its way to the combustion chamber.

The 1969 design, while maintaining the integral intake, did offer improvements in the log volume and larger intake valves. It was also designed to use a larger 1V carburetor. Even with these changes, and the fact that the 250 block was larger, the new head was still basically a bolt-on upgrade for the earlier engines. The main exception to the bolt-on nature of the upgrade was the combustion chamber size. For earlier engines, the head needed to be milled to decrease the combustion chamber size to maintain the static compression ratio.

While the increase to 250 ci certainly improved the performance (horsepower increased to 155), fuel economy suffered quite a bit. For today's builders who are not concerned with fuel economy, a turbocharged 250-ci engine in an appropriately-built race car can reward the driver with quarter-mile times in the mid-10-second range!

Last Variant Upgrades

Other than some minor changes through the 1970s, the last significant change to the engine came in 1980 when the 200 was given a new (but short) lease on life. Due to a shortage of V-6 engines planned for the new Fox Mustang, the 200 block was once again changed to what is now known as the *low-mount starter* version. It's called this because due to another change to the bellhousing bolt pattern, the starter position was moved below the oil pan gasket surface at the bottom of the block. This new pattern, unlike the 250-ci pattern, did not allow other transmissions to be used without an adapter.

While the last cylinder head is considered by builders today to be one of the most desirable of the large log versions, it did have an exhaust gas recirculation (EGR) valve port cast below the carburetor mounting. For classic cars and any vehicle where emissions laws do not apply, this port can be filled or blocked off with a homemade plate (as is more frequently done).

Australia and Argentina Versions

Not mentioned in this history of US inline sixes are the engines designed and built by Ford in Australia and Argentina. In these countries, the integral intake manifold was addressed head on (pun intended) by designing cylinder heads that used separate intake manifolds. While both head designs were based on the original US design and even used some of the original parts, each country took a different approach.

Australia

Australia produced a larger volume of heads than Argentina over the few years of production, and they were more familiar to US builders. Known as the 250-2V, the cast-iron head featured improved intake and exhaust ports along with the aforementioned separate intake manifold. The manifold mounted a 2V carburetor on the 250-ci engine and inspired the name.

Many parts, including the valve cover and exhaust manifold, are interchangeable between the US and Australian cylinder heads.

Argentina

While the Australian heads are much more well-known and are currently available in the US (albeit in very small numbers), the Argentina-produced heads do not enjoy the same following in the US.

Ford engineers in Argentina took a different approach when they introduced their version of the improved cylinder head in 1966. More like the US version than the Australian head that came later, the Argentinian-produced heads are reminiscent of early hot rodder efforts at literally cutting off the log with a band saw so that a separate intake and a new-style exhaust manifold could be bolted in place.

The increased flow on both the intake and exhaust sides along with slightly higher compression gave the Argentina engine 132 hp in 1966. These heads are very rarely found in the US today.

Expectations

There are a few reasons to build a 6-cylinder engine. There are also a few reasons to not build a 6-cylinder engine.

If your dream is to leave twin 50-foot-long burnout marks on your favorite cruising boulevard, you are probably reading the wrong book. If you want to race your obnoxious friend in his new Mustang GT (and win), you might be reading the wrong book.

If you want to have respectable, reliable power from an engine that other people overlook, you are definitely reading the right book. That sentiment also applies if you want to put in some extra effort so that you can surprise more than a few people from a stoplight.

While it is possible to build an engine, put it in a well-built car, and run in the 10s at the drag strip with an inline 6-cylinder, that is not everyone's cup of tea, and frankly, it is much easier to do with a V-8. If, on the other hand, you want an affordable classic that gets attention at shows and keeps your honor intact on the street, you can do that with a solid rebuild and some standard bolt-on parts.

It seems like a lot of people forget that the principles are the same whether the engine is a V-8 or an inline six. The same modifications that improve performance on one will improve the performance on the other. Compression, fuel, spark, and exhaust can all be improved on a Ford inline six. Camshafts, pistons, distributors, and headers are all available. It is even possible to replace that much-maligned cast-iron, integral intake manifold/cylinder head with a new alloy piece based on the Australian 250-2V head. Modern fuel injection, designed as a bolt-on replacement for carburetors, can also increase power and improve starting and drivability to close to modern car levels, which is also important.

With the range of expectations, along with the different budget levels that people have, it is plain to see that the inline 6-cylinder engine can meet the expectations of all but the most demanding drivers. Truthfully, due to lower demand, 6-cylinder performance upgrade parts are typically more expensive than their V-8 counterparts. With that said, keeping the 6-cylinder and modifying it is still generally more economical than transplanting a V-8. Builders must keep in mind that for a successful transplant, other upgrades are generally required, such as fuel and cooling systems, and suspension and braking components. But to be fair, braking upgrades are normally a good idea on any rebuild, regardless of the engine size.

The decision facing many people is whether to keep the 6-cylinder or transplant a V-8. For a lot of new owners, this is the first question asked after buying an old Mustang, Falcon, Maverick, or any of the many other Fords that came with these engines. For owners who have had the cars for a while, it might be a debate of either wanting something new or breathing new life into an old friend. In either case, the decision will be made based on expectations and a budget.

When considering the expected performance level, remember that parts of the powertrain respond equally as well on a 6-cylinder as they do on a V-8. While the original rear axles on many 6-cylinder cars are small, weak, and have few gear ratios available in the aftermarket, V-8 axle assemblies are typically an easy bolt-in upgrade. Likewise, with adapters available for many applications, 5-speed manual transmissions can really wake up a 6-cylinder engine, whether it is stock or modified.

Cost	Low to No Improvement	Moderate Improvement	Substantial Improvement
Low (Less than $500)	Cosmetic maintenance upgrades (plugs, wires, convert to electronic ignition pickup)	–	–
Moderate (Up to $2,000)	–	Bolt-on performance improvements: carburetor, distributor, header, exhaust	–
Substantial ($4,000 to $6,000)	–	–	Full rebuild: pistons, camshaft, new head, head porting

This table shows a decision matrix with very generalized estimates for power and cost. The boxes describe possible combinations of cost and performance and what you might be able to do on a given budget.

Of course, with increased performance expectations, increased budgets are required. The good news is that most upgrades can be made in a stepped manner, building on each other until the ultimate expectations are achieved. To that end, it is important to plan upgrades in a logical, safe manner that will provide the desired performance within the established budget. It often makes sense to spread the upgrades over an extended amount of time for budget reasons. This also means that every year or two, you get to make exciting upgrades that will undoubtedly extend the love affair with your car.

The bottom line regarding expectations is that there are definite limitations to what a 6-cylinder can provide. Expect a reliable, durable engine with stock levels of performance, and you will never be disappointed. If you want noticeable increases in power and are willing to spend extra money and effort, you will likewise not be disappointed. If you want power to rival a mildly modified small-block V-8, be ready to do what it takes, and you still will not be disappointed. If you want more than that, you are on your own (but it can be done).

With this in mind, as you read the rest of this book, take note of the choices you have and begin to formulate your expectations. Then, like a lot of us, consult with your domestic financial manager (for me, my wife) and see if your expectations align with your budget.

While it is a stretch to say that the Ford small six has a rich racing history, it does have *a* racing history, especially in A Class Hydroplane racing in the early 1960s. The A Class included engines up to 150 ci, so the new Falcon Six, which was introduced in the fall of 1959, was immediately a popular choice due to its relatively light weight. Many racers switched to the new engine, and modifications began almost immediately. Ultimately, even companies such as Hilborn were manufacturing parts, but the real treasures are the homemade induction setups that these innovative racers created. Roller camshafts were used even though they weren't popular with the Big Three until the 1980s. High-compression pistons, performance distributors, and homemade headers found their way onto all of these racers.

In addition to the Hydroplane racing, the Falcon Six saw action in the Specials, which were sports cars of the early 1960s. These cars can be found in Group 4 races at vintage events across the country. The Specials were

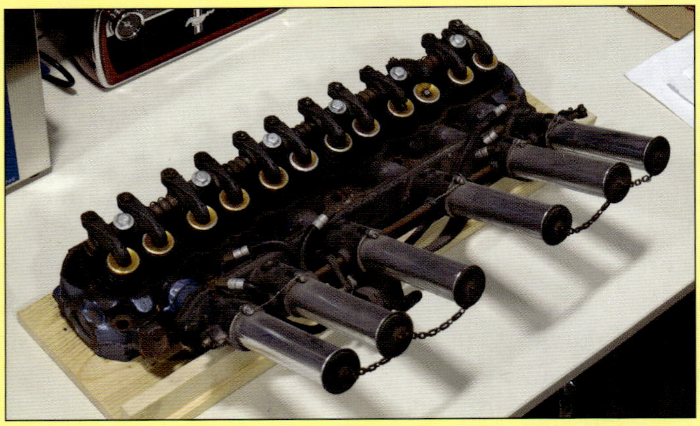

Early on, the small six found its way into various forms of racing vehicles. To alleviate some of the natural weakness of the integral intake manifold, companies like Hilborn produced parts like this mechanical fuel injection manifold. It was up to the builder to remove the stock intake and attach the fuel injection. For this reason, no two setups were ever exactly the same.

Some racers made homebuilt Specials. These cars had production-based running gear, including engines, transmissions, and rear axles. This car, known as the **Philson Falcon,** ***is one of the first such cars to use the new-for-1960 Ford inline 6-cylinder. Charles Bordin of Long Island owns the car today and competes in regional vintage racing events. (Photo courtesy AutoPhotos 2019, Ed Hyman)***

generally homebuilt vehicles from the chassis to the body that used a production suspension, drivetrain, and powerplant of the day. Some of them were successful, and all of them were innovative. Today, when we think of the hot rodders of days gone by, we admire the builders of these cars and others like them.

A type of induction known as slide-throttle fuel injection was used in some racing vehicles. Unlike most throttle bodies that use a round butterfly, the slide throttle had a plate that slid to the side to open multiple ports with one motion. Very small idle-bleed holes were drilled in the plate to allow the engine to idle. It is said that the system had three modes: off, 2,000-rpm idle, and full throttle! It's definitely for racing only.

The Offenhauser 3X1 intake adapter allowed builders to install three stock-style carburetors on the integral intake log. This vastly improved the fuel distribution concerns of the single, center-mounted carburetor. Plus, just look at it! This one belongs to Mark Weber.

The small six found favor early on with Hydroplane racers of the 1960s. Their lightweight and relatively good power made the 144-ci engines a natural for the 150-ci class. This example belongs to Mark Weber of Washington, Michigan.

CHAPTER 2

Engine Removal

If you do not already have a copy of the correct Ford shop manual for your car, get one. Not only will it help you with some of the tricky procedures, such as carburetor setting, it will also give you safety tips to do the job with a minimum of risk.

Safety

No car project is worth risking personal safety. There are several things to remember throughout the removal, disassembly, and rebuild processes. Regarding personal protective equipment, at a minimum, wear goggles when operating air tools or any time you are under the vehicle. If you have to grind any metal with a cutoff wheel, goggles are a must. Grinding of any kind, such as when porting a cylinder head, creates dust and very fine metallic particles. To prevent damage to your lungs, wear a mask. Masks are rated by the size of particles they filter. Get the best mask you can find to avoid long-term complications.

It is also advisable to have a fully charged fire extinguisher nearby. The risk of fire is highest when removing components of the fuel system because they may still contain fuel. When starting the car for the first time, the risk comes from fuel lines and components that may leak, especially when combined with a spark from an inadequate electrical connection.

Other safety risks include the potential for dropping heavy components that may have oil or engine coolant on them. Before lifting, make sure that you wipe off anything that will cause you to lose your grip. There is a possibility of slipping if spills are not properly addressed when they happen. The best defense is a good offense. Whenever possible, have appropriately sized catch containers and drip pans handy and use them. Spills happen, so have a bag of oil-dry nearby to stop the spill from spreading.

When removing the engine from the car, keep these things in mind:

1 Fuel and sparks don't mix. Always start by disconnecting the battery and removing it from the car. Be careful when removing the

The first step in removing the engine is to take out the battery. Disconnect the cables at the battery end, remove the battery hold-down, and carefully lift the battery from the car. Store the battery in a safe place until you are ready to reinstall it unless you plan to replace it. Do not store the battery in an enclosed area because the gases that come off the battery are dangerous.

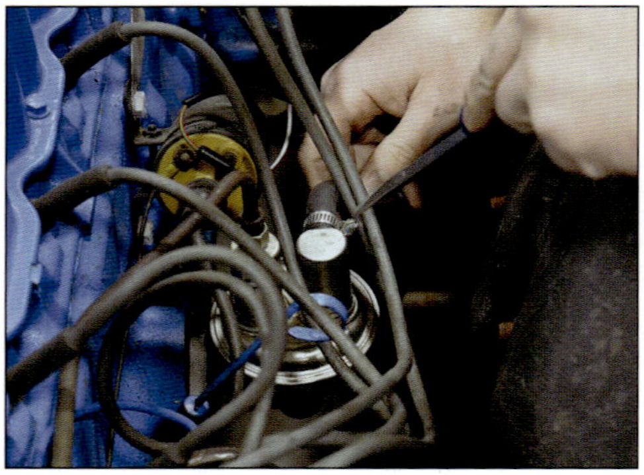

Disconnect the fuel line from the fuel tank at the fuel pump on the engine. If the fuel line has a threaded fitting at the fuel pump, use a line wrench to remove the line and avoid damaging the fuel line fitting. Be prepared to catch the fuel that will come out of the open line. Immediately remove the fuel from the work area to avoid spills or accidental ignition.

fuel lines, fuel pump, and carburetor. Take special care to minimize fuel spillage.

2 Protect your car. While it's not officially a safety issue, be careful to not damage the engine compartment and body panels of your car when removing the engine. Take your time and plan ahead.

3 Because of the weight of the engine, the hoist, chains, straps, and bolts used to remove them are under tremendous stress. Carefully follow the hoist manufacturer's instructions and do not exceed the capability of the equipment you are using.

Take every precaution to prevent damage to the car's fenders and inner fenders. An inexpensive fender cover will not protect the sheet metal from damage by the engine during removal, but it will prevent annoying scratches and marks from belt buckles, tools, and engine hardware.

On the small six, it is tempting to attach the chain to the rear exhaust manifold bolt hole. Do not do this! The most common damage to a stock manifold (and worse, the cylinder head) is the rear ear broken off. Besides the obvious expense of having to repair the head, the cost of the engine being dropped can be measured in emergency room bills. The safest place to attach the chains for the hoist are the left front and right rear cylinder-head bolt locations. You will need longer bolts that allow you to attach the chains.

Attach the lifting chain to the engine and make sure to consider the strength of the component to which you attach the chain. Resist the temptation to use the outer bolt holes for the exhaust manifold in the cylinder head. The ears on the cylinder head are barely strong enough to handle the weight of the engine, especially if the transmission is still attached. If the attaching points fail while supporting the engine, damage to the engine is likely and personal injury to you or a helper is a real possibility.

Remember that the engine (or engine/transmission combination) is very heavy. Before you begin to remove the engine, clear the area around the hoist to prevent trips or falls as you back the hoist away from the car.

4 Engines are still heavy! Due to the weight of the engine, even a slight movement when it is unbolted in the engine compartment or hanging from the hoist that pinches a body part against the car body or any immoveable object can cause very serious injury. Never put your hand or any body part in areas that do not have adequate clearance in case of sudden, unexpected movement.

5 The danger hasn't passed when the engine is bolted to the stand. Always use proper fasteners when attaching the mounting brackets to the engine. Cheap bolts have been known to break, so spend the extra $2 and get good bolts.

Most of these cars weigh 3,000 pounds or more. The engines weigh in the neighborhood of 400 pounds. When you pinch a hand between a 400-pound engine and a 3,000-pound car, serious injury will likely occur. Always be careful if you have to reach into a tight area, and do not do so while the engine is being lifted. Also, remember that if the engine is in a bind, it can jerk violently when it breaks free.

In all seriousness, because of the weight of the engine and the potential for sudden movement, you must always plan ahead, use good equipment, pay attention, and not rush.

While this book is not intended to be an engine removal tutorial, these are the basics. Engine removal only requires you to remove every hose, wire, and tube attached to the engine, then remove each fastener that secures the engine to the car. Simple, right? It really is, but like everything else, it requires you to be methodical. Cars built in the 1960s will be easier than cars built in the 1970s, which will likewise be easier than the vacuum-line nightmares of the 1980s.

Vacuum Lines and Fittings

Vacuum lines and fittings may be brittle, so use care when removing them. You do not want to reuse brittle fittings, but keeping them intact during removal will make replacement easier. Most fittings can be sourced at local auto parts stores, although they may not be an exact match as far as appearance goes. You need to take a lot of pictures when removing vacuum lines for the purpose of rerouting at assembly.

Steel Lines

Steel lines typically attach to the engine with brass fittings. Steel lines are used for fuel, automatic transmission fluid, and vacuum lines on older vehicles. Use a pan to collect any fluids that leak when the fittings are removed, and dispose of the fluids according to local laws.

The good news for owners of older cars is that many lines are reproduced now, so it is very easy to replace rusted, damaged or pinched lines. If the fitting is not already rounded off from a previous repair with incorrect tools, use a line wrench to prevent further damage and get the best grip on the fitting. After years of being attached, brass fittings can corrode and be very difficult to remove.

They are also known to corrode to the steel line. When this happens, the

Take extra care when removing fittings on steel lines. Fittings can seize over time and can round off and cause extra effort to remove without the proper line wrench. This condition usually leads to replacement of a line you may have been able to reuse. Brass fittings are soft, round, and much easier to damage than steel fittings.

most likely result is twisting the tube, and that usually means that it needs to be replaced. Be prepared for this outcome, and buy new lines ahead of time if your budget allows it.

Electrical Connections

Verify that the battery has been disconnected before disconnecting electrical wires and cables. Electrical connections are made in several different ways. The most common connection is through a spade terminal inside a plastic shell. These sometimes have a locking feature on newer vehicles. The locking tabs are easy to break on vehicles this old and may not retain well without the tabs. If you break them, replace them to avoid potential electrical gremlins later. There are some resources online that can help. As is the case with steel lines, reproduction engine harnesses are available for the older models. If your wiring has obvious damage from age or previous repairs, consider replacing the harnesses.

Battery cables generally attach with clamps or bolts at the battery and an eyelet and bolt at the engine block for the ground cable. The positive cable usually attaches via a nut to a stud on the starter relay or solenoid.

After the battery is disconnected, disconnect the cables and wiring at the alternator. These wires become brittle over time, and it is easy to twist the terminal off the wire if the terminal is stuck to the fastening nut. Take a picture to make engine reinstallation easier.

Another danger when removing steel lines is that the fitting can corrode and fuse to the steel line. If this happens and you are not careful, the line can twist as you turn the fitting, which can cause damage that leads to part replacement.

After the battery is disconnected, it is safe to remove the starter. Start by removing the cable-attaching nut. The starter is bolted to the transmission bellhousing. The top bolt is easiest to reach with an extra-long extension on a ratchet. As a general rule, manual-transmission cars have a two-bolt starter, and automatics have three bolts. The starter should stay in place after the bolts are removed, but carefully support it until you are ready to remove it because it is heavy.

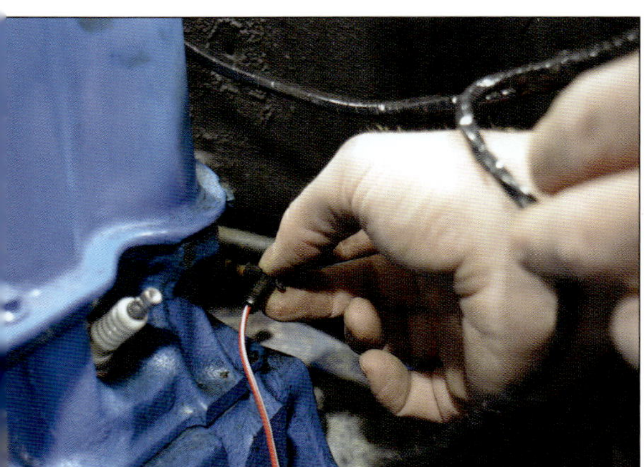

On cars from the 1960s, there are very few connectors on the engine. The connectors are typically eyelets attached with nuts to a stud or press-on connectors that use a friction fit to a stud on a sensor. For the eyelets, take care when removing the attaching nut to avoid damaging the component or the wire. The press-on connectors usually come off easily if they are not severely corroded. Give them a gentle twist before removing.

Coolant Hoses

A variety of hoses, usually for coolant, will need to be removed. Most hoses will be in bad shape and need to be replaced. The easiest and most effective method for removing hoses that are stuck in place is to remove the clamp and slice the hose on the fitting. With a simple twist, the hose should come off easily. Tools are available for this specific purpose, but obviously a sharp blade will do the job. Be careful when doing this because the hoses can often be in awkward locations and the blade may slip. The tools designed for this are safer than a pocket-knife blade because they have a rounded shape to the blade.

Since hoses require a lot of maintenance and are prone to failure, chances are good that yours have been replaced many times over the life of the vehicle. Because of this, chances are just as good that not a single clamp on your engine is original.

This should not be a problem because replacement clamps are readily available. For appearance and function, make sure to get the right-size fitting for the hose. This will ensure the best clamping force and that you will not have extra band sticking up everywhere. Radiator and coolant hoses can be lubricated on the inside with coolant before installing to aid in proper placement.

If an original look is desired or you are doing a restoration, some original-style clamps are available and can be purchased online.

Coolant hoses do not withstand the rigors of containing 200-degree coolant at 14 psi forever. Do not consider reusing hoses unless they were recently replaced expensive reproductions. For daily drivers, quality hoses are more important than originality.

Since you will probably be replacing the hoses, do not hesitate to use a hose splitter to make removal easier. If you do, use a tool specifically designed for the purpose to minimize the risk of injury. You might be tempted to use a pocket knife, but you should not. The risk of slipping and hurting yourself or damaging the car is too high.

Engine Removal

1 *After all hoses, lines, and wiring are removed and the engine is supported by the hoist, disconnect the motor mounts from the frame. It is usually easier to unbolt the mount from the frame in the car and remove it from the engine after it is out of the car.*

2 *If the automatic transmission will remain in the car, you will need to remove the torque converter inspection cover first to gain access to the nuts that retain the torque converter to the flexplate. The inspection plate may be missing if the car has had previous engine or transmission work. It could also be damaged from mishandling or road damage. Reproduction C4 transmission inspection covers are available.*

Engine Removal *continued*

3 ***When the inspection cover has been removed, turn the crankshaft until one of the torque-converter-attaching nuts is showing. Use a breaker bar with the appropriate socket on the damper bolt to turn the crankshaft. Remove the torque converter nut and store it. Turn the crankshaft again until the next nut is visible. Repeat the process with the remaining two nuts.***

4 ***Only bolt the engine to a stand that is rated for the weight of the engine. For these Ford small-six engines, a 1,000-pound engine stand is more than sufficient. Make sure to select the proper size and grade bolts to bolt the engine to the stand. This engine uses 3/8 x 16 bolts and should be at least a Grade-5. Carefully choose the length based on your particular stand and do not use bolts that are too long and require multiple washers for spacers.***

When you are certain that everything has been disconnected from the engine and transmission, it is time to attach the engine hoist and remove the engine mounts. The most secure place to attach the chains is at the left front and right rear cylinder-head bolt holes with extra-long bolts. The engine mounts are typically designed so you can leave them attached to the engine or transmission and unbolt them from a bracket that is attached to the vehicle without the engine falling. For the transmission, when the bolts are removed and the transmission is supported by a jack, you can remove the transmission crossmember so that the assembly can be removed.

If you are just removing the engine and not the transmission, it is important to secure the engine to the engine hoist before it's separated from the transmission. There will be no support at the back of the engine once the transmission is detached, and you must separate the transmission with it in place.

With an automatic transmission, unbolt the inspection plate so that you can access the torque converter attaching nuts. Rotate the engine at the crankshaft until the first nut is accessible. There are four nuts, so after the first one is removed, it is necessary to rotate the crankshaft one quarter turn to get to the next nut. Repeat this for the remaining two nuts.

Support the transmission with a jack and a stand. Remove the six bolts that attach the transmission to the engine. The transmission and torque converter will stay in the vehicle. The flexplate will be removed with the engine and detached later.

If you have a manual transmission, the process is slightly different. After the shifter and linkage are removed, unbolt the transmission from the bellhousing. The bellhousing, clutch, pressure plate, and flywheel will stay on the engine during engine removal and will be detached when the engine is out of the vehicle.

While it may not seem like it, it is sometimes easier to remove the engine and transmission as an assembly. This may be the case if you need to remove the transmission for service. This is especially true if you are not able to raise the vehicle enough to remove the detached transmission from the side of the vehicle. If you elect to remove the engine and transmission as an assembly, take extra care to ensure the engine hoist chain is balanced so that the assembly can be maneuvered while it is lifted out of the engine bay and returned to a horizontal position once it has cleared of the vehicle.

The last step to remove the engine is to put it on the stand. If there is still oil in the engine, it will leak out when the flexplate/flywheel bolts are removed. It is best to drain the oil and as much coolant as possible before the engine is removed. After the flexplate or flywheel is removed, bolt the bracket for the stand to the back of the engine while it is still attached to the hoist. Position the hoist at the right height and slide the stand into place with the bracket going into the tube of the stand. Put the locking pin for the stand in place and remove the hoist chain from the engine.

DISASSEMBLY

As the name implies, the goal of disassembly is to separate the engine into its individual pieces. This sounds easy enough, and in fact is a straightforward process. While there may be builders who insist on disassembling an engine in a specific order, the only real, common-sense rule is that you must remove things in the order you come to them. In other words, you cannot remove the valve cover while there are still vacuum and fuel lines over the top of it.

In some cases, it helps to leave a part in place to aid disassembly of another part. An example of this on the Ford small six is the timing chain. If you leave the gears and chain in place while you remove the connecting rods, it will prevent the rods from contacting the camshaft lobes as the crankshaft is rotated. If the chain is removed, it will be necessary to rotate the camshaft separately as you move from one connecting rod to the next.

We will offer as many tips as possible, so before you begin, take the time to read the entire chapter. Then, follow the step-by-step process to perform the actual work.

Organization

An assortment of containers, bags, buckets, and placeholders will come in handy to keep things organized. Shelving for your engine's components isn't required but aids in keeping the materials consolidated.

Before you start, make sure that you have the tools you will need for

Before a single part is unbolted, get out your phone and start taking pictures. They are easy to take, and you can never have enough. Photos not only document this major step in car ownership but they also provide valuable reference material when you reassemble the engine. The longer that it takes to finish the project, the more valuable the pictures are.

Commercially available racks are designed to make it easy to keep lifters, pushrods, and springs organized in case you plan to reuse them. If camshaft replacement is necessary or desired, replace the camshaft and lifters together because you should not mix used parts with new due to unique wear characteristics on the used parts. It is acceptable to reuse the original parts together as long as you keep them matched.

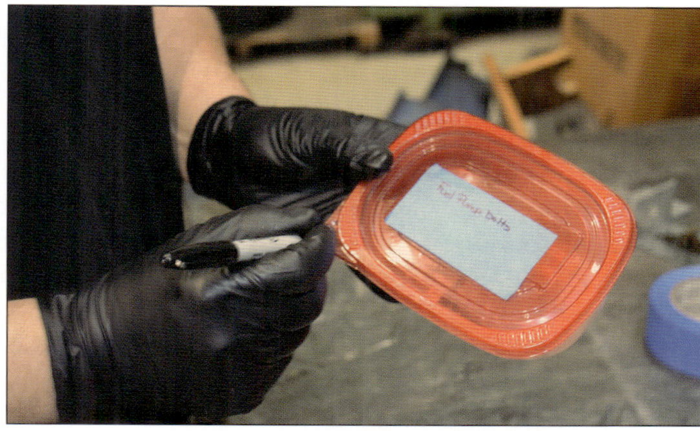

Other than the racks for valvetrain components, the supplies needed for organization can probably be found around the house. An assortment of plastic containers is a good starting point, but don't get the nice ones from the kitchen cabinet! Resealable plastic bags are also convenient for storing hardware that is not too heavy. Label the bags using a wide-tipped permanent marker before you add the parts for easy identification. You can also use tape on some components to label parts and make notes, but remember that tape does not stick to grease.

disassembly. Most of the tools necessary are typical hand tools. Cordless nut drivers and impact wrenches are very popular, and as long as they are used cautiously, they will help to save time during disassembly. The tools that you don't have can be rented from larger auto parts stores—sometimes for free.

If you are disassembling the cylinder head, a valve spring compressor (rental) will also be needed.

For engine reassembly, you will need a piston ring compressor (rental) and 3/8- and 1/2-inch-drive torque wrenches in addition to all of the tools above.

Preparation for Disassembly and Inspection

When the engine is safely on a stand, the inspection and disassembly can begin. With that said, there is some preparation that must happen before the parts start to come off.

The key to a successful reassembly of the engine is a successful disassembly. A successful disassembly happens when everything comes off and is properly documented for reinstallation. Take a lot of photos; your cell phone camera is a cheap and easy way to document the process. Take pictures of the orientation of the parts and any details, such as different-size bolts holding one part

Necessary Tools

Here's a list of tools you will need at a minimum:

- 1/4-inch ratchet and socket set (deep) and extensions
- 3/8-inch ratchet and socket set (deep) and extensions
- Spark plug socket
- 1/2-inch ratchet/breaker bar (crank damper bolt: 13/16 inch; head bolts: 11/16 inch)
- Assorted screwdrivers (Phillips and slotted as needed)
- Pliers
- Combination wrench set (5/16–5/8 inch)
- Line wrench set (for steel line fittings)
- 1/2-inch distributor wrench (may save you some grief)
- Pry bars
- Gasket scrapers and razor blades
- Magnetic pickup tool
- Crankshaft damper remover/installer (rental)

on. Examples of this are the front cover and the oil pan.

Once the parts are removed, put the bolts in a container or baggie and write the name of the part on the bag before moving to the next part. This is a minimum requirement. You may have friends who will try to shame you for being overly organized, but if the project takes longer than about a week, your power of memorization may fail. Something that seemed obvious during disassembly may become a huge frustration during reassembly.

There are commercially available organization tools that make this easier, especially in the area of cylinder-head components, but they are not required and can be made with a little ingenuity. Like most tools, the decision to buy or improvise comes down to the frequency that you intend to need it and your budget.

Most of the disassembly can be done with quality hand tools. In some cases, pneumatic (air) tools, including impact wrenches, can certainly make the job easier but

TECH TIP

Prepare for Fastener Issues

It is a good idea to look at all the visible fasteners before you begin disassembly. Have a can of rust-penetrating spray nearby and use it liberally. Let the spray sit for a few minutes and try to remove the fastener. It may be necessary to tap on the bolt/nut and use a wrench to try to turn it back and forth. Repeated application may be necessary.

Areas like the exhaust manifold and thermostat housing bolts will often be the most challenging due to the harsh conditions they endure. Applying heat from a torch will often help with the exhaust bolts. Then, apply torque in both directions until you feel movement in the bolt.

Thermostat housing bolts and any other bolts related to the cooling system face a different problem. The corrosive environment caused by a lack of cooling system maintenance weakens the bolts to the point that they can be nearly impossible to remove without breaking. Be prepared for this and do not let it discourage you. Know that it is possible and consider that you will need extra time for repairs. If you are taking the engine to a machine shop, it will be well equipped to make those repairs. ■

No matter how careful you are, it is very likely that you will encounter at least one broken bolt. Some broken bolts are easy. If just the head breaks off, you may just be able to grab it with locking pliers and work it out when the component is removed.

Some bolts require a judicious application of heat from a torch, jokingly known as a hot wrench. *If the bolt breaks off flush with the block or head, it is necessary to drill the bolt and use some type of extractor. If you are not comfortable with these techniques, your machine shop will be able to remove the offending bolt.*

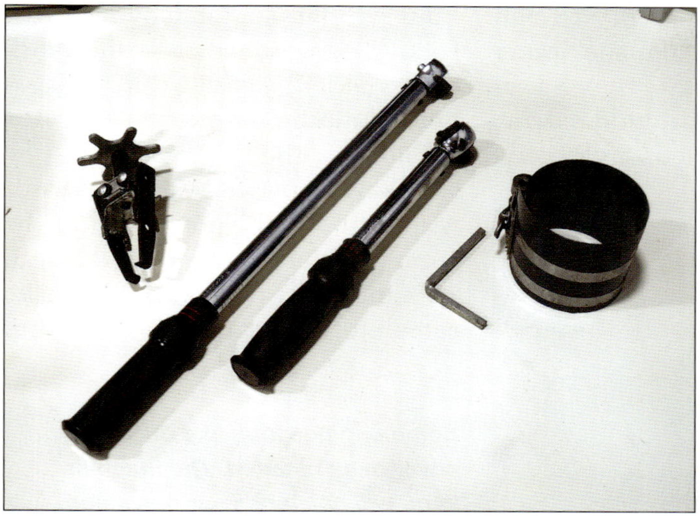

Some special tools are needed to disassemble and rebuild an engine. If you don't have them, they can be rented at many auto parts stores. Some examples are shown: (left to right) a valve spring compressor, torque wrenches, and a piston ring compressor.

Special tools, such as the cam bearing remover/installer, can be tricky to use for beginners. If the machine work will be done at a shop, consider letting the shop remove the old bearings and install new ones.

they must be used with caution. If you are unfamiliar with them, air tools can cause damage if not used properly. Removal is safer than installation, but care must be taken to avoid breaking stuck fasteners. While any broken bolt can be repaired for a price, the inconvenience and cost are disappointments to say the least. Fortunately, we get to demonstrate techniques for removing bolts during this build.

Other tools that are required and may not be in everyone's toolbox are noted in the text, including a valve spring compressor, torque wrenches, and a piston ring compressor. These tools can all be rented at most of the nationwide chain auto parts stores. When you use a new tool, follow the manufacturer's instructions. Planning is key to prevent you from making multiple trips to the parts store for tool rentals.

Finally, some tools should only be used by professionals. An example is the cam bearing installer. Unless you are determined to do as much of the build yourself as possible, some processes are better left to the pros due to complexity, tool availability, convenience, and peace of mind. There is no shame in having the more sensitive processes done by a shop. (We will note these in the step-by-step sections.)

Unless you are rebuilding the engine from your own pampered car, there is an excellent chance that the engine is going to be greasy and dirty. Unless you feel that you need to clean it before you begin, you do not need to clean it before you begin. Machine shops have fantastic machinery for cleaning your engine parts before they begin any other work, and they are going to clean your parts before they begin any work. The exception to this advice is an engine that has so much coolant or oil on it that it will be tricky to handle the parts as you remove them.

If possible, cleaning the engine before removal from the car is the safest and easiest way to do it. Once the engine is out of the car, use a pressure washer to clean it, but make sure to seal all openings into the engine. It does not take long for moisture to start the oxidation process inside the engine. This becomes more of a problem the longer it takes to get the project started.

Unfortunately, for many of us (including the engine featured in this book), the starting point is a found or *gifted* engine. Many people swap the original six for a V-8, which makes it almost easy to find an engine to start with. The downside is that many of these engines were removed and improperly stored while the owner tried to get rid of it.

When all the preparation is done, the tools are gathered, and everything is safe, start removing parts. Follow along as we strip the block and cylinder head down in preparation for machine work.

Begin the disassembly by removing any tubes, hoses, or wiring that did not need to be removed during engine removal. This includes spark plug wires, the carburetor-to-distributor vacuum

Some engines look like they have never been cleaned. The machine shop will hot-tank your block and head before working on them, so pre-cleaning is not really necessary unless you can do it with a spray washer before removal from the car. Take extra care not to get water inside the engine in case it does not immediately go to the machine shop. Some engines are painted orange and still look like they have never been cleaned.

This is the result of not sealing all the openings before storing an engine. The rusty cylinder is most likely the cylinder that had the intake valve open. If the engine was stored uncovered and outdoors, water entered through the carburetor and found its way to the open valve.

By now, all preparations have been made to begin the disassembly. Start by removing any wiring, tubes, or hoses that were not removed during engine removal. Mark the spark plug wires on tape wrapped around each wire. You will probably replace the wire set, but this will help you identify the correct wire for each cylinder.

External Parts Removal (Left Side of Engine)

1 Remove the fuel pump. It is attached with two bolts; remove them slowly. You will feel the tension on the pump arm release as the pump comes loose. Carefully note how the arm comes out and take pictures. When you reinstall the pump, you have to position the arm properly in relation to the cam lobe that moves the arm before you tighten the bolts.

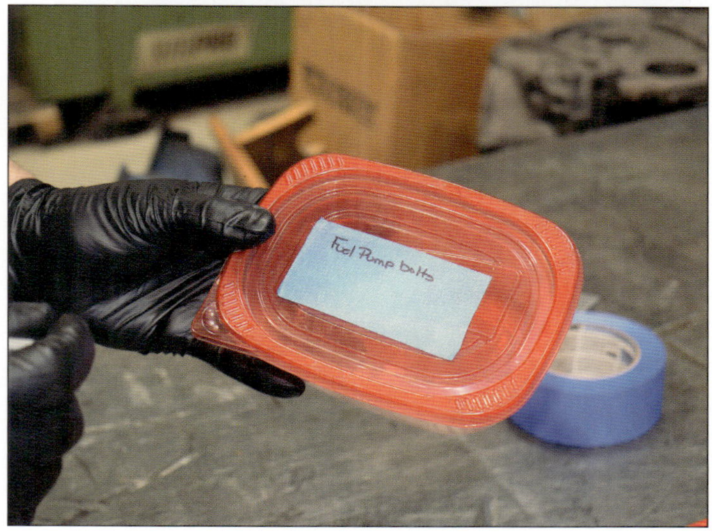

2 From this point on, bag the hardware and label the bag after every step.

3 The ignition coil and bracket are on the same side of the engine. The wiring to the coil should be removed by now. With the bracket still attached to the engine, loosen the screw that tightens the bracket around the coil and remove the coil. Unbolt the bracket and store it. You can replace the bracket with a new dress-up replacement or clean and paint the original.

4 There are special procedures to follow when removing a distributor for repair and reinstallation. Since the entire engine will be disassembled, it is not necessary to mark the distributor before removal. Take a picture of the vacuum advance orientation for reference when reinserting the distributor. If all the wires and the vacuum line have been removed, remove the bolt that retains the distributor hold-down. If the cap is removed, you will see that the rotors turn almost a quarter of a turn while you pull the distributor out. Keep this in mind for reassembly because it will help you insert the distributor close to the right position.

5 *Inspect the distributor gear after it is removed from the block. The distributor is driven by a matching gear on the camshaft. Excessive wear on the distributor may indicate the camshaft is moving fore and aft more than it should. Have your machine shop inspect the cam and thrust plate for excessive wear.*

6 *Remove the right motor mount from the block by removing the two bolts. Motor mounts should always be replaced during a rebuild. Some cars have different left and right motor mounts, so pay attention and take a picture. Mark the old part and keep it for reference until the new engine is assembled. A mount still in the car is shown.*

7 *Spark plug removal is straightforward. It is not necessary to use a plug socket with the engine out of the car, but it does make them easier to handle. When you remove the plugs, study them and take photos to note which cylinder each plug came from. This is useful in assessing the condition of the engine and will indicate how much work needs to be done if you are not planning a complete rebuild.*

line, and oil pressure and temperature sending units.

Now is the moment you've been waiting for: removing parts from the engine! Remember, the order in which most of the external pieces are removed is not critical, but we will make every effort to let you know when it is important, starting on the left side of the engine.

Fuel Pump

Remove the fuel pump by removing the attaching bolts and lifting the pump from the engine. Carefully note the orientation of the pump and take a photo. More than one new fuel pump has been broken when it was installed upside down (it's possible) and the bolts were tightened. This type of mistake tends to happen when the builder is not the same person who disassembled the engine or a long time elapses between teardown and assembly and reference photos are not available. If it will be a long time between teardown and reassembly, seal the opening to the engine with duct tape to keep it clean. Bag the hardware and label it properly.

Ignition Coil

The ignition coil is next. There are several types of coil brackets used on the Ford small six, including aftermarket dress-up pieces. If you can access the bracket hold-down bolts, it is not necessary to remove the coil from the bracket. If you plan to replace the coil (which is a good idea and falls under the category of insurance) or paint and reuse the bracket, remove the coil while the bracket is attached to the engine. This makes it easier to get leverage on the small nut and screw that tighten the clamp that holds the coil in the bracket. Bag the hardware and label it properly.

Distributor

Still on the left side of the engine (as viewed from the driver's seat) remove the distributor. The distributor hold-down bolt can be tricky to reach on the Ford small six. It is located at the base of the distributor where it enters the block. The bolt tightens a retainer that fits the distributor housing and holds the distributor in the block. This bolt must be loosened when it is necessary to adjust the ignition timing by rotating the housing in the block. After the timing adjustment is made, retighten the bolt to hold the housing firmly in place. As you can imagine, the normal vibration of the engine is enough to cause the housing to rotate, thus changing the ignition timing if the bolt is not properly fastened. Plug the opening to prevent moisture intrusion if the teardown will not be completed soon. Bag the hardware and label it properly. With the distributor removed, inspect the gear for signs of excessive camshaft movement.

Engine Mounts

Near the distributor hole is the left-side engine mount. It is held on by two bolts. Remove the bolts and the mount, and then bag and label the hardware. Through the years, different motor mounts were used based on the engine size and model of the vehicle. Make sure that you have the right information when ordering new motor mounts. Replacing the motor mounts is critical because they weaken and wear over time. If a motor mount fails, the engine will tip to one side or the other when the vehicle is in drive or reverse. If you cannot find replacement motor mounts, there are companies that can rebuild them. Bag the hardware and label it properly.

Power Steering Pump

If your vehicle has power steering, remove the pump at this time. Check the pump for leaks. If the reservoir or shaft seals are leaking, replace them if they are available or purchase a rebuild kit. Otherwise, if a replacement pump is available, it would be a good time to replace it. In cases where the pump will just be cleaned and reinstalled, it is not necessary to remove the pump from the bracket. You can remove the pump and bracket together. It is easier to remove the pump from the bracket while it is still on the engine if you plan to replace the pump or clean and paint the bracket.

Considering the economical nature of the 6-cylinder engine, it is no surprise that power steering was a rare option on cars in the 1960s. However, as the marketplace changed in the 1970s, power steering became more popular. Bag the hardware and label it properly.

Spark Plugs

You may be tempted to remove the spark plugs at this time because it is easier to get leverage on stubborn plugs when the head is attached to the engine block. However, leave the plugs in the head until you are ready to remove the head. Remember that any opening into the internal engine area is a source of moisture and is best kept covered or plugged as long

External Parts Removal (Right Side of Engine)

1 *There should not be any fuel lines, vacuum lines, or electrical connectors attached to the carburetor by now. Remove the carburetor by removing the two nuts that attach the carburetor to the carburetor adapter. Hold the carburetor carefully because there could still be fuel in the bowl. Pour the fuel into a suitable container by tipping the carburetor. Tip it in several directions as fuel can come out various passages. Be sure to dispose of old fuel, oil, and coolant responsibly and legally.*

2 *Unbolt the carburetor adapter by removing the two bolts that attach it to the cylinder head. The adapter may be in poor condition on early vehicles due to the coolant passage that runs through it and the inexpensive materials used for parts of this type. For engines through 1968, the adapter is available as a reproduction if you plan to use the original-style 1-barrel carburetor.*

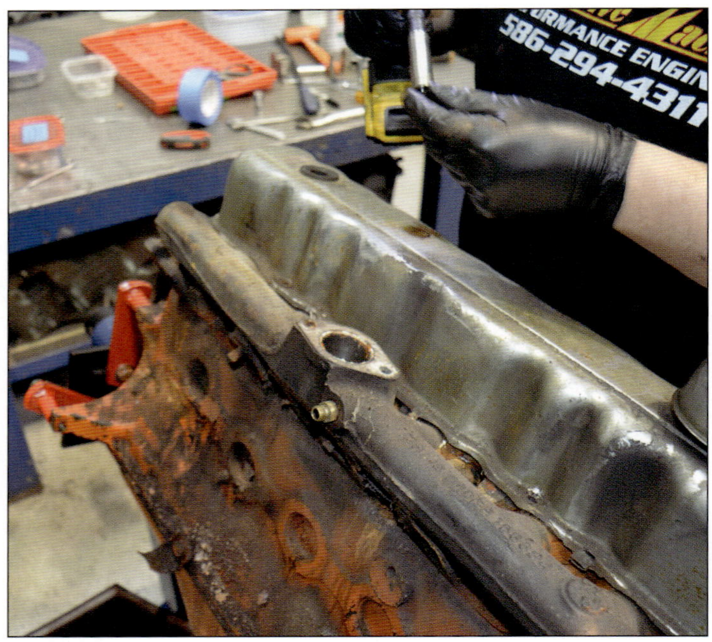

3 *Remove any fittings from the head near the base of the carburetor in preparation for cylinder-head work and to take advantage of the extra leverage available when the head is attached to the block on the stand. Early cars have one fitting, usually brass, that serves as the intake port for the PCV system. Carefully remove it with the correct-size open-end wrench. You should be able to clean and reuse it unless there is excessive carbon buildup.*

4 *At the front of the head (on the right side) is a fitting for the heater hose return. Use the correct-size wrench to very carefully remove the fitting. Due to the corrosive environment, this fitting very often corrodes and can break off in the head. Like anything else that breaks, this can be fixed, but by now you may be tired of fixing broken bolts and fittings.*

5 *The freeze (core) plugs on the side of the block can be an indication of the internal condition of the block. If any of the plugs are rusted or corroded through, expect there to be considerable rust inside the block. This rust can normally be cleaned during the hot-tank process.*

6 *Freeze plugs are driven into the block and held in place as a press fit. To remove them, use a hammer and punch on one edge of the plug. It should spin in the hole enough that you can grab it with pliers and pull it out of the hole. Do not panic if the plug falls into the block. You may need to use needle-nose pliers to pull it back into the hole for removal.*

7 *There are threaded plugs on the block. You can either remove these plugs or let the machine shop remove them. If they come out easily, take pictures for reference and store them until the block is ready to be painted.*

as possible. If your timetable is interrupted, open plug holes can cause rust that was not there before you began.

The right side of the engine can be more challenging than the left because of the years of abuse from the exhaust manifold. Bolts tend to be rusted, and if there was an exhaust leak (likely), everything will be covered in a layer of thick, oily soot. Take your time, be methodical, and be ready for some frustration.

Carburetor

Start at the top of the engine and remove the carburetor. Any hoses or fuel lines not removed when the engine was in the vehicle should be removed at this time. The stock 1V (1-barrel or venturi) carburetor is attached to the stock adapter with two studs. Carefully remove the nuts and washers and lift the carburetor straight up and off of the adapter.

Depending on how long it has been since the car ran, there may still be fuel in the bowl. Be careful not to spill it on yourself, and carefully tilt the carburetor over a receptacle and drain the fuel for safety. Dispose of the extra fuel according to local laws. Bag the hardware and label it properly.

If you plan to reuse the carburetor, this is the time to rebuild it. Rebuild kits are available for any of the carburetors originally installed by Ford. Kits come with detailed instructions, and as long as you are careful, you can rebuild your own carburetor. Make every effort to get the body cleaned out, including all of the internal passages. One weakness of the Autolite 1100 carburetor is the potential for the main body and carburetor top to warp over time. If your carburetor is not useable, it will need to be replaced. (See chapter 7 for upgrade options.)

The purpose of the carburetor adapter is to properly align the carburetor on the head. There is a tube cast into the adapter on early vehicles. Heater hoses attach to each end of this tube. The tube allows hot engine coolant to warm the carburetor base for cold-weather driving. It is sometimes easy to forget that when these cars were new, they were not pampered for the most part and were driven in all weather conditions. The adapter can now be removed from the cylinder head. The adapter is fastened to the head by two bolts.

After the adapter has been removed, block the carburetor opening with duct tape or a similar method to prevent moisture from entering the engine if the teardown will not be completed soon. Bag the hardware and label it properly.

Hose Fittings

There are several fittings on the right side of the engine. A fitting for engines with a positive crankcase ventilation (PCV) valve is located at the base of the carburetor. Because of the advantage of leverage, it is easier to remove the fitting while the head is still on the engine block. There is also a fitting at the front of the head near the thermostat housing for the heater hose outlet. Be careful when removing this fitting. The fittings corrode over time and weaken to the point that most are damaged on removal if extra care is not taken. As with other broken bolts, this can be fixed, but it is less of a headache if you can avoid it.

Freeze Plugs

Freeze (core) plugs are on the side of the block. These plugs serve a dual purpose.

They are used to help remove core sand during the casting process. Core sand must be removed as much as possible to prevent it from causing issues through the life of the engine. This is why they are sometimes referred to as core plugs.

The more common term is *freeze* plugs because it is possible for the water in the engine block to freeze if the proper water/antifreeze ratio is not maintained. When water freezes, it expands. If it expands enough, it can crack the engine block. While they are not strictly designed for the purpose, the plugs are press-fit in the block. The freeze plugs can act as a sort of fuse when they are pushed out by the expanding ice. It causes a mess but potentially saves the engine block from cracking.

The core plugs are easily removed by hitting one side with a punch. This rotates the plug enough that you can grab it with pliers or Vise-Grips and pull it out. Do not be alarmed by the corrosion you may see in the water jacket area unless your machinist is alarmed. Professional machinists can determine the extent of the damage, but it can usually be cleaned up using their equipment.

There are also threaded plugs in the block. It may be best to leave threaded plugs for the machinists to remove. These plugs provide access to oil passages, which must be cleaned using special brushes. Unless you have the brushes and intend to do it yourself, leave the plugs in place and you will not lose them.

Almost all of the components on the front of the engine are periodically replaced due to age or wear. The components are generally easy to remove. In fact, if you have had this vehicle for any length of time, you may have even already replaced some of them.

External Parts Removal (Front of Engine)

1 *Remove any wires or cables that might still be attached to the back of the alternator. Remove the nut from the lower bolt, but do not remove the bolt yet. Remove the top bolt. Carefully support the alternator, remove the bottom bolt, and remove the alternator from the brackets.*

2 *There are two alternator-bracket pieces on early engines to remove. The top piece has only one bolt to allow it to pivot for belt adjustment. The bottom bracket attaches with two bolts. Engines from later years have two bolts for the alternator, but the bracket arrangement may be different.*

3 *Remove the fan, fan spacer, and water pump pulley at the same time. There are four bolts that hold them to the water-pump shaft flange. Hold the fan to counter the leverage of the tool while you remove the bolts. Do not completely remove the bolts until they are all loose.*

4 Water pumps on 144- through 200-ci engines attach with three bolts. The 250 pump has four bolts and a longer snout.

4.5 The water pump impellor on our engine has a straight line of rust across it. This line marks where the coolant level was while the engine was not used. Coolant has anti-corrosion properties, so the portion of the impellor in the coolant did not rust.

5 Remove the thermostat housing on the front of the head, which houses the device that regulates engine temperature. When the engine coolant heats to a preset temperature, the thermostat opens and allows hot coolant to flow into the radiator.

5.5 Because of the heat in the area and the corrosive nature of improperly maintained coolant, thermostat housing bolts take a lot of abuse. Of all the bolts on the engine, these two are the most likely to break. Look no further than our engine for proof.

Alternator

Ford alternators on the inline 6-cylinder engines all had the same dimensions. It is simple to remove the alternator from the engine, especially on vehicles not equipped with air-conditioning. You might be tempted to cut the belt to remove it, and as long as you are safe, go right ahead. Stock replacement alternator belts for these engines are available at the auto parts stores.

Using two wrenches (or a wrench and a ratchet), remove the nut from the bottom pivot bolt, but do not remove the bolt just yet. Next, remove the top bolt from the alternator, being careful to keep the alternator from unexpectedly rotating. Hold the alternator and remove the bottom bolt. The alternator can now be removed. Remove the two brackets from the block. The top bracket has one bolt and is attached at one of the front-cover bolts. The bottom bracket is attached with two bolts directly to the block. Store this hardware and mark the container.

Cooling Fan and Water Pump

The engine cooling fan, spacer, and water pump pulley are all attached by the same four bolts. The bolts are threaded into the water pump pulley flange.

Hold the fan and loosen all four bolts before removing them. Be careful when holding the fan. Apply quite a bit of force as you remove the bolts. There should not be sharp edges on the fan, but check carefully to avoid injury. If these parts have been in place for decades, you will probably need to persuade them to separate them from the water pump. A rubber mallet usually does the trick, but be careful where you strike the parts and do not bend the fan blades.

The water pumps on 144- through 200-ci engines are attached with three bolts. A four-bolt water pump is used on 250-ci engines. The removal process is the same. Remove the bolts and remove the pump. Like most other parts on the engine, the longer the pump has been on the engine, the harder it will be to remove. Our engine had been stored with antifreeze in the block. Antifreeze has some anti-corrosion characteristics and helps parts like the pump impellor resist rust.

Cylinder Head External Components

Before removing the cylinder head, remove any components attached to it. The thermostat housing is attached with two bolts, which are the most likely bolts on the whole engine to break. The combination of heat and coolant tends to be very corrosive if the cooling system is not properly maintained. This severely compromises the bolts, and they break very easily on removal.

If you have not already done so, remove the heater hose fitting from the right front of the cylinder head. You will have extra leverage if you remove it while the head is still on the block. It will likely be corroded and seized in place and will require quite a bit of force to remove. Be careful not to break off the fitting in the cylinder head. If you do, it will need to be removed, but it may be easier than a bolt because it is hollow.

The water temperature sensor is located on the left rear corner of the cylinder head. Remove the sensor before you remove the head to avoid breaking it while handling the head. You may be replacing it anyway, but it is unnecessary extra work if you break it off by accident.

Valve Cover

The first real look into the engine comes when you remove the valve cover. The valve cover is attached with seven bolts. After the bolts are removed, you may need to pry gently on a corner to get the gasket to separate. The valve cover may or may not have been removed in the past. Considering that some of these engines have been on the road since 1960, it would not be a surprise to learn that the engine was previously rebuilt. If you are rebuilding an engine that you have not seen in operation or one that has been in storage for a while, you can get an idea of how well the engine was maintained and the condition it was in when it was last driven. If the area under the valve cover is clean and shows signs of oil, it was probably well maintained. Oil that has turned to sludge indicates that the oil was not changed regularly. If it is dry and has a burnt look, the upper end of the engine may not have been getting enough oil and you will need to make sure the oil passages are cleared properly.

Oil that is milky or light brown means that there was moisture in the oiling system when the engine was running. This could be from short trips where the engine didn't get to operating temperature or a coolant leak due to a crack in the worst-case scenario. Cracks in the cylinder head are not difficult to confirm, but repairing a cracked head is usually not worth the cost and you should look for a replacement. (See the section on cylinder heads in chapter 8 before you buy a replacement head.)

The cylinder head is one component of the complete engine, but it can be thought of as a system in and of itself. The cylinder head has moving components, oil passages, coolant

Cylinder Head Removal

1 *Remove the water temperature sensor from the head before you remove the head. It is easy to break off the sensor in the head once the cylinder head is on the bench. It is not an expensive part, but the time and cost to remove a broken sensor is an aggravation that you do not need.*

2 *Here's something you do not see on a 6-cylinder engine every day. Valve cover T-bolts were designed for racers so that they could quickly remove the valve cover between runs for inspections and adjustments. The look became popular on street cars, even though there was no justification for having them.*

2.5 *Stock valve cover bolts are all the same size, and there are seven of them. Remove the bolts and the valve cover may lift right off. It may also be stuck to the gasket and head, which will require some gentle prying to break it loose. Do not pry too hard. If you bend the sheet metal valve cover, it can be bent back into shape. Take your time here and don't waste your time having to make a repair.*

3 *Remove the valve cover and you will get your first look into the real condition of the engine. Ideally, the valvetrain will be clean and lightly covered in oil. Sludge is an indication of poor maintenance and blocked oil passages. Milky or tan-colored oil indicates moisture while the engine was running, either from a leaking head gasket or a crack in the cylinder head.*

4 *Before you remove the rocker arms, check for excessive movement, which can indicate an issue with the rocker shaft, lifters, or a cam lobe. Remove the bolts that hold the rocker rail pedestals to the cylinder head. Loosen them a little at a time until the spring tension is removed. Then, remove the bolts and the rocker-arm assembly.*

5 *When the rocker-arm assembly has been removed, inspect the ends of the pushrods. This engine has adjustable rocker arms, so the rocker end of the pushrod has a cup. Check the cup for signs of wear that could indicate alignment problems.*

6 *When you remove the pushrods, keep them in order. If there are any issues with the valvetrain, your machinist may want to see the parts that came from each cylinder. Roll the pushrods on a flat table to check for straightness. Bent pushrods need to be replaced.*

7 *Use a torque wrench to remove the cylinder-head bolts. Why use the torque wrench on removal? By setting the wrench to the installation torque, you can tell if any of the head bolts have lost torque through the years. If you have head gasket issues, this could be why.*

8 *When you remove the cylinder head, visually inspect it for signs of problems. The term* blown head gasket *refers to a condition where the gasket no longer completely seals the combustion chamber between the block and the head. Our gasket was in good shape.*

9 ***Sometimes the oil-pump driveshaft comes out when you remove the distributor because it is stuck in the hole at the bottom of the distributor shaft. A good cleaning will fix that. If it was not stuck, it probably stayed in the block. Remove it with a magnetic pickup tool.***

10 ***Use the magnet to remove each lifter from its bore. If one is stubborn, spray it with penetrating oil and attempt to rotate it with a long pair of needle-nose pliers or a screwdriver and try the magnet again.***

passages, and other parts attached to it (external parts were removed earlier). In addition to all of this, there is a complete list of machining operations that will be done to the head. Before all of that, it must be removed from the engine.

Rocker Arms

After the valve cover is removed and before you remove the rocker-arm shaft, check each rocker arm for excessive play that may indicate issues with a cam lobe or lifter. To remove the rocker-arm shaft, loosen the bolts a little at a time until the tension is off the rocker arms. The tension is there because the lifters and pushrods for the valves that are open are exerting pressure upward.

Once the tension is removed, remove each bolt in no particular order. Check the rocker arms for freedom of movement. If the engine has not been driven for some time, the rocker arms might be stiff but may free up with a simple cleaning. Any evidence of a bent or scored shaft means the rocker-arm assembly needs to be replaced.

Remanufactured assemblies by Rocker Arms Unlimited are available in the stock 1.5 ratio or a higher 1.6-ratio stock-style assembly for increased lift.

Pushrods

Make sure that you have a way to keep the valvetrain parts in order before you begin to remove them. The first parts to come out are the pushrods.

Engines with adjustable rocker arms have pushrods with a ball on the lifter end and a cup on the rocker-arm end to match the rocker arm. Engines with nonadjustable rocker arms have pushrods with a ball on each end.

Inspect both ends of the pushrod for signs of excessive wear. If there is excessive wear, the pushrods and possibly the lifters will need to be replaced. Check the straightness of the pushrods by rolling them on a flat surface. Bent pushrods will be evident and should be replaced.

Cylinder Head

When you unbolt the cylinder

head, use a torque wrench set to the torque at which the heads should be installed. This will indicate whether any head bolts have lost torque. Loosen the bolts in the reverse order of the tightening sequence. Loosen them all first. Then, remove them to prevent unnecessary, uneven force on the head that can contribute to warping. It's not likely, but it's better to be safe than sorry.

Before you lift the cylinder head off of the block, make sure that you have a place cleared on the bench to set it down. Do this carefully because the assembled head weighs close to 50 pounds.

With the head off the block, you can start to visually inspect it for signs of the engine's condition. Blown head gaskets are obvious, and burned valves can also be seen. Either of these conditions means that you will have to perform the necessary machine work to correct the underlying cause.

Distributor Driveshaft

If the oil pump driveshaft wasn't removed with the distributor, use a magnetic pickup tool to remove it. The driveshaft inserts on the bottom end into the oil pump and on the top end into a hex-shaped hole in the bottom end of the distributor shaft. The shaft drives the pump from the rotation of the distributor. The distributor is driven by a gear that is cast into the camshaft.

On 144- and 170-ci engines, the shaft is 1/4 inch in diameter. On 200- and 250-ci engines, the shaft is 5/16 inch.

Lifters

The last step to remove the cylinder head before turning the engine over is to remove the lifters from their bores. Do this with a strong magnetic pickup tool. If some of the lifters resist removal with a magnet, spray some rust penetrant in the bore and try to spin the lifter to break it loose. You should be able to remove all but the most stubborn lifters this way.

Harmonic Balancer, Oil Pan, and Front Cover Removal

1 *Engines from the 1960s rarely had accessories such as power steering or air conditioning, but if they did, they required an extra belt sheave on the crankshaft balancer. When these options were installed by the dealer at the time of sale, it was easier to bolt on the extra pulley than to replace the harmonic balancer. Our engine has the extra pulley, but the accessory that necessitated it is long gone.*

1.5 *Before the harmonic balancer can be removed, remove the single, large bolt that retains it to the crankshaft. Be sure to properly store this bolt. It can be cleaned up and reused. If you have an impact wrench, it may be necessary to use it now. It can be difficult to hold the crankshaft to apply the amount of torque needed to remove the bolt.*

2 *Install the balancer puller according to the manufacturer's instructions. Be careful not to thread the puller bolts too far into the holes on the balancer. If you do, they will contact the front cover and may crack it.*

3 *With the tool properly installed, turn the shaft to remove the balancer from the crankshaft snout. Since only one bolt holds it on, the balancer is keyed to the crankshaft. Do not lose the key.*

4 *Turn the engine over on the stand so that you can access the oil-pan bolts. Remove the bolts and pay attention to where each one goes. There are different sizes and lengths at the rear and front of the pan compared to bolts on each side of the pan. Two of the front bolts thread into the front cover from the bottom. They must be removed before the front cover can come off.*

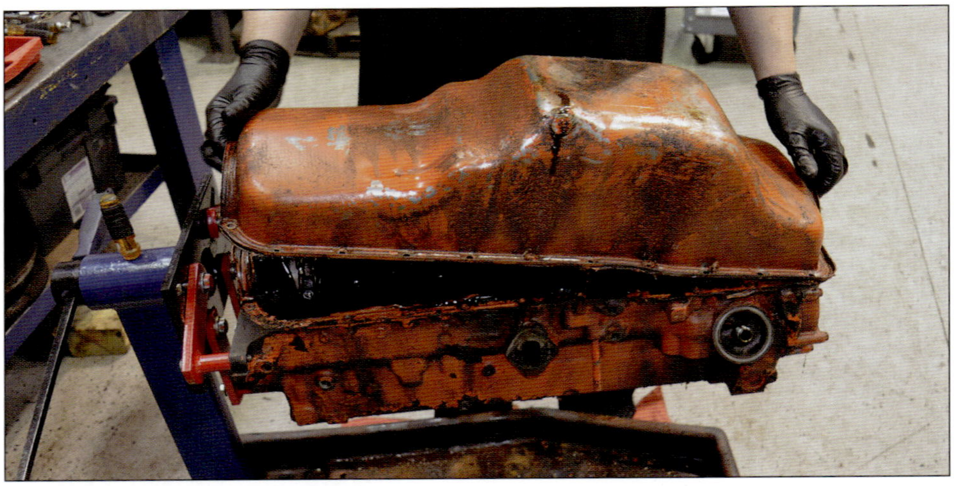

5 *Lift the oil pan off the engine block. However, it may be stuck to the block. If so, try to get a steel scraper between the block and pan. If this does not give enough leverage, use a pry bar. Be careful to not bend the sheet metal. Bent pans, even ones that have been straightened, are very prone to leaks.*

6 *Once the oil pan has been removed from the block, visually inspect the pan and block for damage. A cracked block is expensive to repair and is a reason to find a new block. (This block appears to be okay.) Check the oil pickup screen for blockage. A blocked screen will cause oil starvation and engine damage. This can be caused by poor maintenance or overzealous use of silicone sealers on previous repairs that come loose and end up in the pan.*

7 *At the front of the engine, remove the front-cover bolts that attach to the block. There are various lengths, so take note of where they go. During reassembly, it is pretty easy to match them to the right hole because they should all thread into the block the same amount.*

8 *Gentle prying may be necessary to break the front cover loose from the block. The cover is pretty strong, but avoid aggressively prying on it. Do not break it because the part is not reproduced. Nicks on the edges should not be a concern, but if they happen, file them down so that the gasket will seal properly when you reassemble the engine.*

The last external parts to come off are on the front of the engine. By now, the fan, spacer, pulley, and water pump are off. Be careful when removing the rest of the front components. The balancer is heavier than you would think, and the front cover can be damaged if it is removed too aggressively.

Harmonic Balancer

At the front of the engine, remove the harmonic balancer (damper) from the crankshaft. If the engine is from a car of the 1960s that had power steering or air-conditioning, it will have a two V-belt groove damper. If the air-conditioning was installed by the dealer, the outer belt groove may be a bolt-on cast-iron pulley. If so, remove the three bolts holding it on and remove the pulley.

The balancer requires a special tool for removal. Harmonic balancer removal tools can be rented at many auto parts stores. Remove the bolt that secures the balancer to the crankshaft. Follow the manufacturer's instructions and attach the remover to the balancer. Be careful not to thread the bolts too far in because they can contact the front cover and damage it. Remove the balancer. It is fairly heavy, so take care not to drop it.

Oil Pan

For the next operation, prepare to catch any oil that comes out as you turn the engine over on the stand. A catch pan designed for use on an engine stand is ideal. Turn the engine 180 degrees on the stand to remove the oil pan, which is attached to the block with a set of bolts on each end (at the rear main and the front cover) and a series of bolts along each side.

Pay attention to the locations as you remove the bolts. They are not all the same. If you put them in a pile, it may be difficult to reinstall them at reassembly. Take photos and carefully label the storage containers.

With the bolts removed and stored, lift off the oil pan. It is unlikely that the pan will simply lift off of the block. Of all the parts on the engine, the pan is one of the most likely to stick to the block. Most likely, you will need to use leverage from a small pry bar to pop it loose. Be extremely careful not to bend the flange on the pan. Start small and try to wedge a scraper in first. This might be sufficient to break it loose. Take your time and only use enough force to break it loose.

Front Cover

The front cover cannot be removed until the harmonic balancer and the front oil-pan bolts have been removed. Remove the remaining bolts that hold the cover to the block. Carefully pry off the cover from the block. Inspect the backside of the front cover for evidence that the camshaft has made contact due to excessive end play.

Check the timing chain for excessive slop. A loose timing chain affects camshaft timing and will adversely affect performance. The condition of the chain is for your information only because you should never reuse a timing chain after going through the trouble to get to it.

If the gears are in good shape, replacement chains are available, but we recommend that you replace the set while you are in there.

So far, the disassembly has involved parts that realistically could

Timing Chain

Do not remove the timing chain set at this time. You will avoid frustration when you remove the piston/connecting rod assemblies from the block. If the timing chain is left in place, it will allow the camshaft to turn as you turn the crankshaft. As you turn the crankshaft to get the journal in the correct location (to push the rod out through the top of the cylinder bore), the camshaft lobes can interfere if they do not turn with the crankshaft. ■

Piston, Rod, and Crankshaft Removal

1 *If the engine has previously been rebuilt, the rods and rod caps may be stamped with the cylinder number. This is necessary because they are machined together and match. If they are not already marked, the best way to mark the rod caps and the rods to keep them paired is to stamp the corresponding cylinder number into each piece.*

2 *The rods in our engine were already stamped. This is more evidence that our engine has previously been worked on, and it is an example of what to look for when inspecting the engine for signs of previous repairs.*

3 *Remove the rod-bolt nuts using a torque wrench. This lets you know if any of the bolts have lost torque over time. This information is useful if there was a problem and could help explain why the engine failed (if it did).*

4 *Lift the rod cap off of the rod bolts. Due to tight tolerances, lift the cap straight up. If you lift at even a slight angle, the cap will bind. Do not force the caps off. Take your time and lift them straight off of the bolts.*

5 *Using an appropriate removal tool, push the piston and rod assembly out of the block. There will be a ridge at the top of the cylinder bore caused by the wear of the top piston ring where it always ends its travel. Unless this ridge is excessive, the rings will compress enough to get past the ridge. Catch the piston as it exits the bore.*

6 *Inspect each piston as you remove it from the block. Look for broken rings and damage to the piston in the skirt area or in the lands between the rings. Even if the cylinders do not need to be bored, damaged pistons mean that you will need a new set of pistons.*

7 *Inspect the rod bearings once the rod is removed. They will definitely be replaced but can provide insight into the overall condition of the engine and how it was maintained. If the rod journals require machining, the new bearings will be thicker to make up for the amount removed.*

8 *Now that the rods are all out of the block, remove the timing chain. A bolt holds the camshaft gear in place and a dowel pin keeps the gear from spinning on the camshaft.*

9 *The timing chain and gears will now slide off of the camshaft and crankshaft. Be sure to slide them together to keep one from binding on its shaft. This can occur because the chain is still connecting the gears and will cause the gears to become cocked if they do not slide off equally.*

10 *On the crankshaft, remove the main bearing cap bolts with the torque wrench set to the installation torque. Two bolts hold each cap to the block on the Ford 6-cylinder engine. No four-bolt mains are needed here.*

11 *Most manufacturers cast the main bearing cap number right into the cap. A cast arrow on the cap points to the front of the engine to make reinstallation a simple matter of looking at the numbers. Do not forget to look at the numbers when reinstalling.*

12 *The crankshaft is heavy and has many sharp edges. Before you lift it out of the block, make sure you have prepared a place to put it. When you store the crank, avoid injury by not making it a trip hazard, and do not stand it up where it can be knocked over.*

13 *Inspect the condition of the main bearings. Wear is normal and part of the rebuild process. Excessive wear, especially on the thrust bearing, can indicate other problems. Consult with your machinist regarding potential causes.*

14 *Look at the back of the bearings of both the main and rod bearings. The back of the bearing will be stamped "Standard" or with the oversize amount (0.020 inch, 0.030 inch, etc.). This is the amount of the oversize, if any, that was required the last time the bearings were replaced.*

15 *The camshaft is held in the engine block by the cam thrust plate. Two bolts hold the plate to the block. Remove the bolts and the plate. Check the plate for excessive wear. Aftermarket replacements are available.*

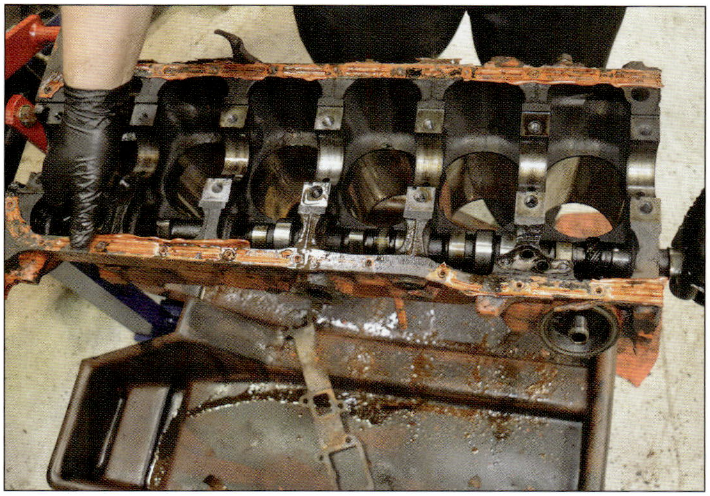

16 *Carefully remove the camshaft from the block. Each time the cam journal clears one of the bearings, the cam will drop a little, so be ready and try to keep it from hitting too hard. A tool made for the purpose or a bolt threaded into the timing-gear hole will provide extra control of the camshaft as it comes out.*

17 *Inspect the camshaft once it is out of the block. Signs of excessive wear on the cam lobes means the camshaft needs to be replaced. This is a good time to upgrade.*

18 *Camshaft bearing removal is a job you may want to leave to the machine shop. The tools are available, and it is a straightforward process, but it can be frustrating if you do not have experience. A certain amount of finesse is needed to feel when the bearing is engaged and can be removed.*

19 *Since there is only one contact point when the last camshaft bearing is removed, we recommend removing the core plug at the back of the block and driving the last bearing out from the backside.*

be removed and replaced in the driveway. In fact, most of the external parts are maintenance items that will need to be replaced on an infrequent basis and do not require rebuilding the engine. It is time to get inside the engine now.

You are on the home stretch. It is time to remove the piston assemblies from the block. If the rod caps and rods are not already stamped with their corresponding cylinder number, do that now using a number punch set. This ensures that you can successfully match the rod and cap to each other during reassembly.

Connecting Rod and Piston Assemblies

Use your torque wrench to remove the rod cap nuts. Set the torque wrench to the rod-bolt installation torque. This lets you know if any of the rod-bolt nuts lost torque over time. Remove the caps and the piston/rod assemblies one at a time to help with organization. To do this, remove the cap and rotate the crankshaft so that the piston is at the top of its travel. Use a rod-removal tool to knock the piston out of the block. Since the block is inverted, be ready to catch the piston (with the rod attached) as it comes out of the block.

With the piston/rod assembly out of the block, inspect it for any broken rings or damage to the ring lands. Undamaged pistons can be reused if the cylinders do not need to be bored, so take care not to cause new damage. If a rod bearing sticks to the crankshaft journal, use a magnet to remove it.

Inspect the rod bearings; visible copper indicates that the engine has been run with inadequate lubrication. Your machine shop will measure and determine if the crankshaft needs to be turned. If so, your new bearings will be thicker to compensate for the amount that had to be machined off.

There is never a reason to reuse bearings. They are, along with piston rings, the main reason for rebuilding the engine.

Remove all the pistons in this manner. Reinstall the caps on their respective rods to make it easier to keep them together.

TECH TIP: Storing the Crankshaft

The crankshaft needs to be stored carefully. There is debate about whether you should stand it up, put it in a cradle horizontally, or just set it on the floor. It all seems to be based on opinion rather than engineering knowledge. Store it in a safe manner to prevent bodily injury from falling or stubbing toes, no matter in what orientation it is stored. The other real storage consideration is rust. If it will be stored for any length of time, keep it oiled to prevent rust on the journals, rear main seal area, and harmonic balancer stub. ■

Regardless of whether you decide to store your crankshaft horizontally or vertically (it will not fall over if it's horizontal, but you might stub your toe on it), you can avoid ending up with rusty parts like these if you coat the crankshaft in oil and store it in a bag. If it is going to the machine shop right away, no special care is needed.

Timing Chain Set

Once the piston and rod assemblies are removed, it is no longer necessary for the crankshaft and camshaft to rotate together, so the timing chain set can be removed. Begin by removing the bolt that retains the camshaft gear to the camshaft. Carefully store the bolt and thick washer and mark the container.

The gear on the crankshaft is not bolted on. Remove the gears and the chain as an assembly by sliding the crank gear off and keeping the cam gear moving with it. At times, it may feel like the crank gear is bound up, but this is likely the result of having it cocked because the chain is not in the same plane as the gear. Be patient and slowly remove the gears and chain.

Crankshaft

The crankshaft can now be removed. Start by removing the main bearing caps. Use your torque wrench to remove the bolts and check to ensure that they all retained the proper torque when in use. Most manufacturers cast the cap number right into the main bearing caps along with an arrow that points to the front of the engine. Ford is no exception. This makes reinstallation in the right order very easy.

Prepare a place to put the crankshaft after it is removed. Carefully lift the crankshaft out of the bearing journals. It should go without saying that the crankshaft is heavy, but just in case, *it is heavy*.

With the crankshaft removed, carefully inspect the condition of the bearings. Wear is normal on bearings; their job is to prevent wear on the machined parts. Excessive wear is an indication of improper maintenance but is generally not a problem because you are rebuilding the engine. If the thrust bearing faces are excessively worn, it could be an indication of transmission issues that need to be addressed.

Finally, look at the backside of the bearings. If they are oversized, you should be able to see the size stamped into the metal. Oversized bearings in an engine means that it has previously been rebuilt. Your machine shop can advise you if machine work is needed and if there is still adequate material to safely perform the needed operations.

Camshaft and Bearings

Remove the camshaft now. A thrust plate holds the camshaft in the block. Remove the two bolts and then remove the thrust plate. If the plate is grooved from wear, it is available from aftermarket suppliers. If you plan to try to reuse the camshaft, be careful not to nick any of the lobes as you remove it.

Special tools are available that thread into the timing-gear hole to help manage the camshaft as it is removed. If you do not have the tool, you can thread a bolt into the hole to give you something to hold onto. As the camshaft journals clear each of the cam bearings, the cam will tend to drop slightly. Be prepared and try to minimize how hard it drops, especially if you plan to reuse the original camshaft.

When the camshaft is out of the block, inspect it for signs of excess wear and check the lobe surfaces. Any evidence of burning or pitting means the camshaft needs to be replaced.

The last thing that must be removed from the block is the set of camshaft bearings. There is a special tool to remove the camshaft bearings that you can rent from the auto parts store. There is a technique to bearing removal that requires some experience to develop the right feel. In most cases, it is easier to let the machine shop remove the cam bearings. If you decide that you want to do as much of the work as you can, closely follow the tool manufacturer's instructions. There are probably a number of videos on the internet that you can reference as well.

Congratulations! The engine block is now completely disassembled.

Head Disassembly

1 ***These are the components that make up the valvetrain on a Ford inline 6-cylinder. Along with the rocker-arm assembly, they include (from left to right) the valve spring, two-piece retainer, valve keepers, and the valve.***

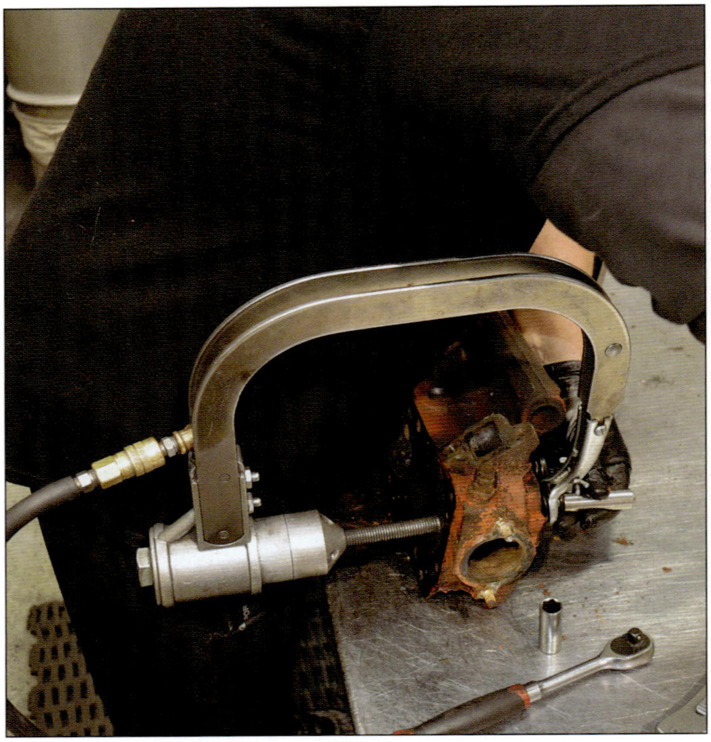

1.5 *If you disassemble the head yourself, the only special tool that you will need is the valve spring compressor. Follow the tool manufacturer's instructions for a manual compressor. We used a pneumatic compressor, which is beyond the means of the average owners who rebuild their own engine.*

2 *Once the spring is compressed, use a magnetic pickup tool to remove the valve keepers. They are held in place by grooves machined into the valve stem and by the shape of the retainer and the tension from the spring. When the keepers are out, release the valve spring compressor, and the spring and retainer will come right out.*

3 *The spring shims in place under the valve springs are another sign that the engine and head have previously been worked on.*

4 *The original-style umbrella valve stem seals are visible here. These seals have no positive retention feature to keep them in place. For this reason, they can ride up and down with the valve stem. These seals become brittle over time, and oil can bypass them and get into the combustion chamber when they lose their effectiveness. Consider upgrading to Viton seals with a spring that seals them to the valve stem.*

TECH TIP

Blue Smoke Could Indicate Leaking Valve Stem Seals

If you need to add oil (more than a quart every 3,000 to 5,000 miles for older engines), leaking valve stem seals could be the culprit. When you start the engine, look for blue smoke that goes away once the engine has run for a little while. This is an indication that oil is leaking past the seals when the engine is off and settling on top of the pistons. When the engine is started, the oil burns off and causes the blue smoke. ■

You may choose to disassemble the cylinder head or leave it to your machine shop. There is really only one special tool needed: a valve spring compressor. These are available to rent or buy, and if you do not do this for a living, we recommend that you rent a manual compressor. The components attached to the cylinder head (valves, springs, retainers, valve keepers, and the rocker-arm assembly) make up the valvetrain.

The rocker-arm assembly has already been removed, so let's focus on the rest of the components. Either way that you decide to go, follow along as we disassemble the cylinder head and prepare it to go to the machine shop.

Valve Spring Retainers

Ford used a two-piece valve spring retainer on the small-six cylinder head. The two-piece retainers are a little difficult to work with and slightly heavy for the job they perform. The retainers are held in place by two-piece keepers. The keepers are held in place in the grooves on the valve stem by the shape of the retainer and tension of the valve spring.

To remove the valve spring retainers, use the valve spring compressor to relieve the spring tension. Once the tension is released, use a magnetic pickup tool to remove the small keepers from the grooves in the valve stem. These parts are replaceable if lost, but they should not have any damage from use, so keep track of them and store them safely.

Valve Springs

Now that the keepers are out of the way, release the valve spring compressor. The spring and retainer will come right off. The presence of valve spring shims indicates that someone has previously worked on the head. With this in mind, make sure to measure the combustion-chamber volumes before milling the head. These heads can safely be milled up to about 0.090 inch maximum. If it has previously been milled, your machinist will need to determine if there is still material that can be removed if milling is necessary to remove any warpage, or if you plan to mill the head for an increase in compression.

Valves

The valves should now come out of the head easily. As you remove them, check for noticeable side-to-side motion. If there is excessive movement, the machine shop may need to replace the valve guides. This is not uncommon and will provide many more years of service. Inspect the valves for obvious damage. Look closely at the backside of the valve. In cases of leaking valve stem seals, excess oil may have burned and accumulated over time and caused significant buildup. If you see this, let it be a warning to keep your engine properly maintained and address issues as they arise.

Finish the cylinder-head disassembly by removing all core plugs with the same punch and pliers technique used on the core plugs in the block.

The cylinder head is now completely disassembled and is ready to go to the machine shop. There is no guarantee that the head will be free of defects, and some can render it unusable, so insist that the machine shop properly inspect it before beginning any work. The extra money to check for cracks is good insurance against the time and money wasted if terminal defects are found later.

MACHINE WORK

Where you choose to get your machine work done might be as important as the work that needs to get done. That may be a little melodramatic, but choosing the right shop is very important. The problem is not so much that some shops won't do quality work as it is their ability and willingness to do what you want to get done.

Surprisingly, many shops tell customers that they cannot work on the old 6-cylinder because they do not have the right equipment. This may be true if you intend to have the crankshaft balanced and the shop does not have a balancer or the one they have is not big enough. A slightly more reasonable objection might be a lack of experience when porting the cylinder head. The truth is that inline 6-cylinders are machined the same as other engine types and require and respond to the same operations as V-8 engines. Do not try to talk a shop into working on your engine, though, if they are hesitant to do it. It may take some searching, but find a shop that is confident it can do what you need.

Performing your own machine work is out of the question for almost all hobbyists. Take one look at the equipment required to do the job, and you will understand that this must be left to the professionals. Doing it yourself is out of the question.

If you are reading this book, you probably do not have the capability and equipment to do your own machine work. Therefore, we will walk you through all the machining operations that will be done on a complete rebuild. It is possible that not all of these operations will be required if your engine has been previously rebuilt. If the machine shop recommends something, you should be prepared to do it.

After reading this chapter, you will know enough to make yourself dangerous, but you will not be an expert. Our hope is to provide enough knowledge that you will be able to make informed decisions when it comes to machine work.

Clean and Inspect Block

1 *While a pressure washer can do a decent job cleaning the outside of the engine block, the only way to thoroughly clean the block is in the thermal degreaser. This machine uses heat and solvent to clean the block better than you could ever hope to do with any other method available to the hobbyist.*

2 *The block is put in the shot blaster to get a final cleaning and prepare it for machine work. This machine uses metal pellets to clean and prep the cast-iron. This is the condition that the block should be in before any machine work is performed.*

3 *Small cracks in the head and block are best found by using a process called Magnafluxing. If a small crack like this is not found before the machine work is performed, a lot of time and money will be wasted. Cracks of this size can leak coolant or combustion gases, either of which will ruin the rebuild.*

4 *To check the deck (top) surface of the block properly, the block must be placed in this fixture. Machining the gasket surface makes sure the deck is flat and prepares it for proper sealing with the head gasket. The requirement for a cast-iron head is 60 to 80 Ra, the term for measuring the surface's smoothness.*

5 *Using a dial indicator, the machinist begins at one point on the deck surface and zeroes the gauge. This is used as the reference point for other points on the surface.*

6 *Every other point on the surface must be no more than the specification for variation. The specification determines how much more or how much less the dial indicator can measure from 0. If all points are within specification, the deck may not be perfectly flat, but it is within the range that can be made perfect with an operation called* decking the block.

7 *The machinist will take the opportunity before machining begins to clean out bolt holes and repair threads by tapping all the bolt holes on the block.*

8 *Checking the cylinder diameter in multiple places can determine if the cylinder wall is tapered from top to bottom. Due to the motion of the piston and side loading, the cylinder is usually widest at the top. The rule of thumb for overbore size is to double the amount of taper. If the taper is 0.014 inch, double that amount is 0.028 inch, so a 0.030-inch-over piston is required.*

9 *Boring the cylinder is the process used to remove any surface damage or imperfections that will cause the piston rings to not properly seal to the cylinder wall. If too much overbore is required to return the cylinder to straight (rather than tapered), a sleeve may need to be installed. Normally, 0.003 to 0.005 inch of stock is left for the honing process.*

The machine shop may use a pressure washer to initially clean the block and remove the worst of the grime from 50 years of abuse. A pressure washer will not thoroughly clean the block, so a stint in a thermal degreasing oven is routine. This machine uses extreme heat and water pressure to clean the block and prepare it for further operations. After the degreasing oven, put the block in a shot blaster. As the name implies, this equipment further cleans the block by blasting it with an appropriate medium. This step removes any rust, and the metal is now ready for inspection and machine work.

The first step in the inspection process is called Magnafluxing. Magnaflux is a brand, but it is also the name of the process by which ferrous (contains iron) metal parts are checked for cracks that are often too small to see with the human eye.

A fluorescent dye that contains small particles of magnetic material is sprayed onto the metal surface. The dye pools up in the cracks, and a handheld electromagnet is passed over the metal. If there are no cracks present, the dye will not react. If there are cracks, the particles in the dye that has collected in the crack will line up due to the magnetic field. When exposed to a blacklight, these particles are visible, and the crack is identified. If there is a crack detected, your machine shop will recommend that the block needs to be repaired (if possible) or replaced.

Next, the machinist will check the main journals of the block for size and alignment. This information will be saved and referred to when the crankshaft is worked on. The machinist will also do a check of the thrust bearing surface on the block. Visible wear is rare but may mean the block will have to be replaced.

The top surface of the block is called the deck. This surface mates to the cylinder head with a gasket in between. It is critical to performance and sealing that the deck is flat. Most machine shops are going to take at least a surface cut off the deck to ensure flatness and promote proper sealing of the head gasket. The reason they check for flatness at this point is to make sure that the block is still good to use. If the uneven surface cannot be repaired with the amount of material available, the block must be replaced.

The machinist can now begin to do some of the inspection steps that most of us are more familiar with. We have all heard owners talk about how their engine was "bored 30 over." For example, the original bore diameter on a 200 was 3.68 inches, and an engine bored 0.030-inch over will have a bore size of 3.71 inches.

Clean and Inspect Crankshaft

The next engine part to get attention is the crankshaft. The crank is cleaned with a jet wash and mineral spirits. If the engine suffers the effects from a lack of maintenance, it may be necessary to remove sludge buildup in the thermal degreasing oven.

After the cleaning, the machinist will check the crankshaft oil passages to make sure that they are clean and free of obstructions. This is an

The crankshaft is cleaned with a jet washer and mineral spirits. In extreme cases, it may be necessary to clean it further in the thermal degreasing oven.

The connecting rods also need to be cleaned. In the process of removing the piston pin, an experienced machinist can get an idea of how much pin fitting may be necessary later.

obvious necessity because oil flow throughout the engine is critical, but maybe nowhere more vital than at the main and connecting rod bearings. It is also important to inspect the holes drilled into the crankshaft counterweights when it was originally balanced. Sludge and debris can collect there, and it could be enough weight to upset the balance in extreme cases. It is also a good idea because you do not want it to become dislodged later and end up blocking an oil passage.

Clean and Inspect Connecting Rods

Cleaning the connecting rods is much like cleaning the crankshaft. Jet wash and thermal degreasing are needed. The piston pins are pressed out at this stage. An experienced machinist can tell by the amount of pressure needed during this step if pin fitting will be necessary. This process is described later.

Clean and Inspect Cylinder Head

After the cylinder head is disassembled, it can be cleaned in the same manner as the engine block. It is very important to Magnaflux the cylinder head, especially in the areas around the exhaust valves. These areas experience the most extreme heat and pressure and are the most likely areas to have cracks. If cracks are found, your machine shop will advise you on the next steps.

Valves

The valves can indicate the condition of the cylinder head. An important test is to measure the diameter of the valve stem along its entire length. It should be the same diameter all the way down. If any of the valves are burnt or bent, replace them. It is also necessary for the machinist to determine why the valve was burnt (likely just needs a valve job due to seat wear) or bent (potential bending of parts due to oil starvation or other bent parts).

The cylinder head is cleaned in the same manner as the cylinder block. The thermal degreasing oven and shot blaster prepare the head for the complete inspection and the machine work to come.

The condition of the valve face can tell the machinist a lot about the condition of the engine. Valves that are burnt due to poor seating or bent due to mechanical interference need to be replaced. The engine builder will also need to determine why these conditions occurred and make sure that they are corrected.

Exhaust valve seats are subjected to extreme wear due to the high exhaust temperatures. Prior to 1974, leaded gas provided lubrication to the valve seats, and the wear was minimized. Since leaded fuel is no longer legal, when using a cylinder head manufactured before 1974, it is important to install new exhaust-valve seats that have been hardened in the manufacturing process.

Valve Guides

The machinist will check the valve guides for wear. When these engines were originally built, the valve guide was not a separate component. The valve guide was machined into the cast-iron cylinder head. An initial test involves seeing if the valve can be moved excessively from side to side in the guide. This movement can also be measured with a micrometer or with a dial bore gauge for extreme accuracy. This is done by measuring the valve guide inside diameter over its length. It should stay the same within tolerances. An experienced machinist will be able to tell by simply wiggling the valve.

Note that the exhaust valve stems are manufactured to a smaller diameter. This allows for a slight bit of expansion when the valve is subjected to the extreme temperatures of the exhaust stroke. For this reason, use an intake valve for the most accurate test when checking for valve movement within the guides.

Valve guide replacement is a common procedure on these engines due to the length of time since most cylinder heads have been serviced.

Valve Seats

The valve seats require inspection as well. Prior to 1974, exhaust valve seats were not hardened. It was not needed at that time because of the lubricating properties of the lead in the gasoline. When it was determined that the health risks of leaded gasoline outweighed the benefits, unleaded gasoline was introduced. The major drawback of unleaded gasoline to the cylinder head was the constant wear that occurred on the exhaust valve seat. Manufacturers responded by using induction hardening in the exhaust valves seats.

Like the valve guides, the valve seats in an original head are not separate pieces; they are machined into the casting. If the seats are excessively worn, they are machined out and new seat inserts are installed. Only exhaust valves require hardened seats. And that concludes the history lesson.

Inspecting the seats involves checking for cracks (including Magnafluxing) and hot spots from exhaust valves not seating properly. Another indication of wear is the valve stem tip height: if the height is more than normal, the valve face can be mushroomed, or the seat may be excessively worn.

Machining

Now we are at the part that almost none of us can do ourselves. The machine work that is needed to return the engine to top performance requires very expensive machinery and extensive training and experience to operate it. If you get a chance, check out the machinery at your machine shop. The size and power of the machines are impressive and completely necessary to perform the delicate grinding and cutting for a rebuild.

Crankshaft Machining

1 *Crankshaft machining begins by checking the size and condition of the main and connecting rod journals. If they are within specification, polishing is likely all that is needed. If they are damaged or otherwise out of specification, they need to be ground to the correct undersize, and new bearings of the correct thickness will be installed.*

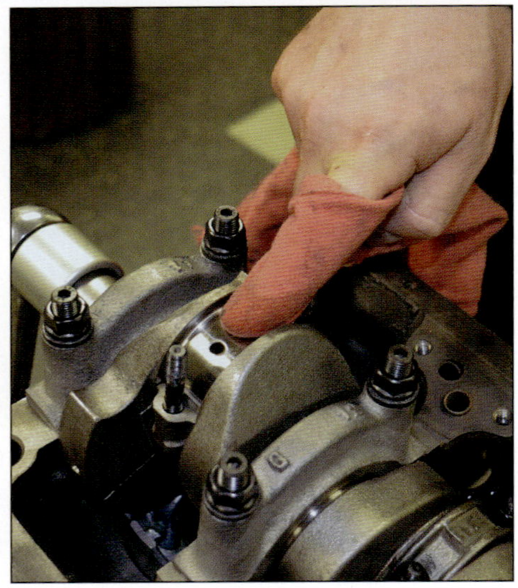

2 *Chamfering the oil passages in the crankshaft helps ensure that the oil flow will be consistent and sufficient to keep the bearings lubricated and hopefully extend the service life. The chamfer process also protects the bearings from any sharp edges that may have been created in the grinding process.*

3 *It is a very good idea to check and tap the bolt holes for the flexplate and the harmonic balancer bolt. The flexplate bolts go through the flange on the crankshaft. If there is debris in the balancer bolt hole, it can lead to improper bolt torque and, in an extreme case, failure of the bolt.*

4 *Special equipment is required for all machining operations on the engine, but maybe none as specialized as the one for decking the block. The block deck must be perfectly flat, precisely tall, and have the exact required roughness for head gasket sealing.*

5 *Many builders choose to have the block zero-decked. In this case, the deck is machined down far enough so that the top of the piston at top dead center (TDC) is flush with the deck of the block. The result of zero-decking the block is that the static compression ratio is increased, and the quench area is reduced to improve combustion.*

6 *Due to years of operation (even normal use), the cylinder walls will become slightly misshapen. If the engine has not been properly maintained, there can also be scoring on the walls of the cylinders. To correct both of these conditions, the machinist will bore the cylinders. Boring results in an oversized cylinder bore that will likely require larger pistons, but this is routine. After boring, the cylinders are honed to the final size and finish.*

7 *Line-honing the main bearing journals is a common procedure to restore the shape and alignment of the crankshaft bearing journals.*

8 *The piston pin is an interference fit, so it is critical that the pin is between 0.001 and 0.0015 inch larger than the bore. This allows the pin to securely retain the piston to the rod and allow proper movement of the piston as it travels up and down the cylinder.*

9 *Connecting rod reconditioning (if needed) begins with removal of the cap bolts and deburring the oil passage and the parting surfaces of the rod and cap. The machinist will use a cap cutter to remove a small amount of material (0.001 to 0.002 inch) from both the rod and the cap.*

10 *With the bolts installed and the cap torqued in place, the crankshaft journal hole, or the "big hole," is honed to restore the correct diameter of the bore. The pin bore is honed on the same equipment.*

11 *A rod heater is used to heat the connecting rod so that the piston pin can be easily inserted through the piston and the pin bore in the rod. Heating the rod prevents damage to any of the components that might occur if extra force has to be applied.*

The machine shop usually starts with the crankshaft. Everything else is dependent on the crankshaft, so it is usually completed first.

Bearing Journals

While it's technically an inspection, the first step is to measure the main and connecting rod journals to determine if they can just be polished, or if they need to be ground to an undersize. Some conditions that require grinding are grooves (normally caused by contaminants or a lack of maintenance) and excessive wear due to age.

If grooves are present, they will adversely affect oil flow control and must be ground out. If there is excessive wear, which is normally due to age, the journals will need to be ground to the next undersize that has an available undersize bearing. Undersized bearings are actually thicker than stock bearings and available in increments of 0.010 inch. This makes it possible to grind the crankshaft journals and retain the same clearance to the main or connecting rod caps and the block.

After the crankshaft is ground, the machinist will ensure that the oil passage holes are properly chamfered. This allows proper oil flow and protects the bearing from sharp edges that can lead to premature failure.

Tapping Threads

An easy step to overlook is checking and tapping the threads for the flexplate and harmonic balancer. The flexplate bolt holes are through holes, so they just need to be tapped for ease of reassembly. The balancer bolt hole is blind. This means that it does not go all the way through. Like some bolt holes in the block, it is possible to have debris in the bottom of the hole that can lead to issues when installing the balancer.

Crankshaft Keyway

While the likelihood of occurrence is low, the machinist should check the crankshaft snout and the keyway for excessive wear. The potential risk is that a loose balancer can cause metal-to-metal wear that can lead to catastrophic failure of the crankshaft. You don't want the balancer separating from the crankshaft at highway speed.

Connecting Rods

The connecting rods on the Ford small sixes are generally strong enough for all but the most extreme (turbocharged or blown) builds. It is still important to have them checked and prepared before reusing the original rods. Replacements are difficult to find, but fortunately after the following operations, your originals should be ready to go.

Flatness

The first thing to check on the connecting rods is flatness. Laying them on a table is not the way to check. If the rod is not flat, it is bent or twisted. Your machinist should determine why that happened, and you will definitely need a new rod.

Piston Pin

The next step is verifying the pin bore and pin interference fit. The pin bore should be 0.001 to 0.0015 inch smaller than the diameter of the pin. If it is too loose, the pin could come out during operation. This will result in a lot of noise at the very least and engine damage at the worst. If the pin is too tight, damage can occur when installing the pin through the rod.

Reconditioning Rod Bores

The connecting rods may need to be reconditioned on the crankshaft bore end. Reconditioning starts with removing the bolts, deburring the thrust faces, deburring the area where the cap contacts the connecting rod, and checking the condition of the oil passage chamfers. Then, the machinist will use special equipment called a cap cutter to remove material from both the rod and cap parting surfaces (usually just 0.001 to 0.002 inch).

When the new rod bolts are installed and torqued to spec, the resulting bore in the rod and cap assembly will be slightly football shaped. Only the height of the bore is reduced in the process; the width stays the same.

To finish the process, a rod hone restores the bore to the original size and a perfectly round shape.

Piston Pin Installation

When both ends of the rod have been checked and reconditioned as necessary, another special piece of equipment called a rod heater is used to—you guessed it—heat the rod. This makes the pin bore expand enough to allow relatively easy fitment of the pin through the piston and rod. The rod heater also has a feature to allow the machinist to set how far the pin is inserted. This makes it possible for the pins to be consistent from one rod to the next.

It is typical to hone the piston pin bores at the same time as the connecting rod pin bores. This ensures that the components match, and the machine is already set up for the connecting rod pin bore, anyway.

Balance and Blueprint

Most car enthusiasts have heard the phrase "balanced and blueprinted," but what does it really mean?

The first part is pretty easy. In fact, I discuss balancing the various components of the engine in this chapter. Balancing the weight of the reciprocating parts of the engine helps to ensure a smooth-running engine. Smooth-running engines are more enjoyable to drive, but perhaps more importantly, they can last longer due to a lack of vibration. (Read this chapter to learn which engine components get balanced and how the machine shop does it.)

Blueprinting is more difficult to understand. Once you learn what is involved in truly blueprinting the engine, the next time you hear that phrase, you can just smile knowingly and let them have their moment.

The term blueprinting refers more to the measurements of the engine and the components. For example, the rods can all be balanced by weighing and equalizing the weights. However, blueprinted rods are precisely checked for length, among other things. The block can be blueprinted as well. The bores are designed to have their centerlines at exact locations, but due to manufacturing processes, they could be very slightly out of position. If the engine is truly blueprinted, the cylinder that is off will be sleeved and re-bored. This is not done with your typical rebuild. Every dimension, from the block to the rocker arms, is precisely measured and corrected or replaced. Blueprinting is a very expensive process, so you can imagine that it is reserved for the most expensive and powerful engines in racing and not your average street build.

By all means, have your engine components balanced. That is a benefit we can all enjoy. ■

Balancing the Engine

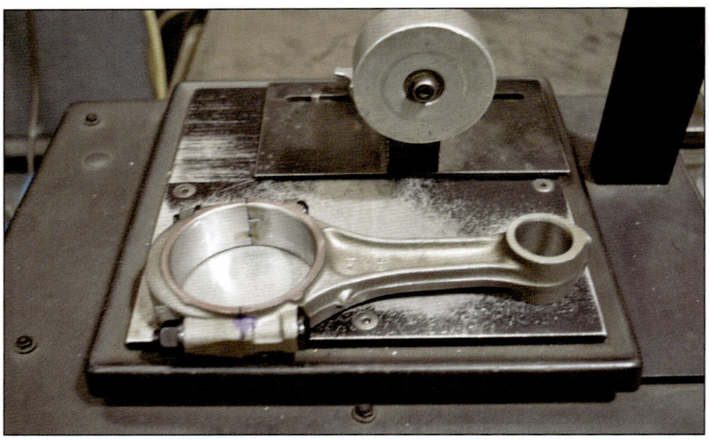

1 ***The balancing process begins by weighing the components of the reciprocating assembly: the connecting rod, piston, pin, and piston rings. It is often not necessary to weigh the pins and rings because there is no good way to add or remove weight from them. The information is recorded so that the heaviest piston can be matched to the lightest rod etc.***

2 ***Connecting rods are measured at the big end and as a total weight. Small-end weight is calculated by subtracting the big-end weight from the total weight. These weights are used to match to the pistons.***

3 *Some machine shops tell customers that they cannot balance the crankshaft for an inline 6-cylinder. However, if the machine is large enough to hold the crankshaft, the machine shop can balance it. Many big-block crankshafts are as long as the inline 6-cylinder crank.*

4 *The crankshaft is positioned in the balancer supported on the two towers. The towers have sensors that measure the imbalance in the crankshaft as it is rotated by the motor-driven belt. The machine indicates to the machinist where to add or remove weight to balance the crankshaft. This is done with the crankshaft still on the machine.*

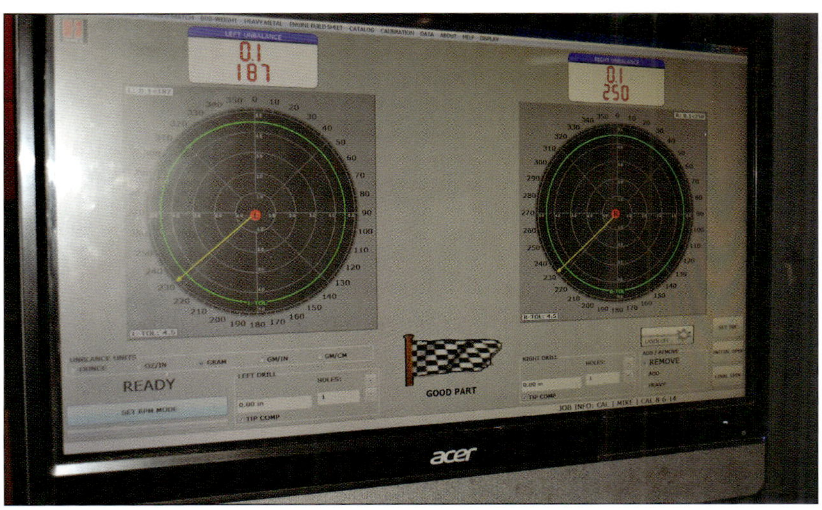

5 *When all of the rotating, checking, and balancing has been performed correctly, the balancer will indicate that the crankshaft is now ready by displaying "Good Part."*

Weight Matching

Balancing the engine begins with weight matching the components of the reciprocating assembly. The reciprocating assembly consists of the rods and pistons, along with the piston pins and the piston rings. The pins and the rings are often not included in the balancing process because you cannot change the weight by grinding off material.

Pistons

The pistons are all weighed, and the information is recorded. The heaviest piston is matched with the lightest rod, and so on, down to the lightest piston with the heaviest rod.

Rods

When done properly, the connecting rod weight is measured in two ways. Measuring the "big end" and recording the information allows the machinist to match all of the rods to the weight of the lightest connecting rod. When the weight of the big end is known, it is subtracted from the total weight of the connecting rod to calculate the weight of the small end.

The balancing act comes when the machinist grinds the correct amount of weight from the big end to get all of the reciprocating assemblies to be the same.

Balancing

The major rotating component of the engine is the crankshaft. If it is not balanced, it can cause vibrations that range from barely perceptible to obvious at most engine speeds. Many owners are told by machine shops that the shop is not equipped to balance an inline 6-cylinder crankshaft. If the shop has a balancer and it is big enough to balance a big-block Ford crankshaft, it is equipped to balance an inline-six crankshaft. The process is actually easier for the shop due to the arrangement of the journals on the crankshaft. Balancing a V-8 crankshaft requires attaching bob weights to do the job. Inline 6-cylinders are naturally arranged to not require bob weights.

The crankshaft balancing process requires a special machine. The crankshaft is mounted on two stands: one at each end of the crankshaft. The crankshaft is spun by a belt toward the center of the crank. The stands on the machine contain delicate sensors that detect imbalance in the crankshaft. After the crankshaft is spun up, the machine indicates where the machinist is to remove or add weight to the crankshaft. It indicates at what angle of the crankshaft and how far from each end. This is done with the crankshaft still mounted on the machine. Then the crankshaft is measured a final time to confirm the balance. Many machinists will repolish the crankshaft end journals where they rode on the stands, although this is not critical.

Block Machining

The first step is decking the block.

Decking the Block

In cases where the static compression ratio needs to be raised, zero-decking the block is an efficient method to increase compression because the whole area of the cylinder bore is milled at once, as opposed to milling the head, which only removes material from the area of the combustion chamber. *Zero* refers to the amount of space between the top of the piston and block deck.

The other effect of zero-decking is improved combustion due to the reduction in the quench area. Reducing the quench area lessens the variation from cylinder to cylinder of the flame activity and causes it to occur in a shorter amount of time. Increasing the quench area has the opposite effect; the flame is slowed down and activity is spread across a larger area.

On the 200-ci engine, many builders choose to zero-deck the block. This is possible on the 200 because the piston does not come all the way to the top of the cylinder bore, but it comes close. It is possible to slightly increase the static compression ratio by decking the block.

On the 250, the piston does not come up as high, so it is not advised to zero-deck the block because too much material would need to be removed. For the 250, pistons are available that slightly increase the compression ratio.

Head Gasket Surface

The machinist will machine the head gasket surface so that the final roughness is suitable for proper sealing with the head gasket. The unit of measurement is the roughness average (Ra). Ra is measured with a profilometer, which is a very expensive tool, and some shops may not have one. The number for the measurement is given in microinches (a millionth of an inch). For a cast-iron head, the block and head should have an Ra of 60 to 80. An aluminum head should have a 50 to 60 Ra.

Boring the Cylinders

The cylinders of most engines of this age will need to be bored. Some can get by with a light honing procedure to restore the correct crosshatch pattern that allows the piston rings to function as designed. Worn engines tend to have smooth cylinder walls that hinder the operation of the piston rings. Engines that have experienced some type of damage or an extreme lack of maintenance can have scoring in the cylinder walls. If the scoring is too deep, it may be necessary to sleeve the cylinder.

Sleeving involves machining the cylinder to accept a cylindrical sleeve that restores the original size of the cylinder and can be machined to match the remaining cylinders. To determine what work is necessary, the experienced machinist will perform a visual inspection and take measurements of the cylinder bore diameter. Since piston motion is repeatable with every power stroke, the most important measurement is at the top of the bore and below the ridge formed by years of piston-to-wall wear. This measurement will determine if the cylinder can be bored enough to correct any imperfections.

Another rule of thumb is to measure the taper, which is the difference in diameter of the cylinder from the top to the bottom. To calculate how much overbore is needed, double the taper amount. For example, if the taper is 0.014 inch, double that, and you get 0.028 inch. The next available piston size is 0.030-inch oversize. The cylinder will be bored to within 0.003 to 0.005 inch of that number to leave material for the final honing.

On the small-six engine, most builders are very comfortable with a 0.030-inch overbore. Even 0.040 inch is generally no problem. This engine can be over-bored to 0.060 inch when the conditions warrant it, but this will likely be the last time it can be bored. Generally, it is not advised to go beyond 0.060 inch. There may be builders who say they have gone more and the engine survived, but the advice we give is to save you from potential grief later.

Tapping All Bolt Holes

This is a good time for the machinist to tap all bolt holes to ensure that there is no debris inside and that all of the threads are in good condition so the reassembly will go smoothly. If debris is left in the bottom of a bolt hole, it is possible to get false torque readings that will cause the attached part to not fully engage the block. This can lead to failure due to vibration and movement that is not supposed to occur.

Align-Hone the Main Journals

In some cases, the main bearing journals and the cam bearing journals may need to be align-bored or align-honed. The difference in the two processes is the amount of material that can be efficiently removed. Many times, if it is needed, align-honing is sufficient to return the alignment of the journals to original.

Align-honing may be necessary if the engine has been subjected to hard usage or if it has overheated. Another reason for align-honing is to repair damage caused by damaged bearings. It is also necessary to align-hone the main bearings when main cap studs are used in place of main cap bolts. The added clamping force of the studs may cause changes to the shape of the bore for the crankshaft journal.

Before align-honing is performed, the main caps need to be de-burred, and the face of each cap needs to be machined where it contacts the engine block. Normally, 0.003 inch is sufficient. If there is damage due to a spun bearing or a main bearing cap is being replaced, align-boring is required.

Block Cleaning

When all machine work has been completed on the block, the block must be thoroughly cleaned. The machinist must ensure that all oil passages are clean by running brushes through them and flushing them. Proper cylinder cleaning consists of scrubbing the block, including the area under the cylinder facing the crankshaft, with hot, soapy water. The importance of cleaning the block cannot be overstated. It is said that engines will forgive slight variations in crosshatch or cylinder roughness, but no engine will tolerate dirt.

Honing the cylinder walls leaves two types of debris: honing stone residue and cast-iron dust. Think of these as the best lapping compound in the world waiting to ruin all of your expensive machine work. To clean the block, the machinist should rinse with hot water, dry the block, and apply a light coating of oil to prevent rust. Your machine shop should do all of this before returning the engine to you.

Camshaft Bearings and Core Plugs

Camshaft bearing bores sometimes need align-honing as well, but not nearly as frequently as the main bearings.

The camshaft bearings must be inserted in the correct order. The small six has four bearings, and the smallest are in the back. With the largest in front, it is possible to insert the camshaft. There are oil-passage holes that must be aligned properly as well. A special tool is required to install the camshaft bearings.

Core plugs and threaded plugs are the last parts to be installed during the block machining process. There are special tools to install the core plugs, but a properly-sized socket can be used in a pinch. A light film of sealer applied to the contact surface helps sealing in the case of imperfections in the block casting.

Finally, the shop may decide to clean the oil from the exterior surfaces and apply a coat of primer to further protect the block from beginning to rust.

TECH TIP

Cylinder Bore Finish

Cylinder bore finish is very important in terms of how well the piston rings will function and how long the engine will last. The main consideration is the crosshatch angle. The crosshatch results from the final honing process that establishes the final surface on which the piston will travel up and down. The correct angle for the crosshatch is 45 degrees. The angle is controlled by how fast the hone turns and how fast the machinist moves the hone up and down the cylinder wall.

If the machinist moves the hone too fast, the angle will be too steep, and oil can run down the cylinder wall faster than it should. This results in not enough oil on the walls and leads to the rings scuffing the cylinder walls.

If the hone is moved too slowly, the angle will be flat and have the opposite effect on oil retention. Oil does not run down quickly enough. This leaves an oil film on the cylinder wall that can cause the piston rings to hydroplane and not seal properly. If this happens, excess oil consumption is the most likely consequence. ■

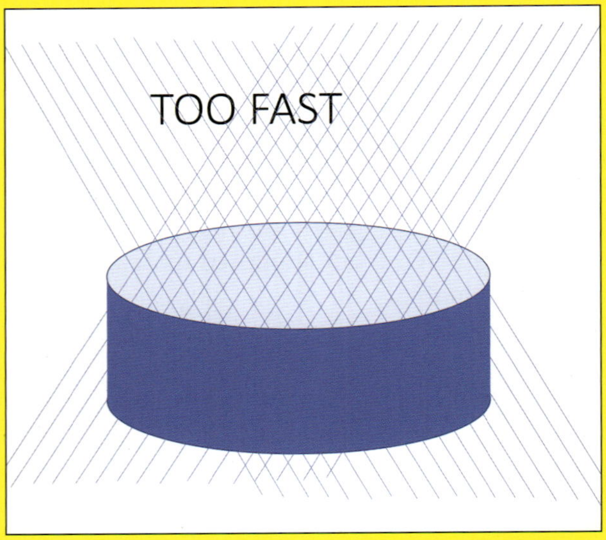

If the machinist moves the hone up and down too fast, the crosshatch pattern will be too steep. In this case, the oil may not stay on the cylinder wall as well as it should, and the cylinder can experience higher-than-normal wear.

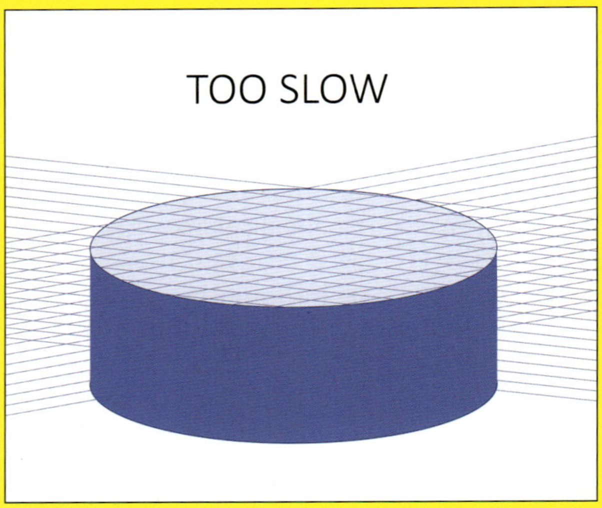

If the machinist moves the hone too slowly, the crosshatch pattern will be too shallow. If the pattern is too shallow, the oil will not be removed from the wall quickly enough and cause the rings to not seal properly.

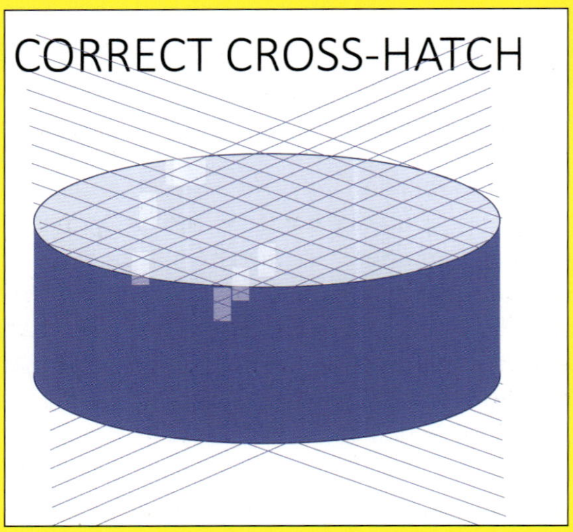

A properly honed cylinder wall has a crosshatch pattern that is nearly at a 45-degree angle. The correct angle is achieved by turning the hone at the correct speed and moving the hone up and down at the correct corresponding speed.

Like the main bearing journals, the camshaft bearing journals occasionally need to be align-honed. It is not nearly as common as crankshaft honing. In fact, replacing the cam bearings in a small-six Ford is usually a simple matter of installing new stock-size bearings.

Cylinder Head Machining and Assembly

The cylinder head is a crucial component in regard to how well your rebuilt engine will perform. Even a stock rebuild must be done correctly to ensure smooth operation, optimum performance, and long-term reliability. The machining process is critical to make sure all valves operate and perform evenly. Uneven assembly can cause unbalanced performance that can lead to rough operating and uneven wear.

Machining

As stated in the previous chapter, the cylinder head is a component comprised of many smaller components. Next to the block, no other part of the engine receives as much attention as the head. A properly rebuilt head will provide years of dependable service. An old adage said that you can put a new head on an old block, but you should not put an old head on a new block. So, if you are rebuilding the engine block, you should definitely have the head rebuilt as well.

Valve Guides

Before beginning the work on the guides in the head, determine the size of the valve stems to be used. Stems on new valves may be slightly different than the original stock valves. This is no problem, but the exact size of the stem needs to be known to accurately hone the new guides. If the size is not correctly measured, issues with the valve seat may occur in addition to increasing the likelihood of excessive oil consumption and premature wear.

Proper installation of replacement valve guides is critical to establish the baseline for all other machining operations related to the valves. (The inspection process has been previously discussed.) If new valve guides are needed, the process begins on a guide and seat machine. This machine allows the machinist to accurately bore and hone the original valve guide to accept the new guide, which is usually made from bronze or steel.

After boring and honing the valve-guide hole, the guide is installed with a guide driver. Once the guides are correctly installed, they must be honed to precisely fit the valve

Cylinder-head machining starts with the valve guides. The guides must be straight and correctly sized. The valve guides in an original cast-iron head are drilled into the casting. If the valve guides need to be replaced due to excessive wear, the machinist will drill out the old guide and install a new guide.

The new valve guides are placed in the head and installed with a valve guide driver. The valve driver tool may be pneumatically operated, or the machinist may use a mallet to drive in the guides. In either case, the correct alignment of the guides is critical because the rest of the valve operations are dependent on the guide.

Knurling the Valve Guides

TECH TIP

There is a process called knurling the valve guides. Most of us are familiar with the term *knurled*. It means there is a relatively deep crosshatch pattern in something like an air cleaner hold-down nut to provide grip.

In the case of the valve guides, the inside of the guide is knurled, which forces some material up, decreasing the diameter of the guide. Then, the knurled surface can be reamed to the original diameter. For a stock rebuild, this process is acceptable. The knurling even helps the guide retain some engine oil in between shut down and restart to extend the life of the guide and the valve stem. On engines with a performance camshaft, knurling is not recommended. New performance valve guides are recommended to handle the pressure and side loading on the valve. ■

stems. Stem-to-guide clearance specifications are 0.001 to 0.0015 inch for the intake valves and 0.0015 to 0.002 inch for the exhaust valves. Remember, due to the extreme heat, the components of the exhaust valvetrain will experience more expansion than the intake valves. For this reason, it is not unusual to see exhaust valve stems that are 0.0005 inch thinner than intake valves from the same company. This needs to be accounted for when establishing guide clearance.

Valve Seats

The valve seats can be replaced (if needed) after the valve guides are installed. Properly installed guides make it possible to accurately install new seats or to grind the valve seats. If the valve size doesn't change and the intake valve seats are in serviceable condition, it is not necessary to install a new valve seat.

On vehicles built after 1974, the exhaust valve seats are hardened for use with unleaded fuel and therefore do not have to be replaced if they can be ground and the size of the valve is not changed.

On heads made before 1974, the exhaust valve seats should be replaced with hardened seats. If the seats are being replaced, the seat size is chosen based on the valve size. The original seat is counterbored, and the new seat is installed with a seat driver and a hammer.

The new seats are then cut to size, and the valve job is performed. The term *valve job* refers to the process of grinding the seat and the valve to make sure the valve properly sits in the seat and that the flow characteristics are correct.

For a stock valve job, the angle on the seat of the valve contact point is ground to 44 degrees. Generally,

Like the original valve guides, the original valve seats were cast into the head. If the seats are in good condition, the machinist can do the valve job without replacing the seats. On heads made before 1974, the exhaust seats are not hardened, so it is always a good idea to install hardened seats on older heads.

The original valve seat is countersunk, and the new seat is driven into the head. Measurements must be made to ensure the correct seat diameter is used and that the new seat does not go so deep or wide that it intrudes into the cooling passages of the head.

Years ago, valve jobs were done with grinding stones and the valve guide was used as an index. The valve guide is still used to align the tool for cutting the seat, but machine shops have been cutting the seat surface rather than grinding for a while now. All of the angles can be cut at the same time to result in more consistent valve jobs than they could get from grinding individual angles.

Positive valve stem seals have become popular and are recommended when rebuilding the head on a Ford small six. To install the positive seal, the machinist will cut the top of the valve guide to create the correct diameter for the guide to seat on. The same cutter can be used to cut the spring seat in case aftermarket springs are being used.

this is the only angle cut in the seat for stock valve jobs.

A traditional performance valve job, called a three-angle valve job, uses a 45-degree angle at the contact point. A 30-degree cut is made on the combustion chamber side to help with flow out of the intake valve and into the exhaust valve. For the same reason, a 60-degree cut is made on the bowl side of the seat. The combination of a 30- to 45- to 60-degree angle provides a gradual, somewhat-rounded, path for gases to follow.

Specialized equipment is required to resurface the head-gasket surface on the cylinder head. The surface must not only be flat but it must also have the correct roughness average (Ra) to allow the gasket to properly seal.

These days, a performance valve job typically involves more angles for even better flow characteristics. The contact angle is still 45 degrees for the intake and exhaust valves. The intake seat may have a topping angle that is very shallow, then typically 35-, 45-, and 57-degree angles. Increments of 7 to 10 degrees are common.

On the exhaust side, a good performance valve job has what is known as a *radiused* seat. A single cutter is used instead of individual stones for each angle. The cutter has even more distinct angles, but they are very gradual, and for all intents and purposes, they form a radius rather than a series of angles.

As for the valves themselves, it is common practice to grind the valve-seating surface to confirm the correct angle and to remove any marks that may have occurred during handling.

Another operation that may be done to intake valves is known as *back-cutting* the valves. This improves airflow by creating another angle that performs the same way as the angles on the valve seat.

Positive Valve Stem Seals

Original, umbrella-style valve stem seals are not very effective. They tend to pick a spot on the valve and ride up and down as the valve moves. The term umbrella is used because they block some of the

The exhaust manifold gasket area should also be resurfaced. Over time, the exhaust manifold gasket surface becomes pitted and can even warp due to the heat and corrosive gases. Resurfacing this area means that a new gasket will seal the surface even better than when it was new, considering that Ford did not install a gasket on the early engines.

When the machinist cc's the chambers, the volume of each combustion chamber is measured in cubic centimeters. To do this, they seal off the chamber and measure how much liquid it takes to fill the chamber. When all values are known, the machinist can mill the head until the chambers are roughly equal to the smallest chamber. This process helps to get the compression ratio consistent through all the cylinders.

TECH TIP

Bolt Hole Repair

Occasionally, bolts holes are so damaged that it is necessary to repair them. In many cases, the repair is no more complicated than running a tap through the threads to restore minor cross-threading damage.

If the threads are too badly damaged for that, it may be possible to fix it with a Heli-Coil. This is the brand name commonly used as the generic name for the product that is designed to restore badly damaged threads.

The process involves drilling the hole to a larger diameter and tapping it to establish threads. Next, a special insert with external and internal threads is threaded into the new hole. Everything is sized so that the internal threads are the correct size for the hole being repaired. This type of repair is used for thermostat-housing bolt holes.

In the worst-case scenario, a piece of the casting around the bolt hole is broken off. This happens frequently on the cylinder head at the front and rear exhaust manifold bolt holes. In this case, the area has to be built back up, most effectively by brazing the missing area with brass or a similar material. The area can then be shaped, drilled, and tapped to restore the bolt hole. Care must be taken to get the hole located as close to the original as possible. In the case of the exhaust manifold, the holes in the manifold are slightly oversized, so there is a slight amount of room for error. ■

Bolt-hole repair is typical for these old engines. The degree of work needed ranges from simply running a tap through the threads, installing a Heli-Coil, or building up the area and reshaping before drilling and tapping new threads in severe cases.

oil that splashes around. They are included with many engine gasket sets. A much better alternative is the positive seal, which requires cutting the valve guide to accept the seal. The seals remain locked in place on the top of the guide. The same cutter that cuts the guide for the positive seal will also cut the valve spring seat to accept aftermarket springs. Not everyone chooses positive valve stem seals, but if you are given the option, they are highly recommended.

The machinist will check the pressure of each spring to make sure they are all consistent within a few pounds. Old springs will weaken over time, so be prepared if the machinist recommends a new spring. The height at which the springs are checked is not critical, but they all need to be checked at the same height.

Resurface Head Gasket Surface

After the other machining operations are done, the head gasket surface should be resurfaced. This cleans up any minor nicks or damage and leaves a suitable surface for the head gasket to seal with. Similar to the cylinder block, the machinist will leave a finished surface with the correct Ra, or smoothness, for the type of material used.

Resurface Exhaust Manifold Gasket Surface

The exhaust manifold gasket should also be resurfaced at this time. Like all other components that come in contact with exhaust gases, the cylinder-head gasket surface tends to fare poorly through the years due to the heat and corrosive gases. Resurfacing this area makes it possible to obtain a good seal at the exhaust manifold or header.

As with the block, the last step in the cylinder-head machining process before assembly can begin is to wash the cylinder head with hot, soapy water to remove shavings and debris. Cleaning also removes unwanted oils and lubricants left from other operations. Dry the head with compressed air to help prevent rust from forming.

Assembly

The first step in assembly of the cylinder head is to make sure that you have a clean work area. Clean up the dirt, old grease, and any other possible debris or contaminants, and remove anything from the area that will get in the way. The cylinder head is very heavy and severe injury is possible if you drop it. Minimize

CC'ing the Chambers

You may hear the phrase "cc'ing the chambers." This describes the process of measuring the volume of all the combustion chambers in cubic centimeters (cc) and then milling the gasket surface of the head to bring all of the chambers as close to the size of the smallest chamber as possible. It is important that the volume of all cylinders is as consistent as possible. Any cylinder not matched to the rest will have a different compression ratio and can cause engine issues.

The only special tool needed to cc the chambers is a piece of Plexiglas appropriately sized to cover the combustion chamber. Drill a hole in a corner of the Plexiglas and chamfer the top surface of the hole.

To measure the volume, flip the head over so that the chambers are up and as level as possible. Coat the seating surface of the valve with petroleum jelly and place the valves in the valve guides. The petroleum jelly will seal the chamber during measurement. Put petroleum jelly in a complete ring around the combustion chamber to seal the Plexiglas.

Fill a syringe with precisely 100 cc's of a fluid, such as transmission fluid. Inject the fluid into the chamber through the hole in the Plexiglas until the chamber is full and not overflowing. Read the amount of fluid left in the syringe. Subtract this from 100, and you will have the volume of fluid that it took to fill the chamber.

Note the volume and measure the rest of the chambers in the same manner. Give these measurements to the machinist, and he or she will size the chambers accordingly. ■

the risk by giving yourself plenty of room to work.

Valve Spring Pressure Test

You probably do not have a valve spring pressure tester, so make sure that the machine shop checks the springs to ensure that the pressures are the same (within a few pounds). This can be done at any height, but all the valves must be the same height. It is especially important to check used springs because they are more likely to weaken over time.

Organization

A bit of good advice is to lay out all the parts in the order they will be needed. Clean the valves, springs, retainers, and keepers to remove shipping coatings and any other contaminants that might be on them. Count the parts to make sure you have the right number of parts. Verifying that you have all the parts on hand will prevent potential frustration if you have to stop during the process to dig through your boxes.

Valve Tip Height

Without using oil, insert the valves in the head. Check the tip heights and make sure they are all within specification (1.800 to 1.840 inch). The valve stem tip height is crucial to getting the correct valve-

Insert the valves into the head with no oil. Check the tip height of the valve. The tip should be at 1.800 to 1.840 inch above the spring seat surface. This measurement is important because it is part of the valvetrain geometry. Correct, consistent geometry helps provide even power in each cylinder.

Install the retainer and the keepers. Measure the distance from the spring seat on the head to the spring seat on the retainer. This is done with a spring height gauge, or if the appropriate gauge is not available, a telescoping gauge can be substituted. This distance is the spring installed height.

Put the spring in the pressure tester and compress it to the installed height. Measure the pressure. This is the spring's closed pressure (the pressure when the valve is closed).

After all the spring heights and pressures are measured and verified, remove all of the valves and keep them in order. Oil the valve stem and the valve face.

train geometry. If the tip height is too short, it can be corrected by cutting the seat deeper or getting a longer valve. It is much easier to recut the seat than to get a longer valve. The seat can only be cut a certain amount; otherwise, you run the risk of shrouding the valve face.

If the tip height is too long, it is easier to fix. Butt the valve stem tip to shorten it. That is a fancy word for grinding the tip.

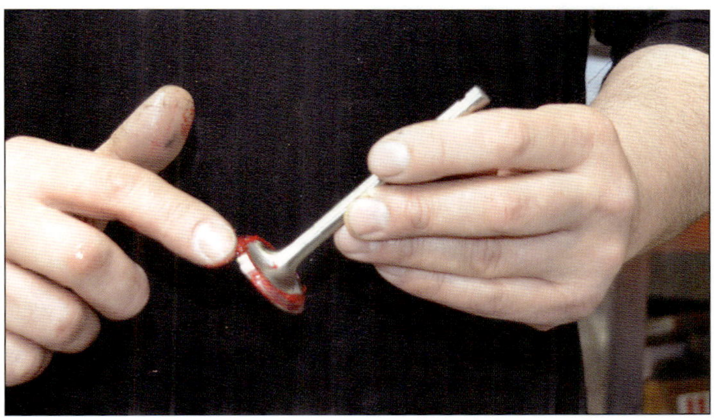

If the engine will not be started in the near future, apply grease to the valve contact area to prevent rust.

Spring Installed Height

Check the installed height of the springs using a telescoping gauge (or preferably a spring height gauge) with retainers and keepers installed on the valve in the head. The gauge goes in place of the spring. Measure the distance from the spring seat on the head to the spring seat of the retainer. Now, put the spring in the pressure tester and (at the previously measured height) measure the closed spring pressure.

Spring Open Pressure

The camshaft lobe lift is provided by the manufacturer. Valve lift is the lobe lift with the rocker-arm ratio (stock is 1.5:1) considered. Multiply the lobe lift by the rocker-arm ratio to get the valve lift. Compress the spring this distance more than the closed spring pressure to get the spring open pressure.

These numbers are used to make sure that you are in the range required by the camshaft manufacturer or that you are in the stock range.

If the pressures are too high, it will result in premature wear due to the extra pressure of the lifter on the cam lobe. If the pressure is too low, valve float will occur at high RPM because the spring will not close the valve quickly enough.

Coil Bind

Next, check for coil bind. Start at the open height and compress the spring to coil bind. Subtract the height at bind from the open height. The minimum for this measurement is 0.100 inch.

Confirm that the valve spring retainer will not come into contact with the valve stem seal and damage the seal. With the retainer and keepers in place (no spring), measure the distance from the bottom of the retainer to the top of the valve guide. Compare this distance to the valve lift distance. A safe value is 0.100 inch more distance than the valve lift.

Insert Valves

If everything checks out, pull out the valves and oil the guides and valve stems. Keep the valves in order! Put grease or oil on the valve face to prevent rust. Install the valves back in the same locations and install the seals. If you are using positive seals and the seal fits through the shims (if needed), the installation order does not matter. If the seal does not fit through the shim, install the shim first and then the seal.

Install the shims now if they are needed based on the open or closed spring pressure readings. The shims balance the pressures on all of the springs for consistent performance.

Install Springs

Install the springs and retainers and compress the spring with a spring compressor. Follow the tool manufacturer's instructions. Install the keepers and ensure they are properly seated. Release the spring compressor. Repeat the process on the remaining springs.

Visually inspect all of the keepers for proper seating in the retainers and use the spring compressor to reinstall any keepers found to not be seated properly. As a last check, lightly rap the valve stem tip with a plastic-faced hammer to seat all of the components.

Finally, install the core plugs and the threaded plugs with sealer.

Finish the valve assembly process by inserting a valve retainer in the spring. Then, compress the spring. Carefully insert the keepers to lock the retainer in place. The spring pressure holds the retainer against the keepers for a strong lock.

Finish the cylinder-head assembly process by installing the core plugs and threaded plugs. Apply sealer to prevent vacuum leaks.

Assembly

Obviously, assembly is the reverse of disassembly. So far, you developed a perfect plan, found the best machine shop to do the highest-quality work, and purchased all of the finest parts. Every step up to this point has been equally important in a successful rebuild. Do not let down your guard now that you are on the home stretch!

There are many good brands of assembly lube on the market, but you probably will not find them at your local parts store. You can readily purchase them online, but you should plan ahead. A good engine-assembly lubricant will cling to engine parts during assembly and dissolve in engine oil when the engine is eventually run.

Now that you have all of the pieces back from the machine shop, it's time to execute the final part of the plan. Before you begin, perform some housekeeping to make sure that the reassembly goes smoothly.

Clean up the area where you are going to work. Seriously. Besides being a safety hazard, a disorganized and dirty work area is the downfall of the rebuild. Professional engine builders have a clean room, where the reassembly of each engine is performed. Clean rooms are not used for any other purpose than engine reassembly. They are kept meticulously clean because dirt, debris, and foreign objects can ruin an engine before it ever gets started.

While you probably cannot convert your guest bedroom into a clean room, you can take extra measures to clean the area you are going to use for the rebuild. If you are fortunate enough to have dedicated garage or shop space, fantastic! Use it to your advantage, but make sure it is as clean as you can get it before you bring your freshly machined parts home.

Be aware of how much wind from fans can stir up dust and debris in your shop. This can certainly be minimized by a thorough cleaning. If you have to do other work in the assembly area while the rebuild is in process, be sure to cover all of your parts to avoid getting them dirty.

A lot of parts came out, and a lot of parts have to go back in. If you pile them all up, it looks intimidating. However, if you follow the steps and take out parts as you need them, it is not too bad.

Cleanliness is very important. You may not have a clean room in your garage or shop, but make every effort to work in the cleanest environment that you can.

Begin the reassembly by installing the camshaft. The camshaft has to withstand incredible friction until the engine is running and the cam gets broken in. Be sure to properly lubricate the cam before installing it in the engine.

Remember, oil filters are designed to remove the smallest of particles from the engine oil to prevent them from getting into bearing surfaces and causing premature wear. If you are not careful, you can install the bearings with these contaminants in place and start the wear process immediately. Have we stressed the importance of cleanliness enough?

Engine Stand

Carefully follow the engine stand manufacturer's instructions and reinstall the block on the engine stand. Reassembly is not as sloppy as disassembly. However, take care during assembly to avoid spilling fluids that could cause a potential slip or fall.

Short-Block

The short-block is the part of the engine that you expect to last the longest. There is no routine or scheduled maintenance for the engine internals. For this reason, it is important to take your time and assemble everything very carefully.

Camshaft

Begin the reassembly by installing the camshaft. Coat the cam lobes and bearing journals liberally with assembly lube. Very carefully insert the camshaft into the block. Take extra care to not nick any of the lobes or journals. Once the camshaft is inserted in the engine block, install the thrust plate and torque the bolts to specification: 12 to 15 ft-lbs.

Tools for Engine Reassembly

The tools needed for reassembly are the same as for disassembly. Do not attempt to reassemble the engine without torque wrenches. As a refresher, here is a simplified list of the tools detailed in chapter 3:

- 3/8- and 1/2-inch-drive torque wrenches
- 1/4-, 3/8-, and 1/2-inch ratchet and socket sets (deep) and extensions
- Spark plug socket
- 1/2-inch ratchet/breaker bar (crank damper bolt: 13/16 inch; head bolts: 11/16 inch)
- Combination wrench set (5/16–5/8 inch)
- 1/2-inch distributor wrench
- Magnetic pickup tool
- Crankshaft damper remover/installer (rental)
- Piston ring compressor (rental)

Crankshaft Installation

1 *Before placing the crankshaft in the block, install the upper bearing halves for the main bearings. Do not lubricate the backside of the bearing.*

2 *The thrust bearing must be placed in the right location. On a four-main engine, it goes on the number-3 main bearing. On a seven-main engine, put the thrust bearing on the number-5 journal.*

3 *Install the upper half of the rear main seal. Instead of placing the seal flush to the block, rotate it slightly so that about 1/4 inch sticks up on one side. This helps avoid leaks by not lining up all of the seams of the seal and the rear main cap.*

4 *Carefully place the crankshaft in the block and onto the upper bearing halves. Since the crankshaft rides on a thin layer of oil, very little effort is required to rotate the shaft. Test frequently to make sure it spins easily.*

5 *If you have chosen to use main bearing studs, thread them into the block now. Follow the instructions provided with the stud kit. Be sure to apply any lubricant provided by or recommended by the manufacturer.*

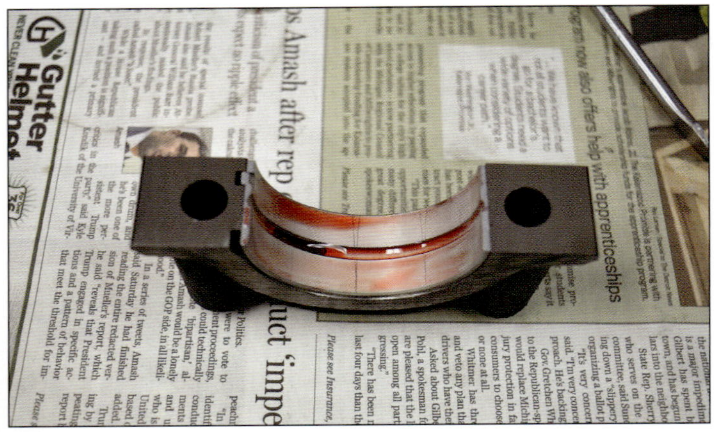

6 *Place a bearing half into one of the main bearing caps. As with the upper half, do not lube the backside of the bearing. After it is in the cap, apply lube to the surface that faces the journal. Place the cap on the crankshaft. If you are using bolts, tighten them finger tight.*

7 *Repeat for the remaining caps and do not forget to put the thrust bearing in the right place. Remember to spin the crankshaft frequently to make sure that there is no interference and it spins freely.*

8 *Torque the bolts to the Ford specification of 65 to 70 ft-lbs in three steps. There is no specified order to tighten the caps, but the cap with the thrust bearing is torqued last. Do not tighten the last cap until after crankshaft endplay is checked. Keep test spinning at each step.*

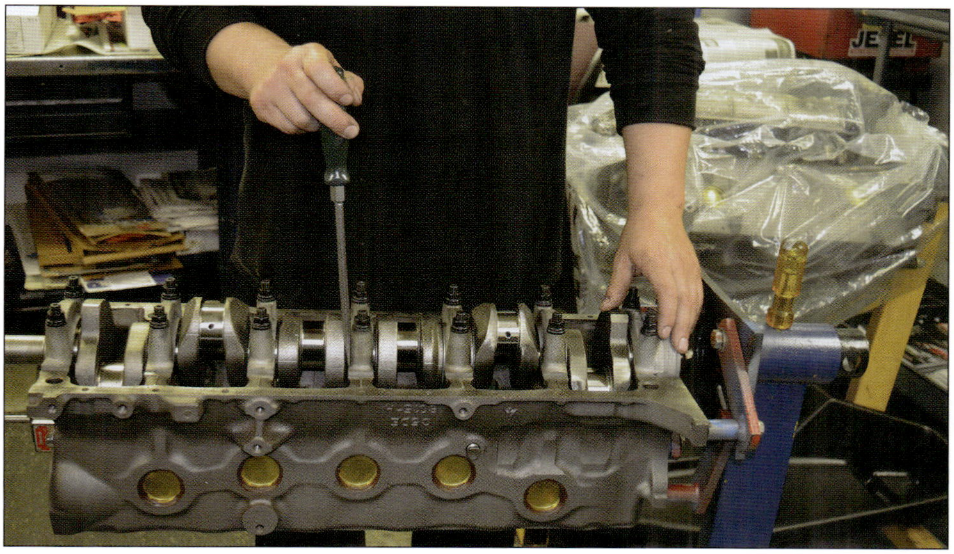

9 *The thrust bearing is used to keep the crankshaft from moving back and forth in the engine. Do not be tempted to skip checking the crankshaft endplay. Excessive endplay can damage parts from the harmonic balancer to internal transmission parts. Align the upper and lower thrust bearing halves by gently prying the crankshaft forward from the rear of the engine. Next, pry from the front of the engine toward the rear. Torque the cap to specification.*

10 *Check the crankshaft endplay by mounting a dial indicator on the front of the engine with the pointer touching the crank snout. Gently pry the crank back and zero the gauge. Now, pry forward and read how far the crank moved. Movement should be 0.004 to 0.008 inch.*

Bearings

Next is the crankshaft. The upper bearing shells go into the saddles without assembly lube. Do not put any lubrication between the bearing and the block. Bearings are precisely manufactured, and the extra thickness of lubrication will cause slightly more crush than desired. Besides, there is no relative movement between the two surfaces, so it simply is not needed. Once the upper bearing shells are in place, apply engine oil to the surface of the bearing where the crankshaft journals will rest. The thrust bearing looks different from the other bearings and must be installed in the proper location. On a 144 or 170 (or the rare four–main bearing 200), the thrust bearing is in the third main bearing cap. On a 200 or 250, the number-5 main bearing is the thrust bearing.

Rear Main Seal

Install the upper half of the rear main seal and carefully install the crankshaft. Turn the crankshaft frequently to ensure that it turns freely at every stage of the installation process. The crankshaft does not actually rotate on the bearings. When the engine is properly built and running correctly, the crankshaft spins on a thin layer of oil between the journals and the bearing surfaces. For this reason, the turning force required to spin the crankshaft should remain relatively constant during the assembly and torque steps.

Main Bearing Studs

When you planned your build, you decided if you would use new main bearing cap bolts or studs. If you are using studs, install them now. Follow the manufacturer's instructions and install the studs by threading them in almost to the point of bottoming out.

Main Bearing Caps

Install the lower main bearing shells into the bearing caps. As with the upper shells, do not apply assembly lube to the back of the bearing, which is the surface that will contact the main bearing cap. Apply engine oil to the crankshaft journal side of the bearings and install the caps in the correct order from front to rear. Do not forget to spin the crankshaft one turn or so to ensure that it still spins freely.

Insert the main bearing cap bolts, or if using studs, insert the nuts provided with the kit. Torque the main caps in three stages and follow Ford's torque sequence. The torque values of the three stages for main bearing cap bolts are: (1) 40 to 45 ft-lbs, (2) 55 to 60 ft-lbs, and (3) 65 to 70 ft-lbs.

Ford did not specify the order in which to tighten the caps, other than installing the cap with the thrust bearing (for four-main engines, the number-3 cap; and for seven-main engines, the number-5 cap) last.

Torque the bolts by setting the torque wrench to the first setting (40 to 45 ft-lbs) and turning the bolt clockwise with the wrench. Turn the wrench slowly and smoothly as the resistance builds. Be prepared to stop torqueing when the wrench indicates that you have reached the setting. Some wrenches click; digital wrenches have a readout. It is not necessary to click the wrench twice. Spin the crankshaft after each torqueing stage to ensure that it still rotates freely and smoothly.

Thrust Bearing Main Cap

The cap with the thrust bearing is last because you must check the crankshaft endplay. This step is meticulous, and you might be tempted to skip it, but don't. It is very important to a long-lasting engine.

The term *endplay* refers to the amount of movement measured from center in one direction and then in the other direction. As you can imagine, the crankshaft cannot be allowed to move much in either direction. It is the job of the thrust bearing to keep it in place.

First, install the cap bolts finger tight. Using a prybar at the rear of the engine, pry the crankshaft forward. While holding pressure on the crankshaft, pry backward on the main bearing cap. This aligns the upper and lower sections of the thrust bearing. With the pressure still on the crankshaft, tighten the bolts.

To measure the endplay, install a dial indicator on the crankshaft with the pointer parallel to the crankshaft. Pry the crankshaft to the rear of the engine and zero the dial indicator. Pry the crankshaft forward and read the distance it moved. If this measurement exceeds the specification (0.004 to 0.008 inch), the thrust bearing may have to be exchanged. You may also need the machine shop to check all tolerances again.

Piston and Connecting Rod Installation

1 ***Before installing the rings on the pistons, take time to check the ring gap. Place the ring (one at a time) into the cylinder and align it with the top of the piston. Remove the piston and measure the gap with a feeler gauge. A narrow gap can be adjusted by filing. A wide gap will require a replacement ring.***

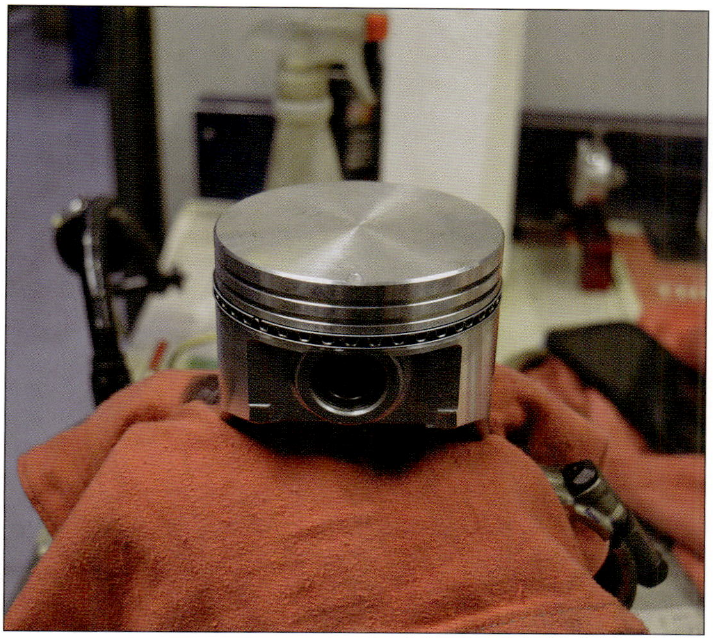

2 *The oil control ring is in three pieces and goes in the lowest groove on the piston. Take care not to scratch the piston and (using two hands) spread the rings and lower them into the groove. Do not twist the rings onto the piston because scratches can occur.*

3 *The lower compression ring goes in the middle groove and is slightly harder to install. Be careful when spreading it, and do not scratch the piston as you put the ring in place.*

4 *The upper compression ring goes on last. The only groove left is the top groove. Carefully spread the ring and lower it into the groove.*

5 *Check the piston-ring side clearance with a feeler gauge in multiple locations around the piston. If the clearance exceeds the specification, the ring will not seal properly. If this is the case, the piston will need to be replaced.*

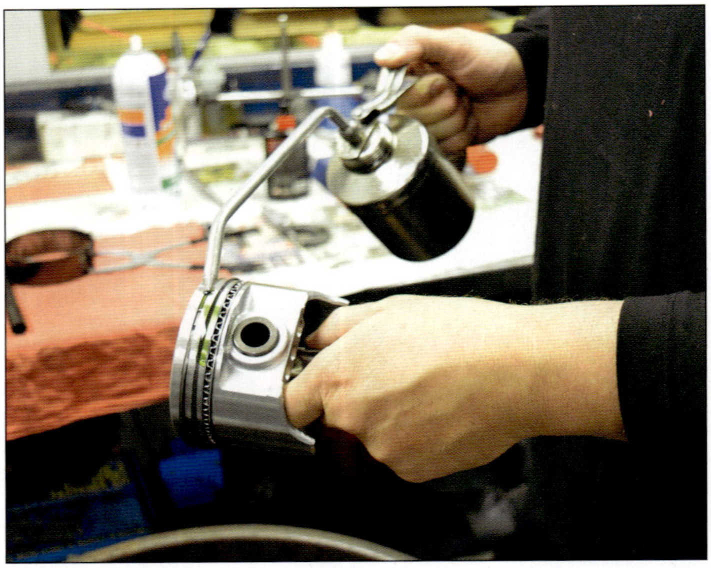

6 ***The piston and rod assemblies are ready to install in the engine. The rods should be stamped to indicate the correct cylinder. Liberally coat the piston skirt and the rings with motor oil before attaching the ring compressor to prevent scratches on the cylinder wall.***

7 ***Note the location of the notch on top of the piston. This notch should be toward the front of the engine.***

The piston pins must be installed with special equipment, so it is best to have the machine shop assemble the pistons to the connecting rod. The tolerance is very tight. The piston pin-to-piston specification is 0.0003 to 0.0005 inch. (See chapter 4 for the steps.)

With the pistons installed on the connecting rods, the piston rings come next. Remember to keep the pistons, connecting rods, and rings together in sets corresponding to the correct cylinder. Before installing the rings, check the gap. This process may seem tedious, but it is critical to get the best performance and longevity from the engine.

Piston ring gap is the term that describes the space between the ends of the rings when the piston is installed in the cylinder. The best way to check the gap is with the ring in the cylinder. Carefully put the ring in the cylinder and use a piston (turned upside down) to evenly position the ring in the bore. Remove the piston, and you will see the gap in the piston ring. Measure the gap with a feeler gauge.

The upper and lower compression rings (the two top rings) should have a gap between 0.020 and 0.030 inch. The oil control ring can have a gap between 0.015 and 0.055 inch. If the gap is too narrow, it can be adjusted with a ring-gap filing tool. If it is too wide, you will most likely need to exchange it.

Installing the rings on the piston involves spreading them out and lowering them onto the piston and down to the appropriate land. The land is the area on the side of the piston above and below each of the ring grooves.

The oil control ring goes on in three pieces in the lowest ring groove. The lower compression ring is in the middle groove, and the upper compression ring is in the top groove.

To install the compression rings, many builders use both hands to spread the ring just far enough to fit over the piston and then lower it into position in the right groove. Take extra care not to scratch the piston lands.

An alternative method (not preferred) is to twist the ring until one end can be inserted in the groove, then expanding the free end and rotating it down into the groove. Some think that this method may leave permanent twist in the ring that could affect its performance over time.

After the rings are installed on the piston, check the side clearance, which is the amount of space between the piston ring and the surface of the land on the piston. Use a feeler gauge to check the clearance around the circumference of the piston. If there are any areas where the measurement exceeds specification, replace the piston. The top compression ring side clearance can vary by year, so refer to the shop manual for exact specifications. The clearance is 0.0019 to 0.0036 inch for the top compression ring and 0.0020 to 0.0040 inch for the bottom compression ring. Ford listed the specification for the oil control ring side clearance as "snug."

Now that the piston and rod assemblies are complete, they can be installed in the block. Be sure to put the pistons in the correct cylinder based on the numbers stamped into the rods and caps. Make sure that the rings are properly spaced around the circumference of the piston. Coat the pistons and rings with engine oil to prevent scratching the cylinder bore during installation.

Follow the tool manufacturer's instructions and use a ring compressor to compress all of the rings within the piston. The notch on the top of the piston faces the front of the engine block. Position the assembly (with the ring compressor in place) into the cylinder bore. Take extra care not to scratch the cylinder wall. Put some form of sleeve on the rod bolts to avoid scratching the crankshaft journals as well.

Now, using a tool such as a hammer handle, tap the top of the piston and push it into the cylinder. If the ring compressor is properly used, the piston will go in with little effort. Install the upper shell of the connecting rod bearing into the connecting rod and oil the crankshaft journal side of the bearing. Guide the connecting rod over the crankshaft journal and install the corresponding cap with the lower shell installed and oiled on the crankshaft journal side of the bearing. Tighten the nuts finger tight. With the connecting rod cap installed, check the side clearance of the rod to the crank journal. The specification is 0.0035 to 0.0105 inch. If the side clearance is within specification, torque the rod bolt nuts to 19 to 24 ft-lbs. Repeat the steps for the other five pistons.

Lubricate the timing chain and the two gears. Put the chain on the camshaft gear (the larger gear). Place the crankshaft gear in the chain and align the two dots on a stock chain. While keeping the dots aligned, place the chain and gears onto the camshaft and crankshaft. The crankshaft will need to be turned so the gear will slide onto the keyway in the crankshaft snout.

Timing Chain

The basic method for installing the timing chain and gears is very straightforward. Lubricate the chain and gears with motor oil. Next, put the chain on the camshaft gear (the larger gear). Hold the gear in the air with the chain in place and rotate the gear until the timing dot is straight down (at the 6 o'clock position). Place the crankshaft gear in the chain with the timing dot straight up and aligned with the dot on the camshaft gear. Position the gears on the camshaft and crankshaft with the timing dots still aligned and push them carefully into position. Install the camshaft gear bolt and washer and torque to specification: 35 to 45 ft-lbs.

The preferred method, especially for any level of performance build, is to precisely set the timing of the camshaft relative to the crankshaft by a process known as *degreeing* the camshaft. In this process, the timing of the valves' opening is precisely set in relation to the pistons rotating to top dead center (TDC). Using the dots on a stock timing chain set will get the timing set close enough to work for a stock engine.

When building the engine for more performance, the builder should make every effort to get as much power as possible from the components being used—in this case, the camshaft. (See the sidebar for the step-by-step procedure.) There is an indexed, double-roller timing chain set available for the 200-ci engine. So far, no company has produced a similar timing chain set for the 250.

The Importance of Degreeing the Camshaft

Degreeing a camshaft is the process of synchronizing the position of the camshaft with the position of the crankshaft. The relationship between the camshaft and the crankshaft controls the timing of the valves opening and closing with respect to the position of the piston. Ensure that the camshaft timing is precisely where you want it, and you will not be disappointed with the performance.

It is natural to ask, "Why can't I just align the dots on the stock gearset?" The reason is very simple. In the engineering world, there is a condition called tolerance stack-up. This happens when each of the components that interact with each other are made to specification. Being within specification means that the part is manufactured with tolerances. However, it may be toward one end or the other of the tolerance. Regarding the timing chain set, this means that the crankshaft may be at one end of its tolerance, while the camshaft is at one end of its tolerance. The two parts are connected by the timing chain and gears, and they can be at one end of their tolerances. If you just align the dots, you have no idea if the camshaft timing is correct. Degreeing the camshaft takes out the guesswork.

Centerline and Duration-at-0.050-Inch Methods

There are two popular methods for degreeing a camshaft: the centerline method and the duration-at-0.050-inch method. Machine shops can generally perform either method. The duration-at-0.050-inch method is more accurate than the centerline method, but the centerline method is easier to do, and for most builds (especially inlines for the street), it is more than adequate. Because the centerline method is easier and effective, we will concentrate on it.

Centerline

The centerline method starts with the assumption that the cam lobes are symmetrical. In reality, cam lobes usually open the valve with a more aggressive slope than closing. But for a street engine, this method will be far more accurate than not degreeing at all.

Here are the basics of the centerline method. Camshafts are ground with a certain distance between the intake and exhaust lobes. This distance is measured in degrees and is referred to as the lobe center or lobe separation angle (LSA). A range of 104 to 114 degrees is typical. The centerline method finds the camshaft centerline by taking measurements before and after TDC, then dividing the distance between the two points. The camshaft timing can be advanced or retarded by moving the centerline of the intake lobe closer to or farther from TDC. There's a better explanation below.

If it is necessary to adjust the camshaft timing, owners of 170- and 200-ci engines are in luck because there is a double-roller, indexed timing chain set available. For 250 owners, there are offset crankshaft keys that will adjust the position of the crankshaft gear by a set amount. If the camshaft is located with a dowel pin, eccentric bushings are available that are used to change the position of the camshaft gear. Ideally, you will degree the camshaft again to ensure the accuracy of the adjustment.

Several special tools are required to degree the camshaft:

- A degree wheel or a piece of properly sized degree tape installed on the stock damper.
- A pointer mounted to the engine that points to the degree wheel or balancer markings.
- A dial indicator with sufficient travel in 0.001-inch increments mounted with a magnetic base or bolts.
- A positive piston stop to locate TDC. It is possible to make your own with an old spark plug by drilling and tapping for a bolt. The stop is used to set up the degree wheel, then it is removed.
- Two solid lifters. If you have nonadjustable rockers, you will need two adjustable pushrods: one for the intake and one for the exhaust.

Before setting up the degree wheel and other tools, install the gearset with the dots aligned. Install the solid lifters and the pushrods for intake and exhaust in the number-1 cylinder only. Adjust the rocker arms to zero lash. The pushrods should spin with light pressure from your fingertips. Turn the crankshaft so that both valves are closed and the piston is at TDC.

Install the degree wheel to the harmonic balancer and make sure that the crankshaft still turns without interference. Next, attach the pointer so it points to 0 on the degree wheel. The pointer can be homemade. A wire coat hanger works well because it can be bent to the right shape. Install the positive piston stop in the number-1 cylinder. Turn the crank counterclockwise 15 to 20 degrees and turn the piston stop in until it touches the piston. The stop prevents the piston from getting to TDC.

Install the degree wheel. Make sure that the wheel does not contact any engine parts and can rotate freely.

Install the pointer. If you plan carefully, you can have 0 degrees on the degree wheel near a location that makes mounting the pointer convenient.

Locating TDC is critical for degreeing the camshaft. With the piston stop in place, rotate the crankshaft clockwise by hand until it contacts the stop, and record the reading at the pointer. Now, rotate it counterclockwise until it stops, and record the reading. Add the readings and divide by two. This is TDC in degrees. Loosen the degree wheel without disturbing the crankshaft position or the pointer and rotate until the pointer is at zero. To validate the measurement, turn the crankshaft in one direction and record the degrees when you contact the stop. Now, turn the crankshaft in the other direction until the stop. Both readings should be the same distance from zero. If so, you have TDC and can remove the stop.

Where you set the dial indicator may vary based on the tools available. Many camshaft manufacturers recommend taking the readings from the top of the lifter. This is possible if your dial indicator has a long enough reach. If not, other camshaft manufacturers recommend taking the reading from the top of the valve spring retainer. It is more important to degree the camshaft than it is to argue over where to put the dial indicator. As you can see in the photos, it can also be done without the head on the engine. This does not allow consideration of deflection from the various valvetrain components, but it is certainly accurate enough for the power levels that these engines can achieve.

With the dial indicator in position, rotate the engine clockwise until the intake valve is fully closed. You will note when the indicator stops moving. Set the dial indicator to zero. The lifter is on the base circle of the camshaft lobe.

The degree wheel should now show the number-1 piston

You can find TDC by alternatively using a dial indicator setup. While it is very precise, it is not the only way to find TDC.

The Importance of Degreeing the Camshaft *CONTINUED*

at TDC, and the dial indicator should show the intake valve for cylinder number-1 fully closed.

Finding the camshaft centerline is the whole point of degreeing the cam, so here we go. Rotate the crankshaft until the dial indicator reads maximum lift. Set the dial indicator to zero, and then continue rotating the crankshaft to 0.100 inch past maximum lift to remove any slack in the timing chain. Take all measurements after turning the crankshaft in a clockwise direction to avoid false readings caused by slack in the chain.

Continue rotating the crankshaft until the dial indicator reads 0.050 inch before maximum lift. Record the reading on the degree wheel. Rotate the crankshaft again until the dial indicator reads 0.050 inch past maximum lift and record the number on the degree wheel. Add the numbers together and divide by two. This number is the camshaft centerline in relation to the crankshaft. If the camshaft is ground straight up (no advance designed in), it should match the lobe center provided by the manufacturer. If so, you can proceed to advance or retard the cam timing as required by the methods mentioned earlier.

Most cams in street engines will provide better bottom-end power if the cam is advanced 4 degrees. For example, Clay Smith cams are ground straight up, so you need to advance the camshaft timing by 4 degrees. This changes the camshaft centerline, say, from 112 to 108 degrees.

A hard concept to keep straight is that the LSA is different from the camshaft centerline. Advancing the cam timing does not affect the LSA or the characteristics of the camshaft. ■

Engine Painting

If the engine has not already been painted, do that now. You can even put the engine together for painting without gaskets and finish the assembly at a different time. It is easiest to paint the engine after it has been partially assembled. In this way, you can get the best coverage and not cause damage to freshly painted parts during assembly. There are spray paints specifically formulated for engines that resist heat, fuel, and oil. For most builders, these paints are more than adequate. Many colors of primer and paint are available. For the best results, start with a primer and finish with the color of your choice. Follow the steps below to achieve the best results.

After the basic assembly is completed, you can paint the engine. Use an appropriate cleaner/degreaser to remove any leftover oil used to protect the parts from rusting. After the engine has been cleaned, mask off any surface that does not require paint and block any passages into the engine. There were different colors and even different shades of blue used by Ford over the years. For a concours restoration, research the color that you should use to paint the engine. If you are not performing a concours restoration, choose the color you like.

Using an appropriate cleaner, clean all surfaces of the engine that will be painted. The machine shop will return the parts cleaned, but they may still have oils and lubricants on them that will hinder paint adhesion. Carefully mask off all machined surfaces, and take care to paint all bare metal that will be exposed after the engine is assembled to avoid premature, unsightly rusting. Use rags to fill holes, such as the distributor bore, but be careful not to block areas that need to be painted. When the entire engine has been prepped, begin to paint and follow the paint manufacturer's instructions.

Take a lot of pictures. If you drive your car on a regular basis, this is probably the best the engine will ever look!

It is now time to start assembling the parts to the exterior of the engine. So far, you have been working carefully so the engine will run right for a long time. Beginning with the front cover and oil pan and finishing with the valve cover, you should work just as carefully because these are the parts that people will see. You've worked this hard, so take

Front Cover Installation

1 *Install the new front crankshaft seal with a specialized seal installer. If you do not have this tool, a carefully chosen socket can be used with the same result.*

2 *Apply a thin layer of gasket sealer to the front cover and place the gasket in place on the cover. Lubricate the snout of the crankshaft with oil and install the front cover.*

3 *The bolts used to attach the front cover are several different lengths. Install the bolts in the proper locations and torque them to 7 to 9 ft-lbs. Do not overtighten the bolts.*

the extra time to have an engine that looks as good as it runs.

Remove the old front crankshaft seal from the front cover. If it has not already been done, thoroughly clean the front cover and make sure that any old gasket material has been removed from the gasket surface. Install the new front crankshaft seal by carefully tapping it in place. There are specially designed tools for installing seals of this type, but a carefully chosen socket can be used in a pinch. Apply gasket sealer to both gasket surfaces, the block, and the front cover, and then position a new gasket on the block. Apply assembly lube to the crankshaft seal and crankshaft snout. Install the front cover on the engine and attach the fasteners. Remember that the fasteners are not all the same length.

Oil Pump and Oil Pan Installation

1 *With the engine flipped back over, install the oil pump to the block. Pour some oil in the pump to help prime it for the initial start-up. Bolt the pump on and torque the bolts to 12 to 15 ft-lbs.*

2 *Depending on the age of your oil pickup tube/ screen, it could be the reason that your engine needed a rebuild. When the screen is blocked by debris, oil cannot be pumped through the engine. Install a new screen with a gasket and torque the bolts to 12 to 15 ft-lbs.*

3 *Use gasket sealer on both the block and the pan rails. Position the side-rail gaskets to the block and place the front and rear oil-pan seals in position on the front cover and rear main cap. Apply a small amount of sealant to each end of the front and rear seals.*

4 *Place the oil pan on the engine and install the bolts. Refer to your notes because there are different-size bolts used to install the pan.*

Refer to your disassembly notes if necessary. Torque the bolts to 7 to 9 ft-lbs.

Rotate the engine on the stand so the crankshaft is visible. If you are reusing the oil screen and pickup tube, thoroughly clean them and blow them out with compressed air. Always install a new oil pump when rebuilding your engine. There is a very slight chance that you can get a defective pump out of the box, but there is a much better chance that your old pump is worn out and not up to the task anymore. Pour some oil in the new pump and turn the shaft to help in priming the pump later. Install the pump to the block and torque the bolts to 12 to 15 ft-lbs. Install the pickup tube and screen to the pump with a new gasket and torque the bolts to 12 to 15 ft-lbs.

Ensure the oil pan gasket surfaces of the block and the pan are clean and that the pan rails are flat. Reproduction pans are available for the 144- through 200-ci engines in the early cars if there is too much damage to the original. The early 250 pans have just become available as well. If there is damage and you intend to reuse the pan, make sure there are no dents that will cause clearance issues in the engine. If there are, repair the damage before installing the pan.

Apply sealer to the block and pan surfaces and position the side oil pan gaskets to the block. Install the front and rear oil pan seals at the front cover and the rear main cap, respectively. Make sure the tabs are positioned correctly relative to the side gaskets. Position the oil pan on the block and attach the bolts. Remember that the bolts are not all the same. Refer to your disassembly notes to make sure that you get them in the right locations. Torque the bolts (from the center out in both directions) to

Front Engine Accessory Installation

1 *Install the crankshaft damper to the front of the engine by aligning the damper with the keyway on the crankshaft snout. If the key has been lost, it must be replaced. Use an installation tool to fully install the balancer onto the crankshaft. Install the bolt and washer and torque to 85 to 100 ft-lbs.*

2 *Apply sealer to the water pump and place the gasket on the pump. Install sealer on the block side of the gasket. Be careful how much sealer you use. Excess sealer can dislodge and end up blocking a cooling passage or interfering with thermostat operation.*

3 *Install the water pump bolts and torque to 12 to 15 ft-lbs. Use thread sealer on the bolts because the bolt holes go through to the coolant passage. Remember from disassembly that the alternator bracket will use one of the water-pump bolts when you install the front accessories.*

specification: 7 to 9 ft-lbs. Return the engine to the upright position.

After the paint has dried, begin attaching the rest of the components to the engine. Take care not to damage the new paint job.

Align the keyway in the crankshaft damper with the key on the crankshaft and install the damper using the harmonic balancer installer. Torque the bolt and washer to specification: 85 to 100 ft-lbs. If there is a separate accessory drive pulley, install it at this time.

Apply a light film of gasket sealer to the water pump and the block and position the water-pump gasket on the block. Install the water pump and bolts and torque them to 12 to 15 ft-lbs. Install the fan spacer and cooling fan to the water pump flange. If the alternator, power steering pump, and air-conditioning compressor were removed from the vehicle, you

TECH TIP

Harmonic Balancer Bolt Torque

Installing the harmonic balancer bolt with the engine out of the car can be a little tricky. If you try to torque the bolt using a torque wrench while the engine is on a stand, you will quickly realize that you are just turning the crankshaft. It is easier to do the final torque setting after the engine is installed in the car but before the radiator is installed. It is also easier to install the bolt with an impact wrench, either pneumatic or cordless. Just be sure you set the final torque with a torque wrench. ■

Left Side of Engine Installation

1 *After refreshing your memory with your disassembly notes regarding the position of the fuel-pump lever, install the pump with a new gasket. Depending on the position of the lobe on the camshaft, the pump might not seat flat. Slowly and evenly tighten the bolts, and the lever will move to the right position. Torque the bolts to 12 to 15 ft-lbs.*

2 *It is very important to prime the oiling system prior to initial start-up. Another way to help the process is to partially fill the oil filter before installing. The filter sits at an angle, so you will not be able to completely fill it. You may choose to install the filter after the engine is installed in the vehicle.*

3 *When you install the oil filter, dip your finger in engine oil (or use an oil can) and put a light film on the filter O-ring. This lubricates the seal and makes it easier to remove at the next oil change. Tighten the filter by hand. If you install it too tight, it will be very difficult to remove.*

4 *Replace the coil with a new one. You may want to replace it with a concours-correct piece or upgrade to one that will provide more spark power. Install the bracket to the engine and place the new coil in the bracket. Torque the bolts to 12 to 15 ft-lbs.*

5 *New motor mounts are a must. Do not reuse them. If you have difficulty finding replacements (vehicles with 250 engines, for example), there are companies that will recondition your originals. Torque the bolts to 18 to 25 ft-lbs.*

6 *In preparation for installing the lifters, lubricate the lifter bores with engine oil. A can with a long nozzle makes this much easier.*

7 *Use a magnetic pickup tool to install the lifters in the lifter bores. If you are reusing original lifters with the original camshaft, you must place them in the correct order. If not, the wear patterns on the cam and lifters will not match, and serious damage will occur pretty quickly.*

See chapter 4 on machining for step-by-step directions of the cylinder-head reassembly. The head will be installed as an assembly with the exception of the rocker-arm assembly.

Modern head gaskets are made of composite materials that seal better than the original steel-shim head gaskets. Many head gaskets now have sealing material printed right on them to minimize coolant and oil seepage from between the head and block. Compressed thickness varies by manufacturer, but most are between 0.045 and 0.050 inch. This is important for compression-ratio calculation.

can reinstall them at this time, using your notes as a guide.

The left side of the engine is very visible when you open the hood. Take your time here and pay attention to the details so that you can be proud of the appearance. Remember that this is where the fuel pump and distributor are located. Besides looks, there are some important parts related to the performance of the engine.

Fuel Pump

Use a new gasket and install the fuel pump. Check your notes for proper positioning of the pump lever. As you tighten the bolts, there may be some resistance depending on where the fuel pump lobe is on the camshaft. Torque the bolts slowly and the lever will move as needed to seat the pump to the block. Torque the bolts to 12 to 15 ft-lbs.

Oil Filter

Fill the oil filter about 3/4 full of engine oil to help prime the oil pump later. Dip your finger in oil and lubricate the O-ring on the filter to keep it from sticking to the block and making removal difficult at the next oil change. To keep from spilling oil, you may want to rotate the engine on the stand partway so that you can keep the filter upright while installing it to the engine. Only tighten the filter enough to fully seat the O-ring.

Coil

Invest in a new coil. Install the coil bracket and coil in the original location. Torque the bolts to 12 to 15 ft-lbs. The stock ignition system is marginal at best. Give it every advantage you can and install new components.

Motor Mounts

Position and install the motor mounts (both sides). On early engines, there is a left and a right bracket. Make sure to install them correctly. Torque the bolts to 18 to 25 ft-lbs. Check the service manual for your particular application because there are slight differences among years and models.

Lifters

They are not an external part, but now is the right time to install the lifters. Many builders soak hydraulic lifters in engine oil overnight to ensure that the lifters are filled with oil and not air before starting the engine. With the engine upright, install the valve lifters. Coat the entire lifter with engine oil and apply assembly lube to the bottom of the lifter and lower it into the lifter bore using a magnet. If you are reusing the lifters and camshaft, make sure you have kept them in the right order and that you reinstall them in the right positions. Do not use old lifters with a new camshaft. The wear pattern on the lifter will damage the new camshaft lobes and you will have to replace the camshaft along with the lifters.

It is a good idea to install the distributor later (after the head is installed) so that the oiling system can be primed before initial start-up.

Cylinder Head and External Parts

The cylinder head needs to be assembled before it is installed on the block. (See chapter 4 for the steps in reassembling the valvetrain in the head.)

Originally, Ford used steel-shim head gaskets that required a sealer on the block and the head when building a 144 or 170. For the 200, Ford did not use sealer. Modern gaskets are made of composite materials and typically have sealing rings printed right on them that make head-gasket sealer unnecessary.

Cylinder Head Placement

1 *If you are using studs, use two as guides when installing the head. If you are using bolts, find two long bolts of the correct size and cut the heads off to use as guides. Install the head gasket over the guides. Pay attention to any guidance from the manufacturer such as "front," etc.*

2 *Now you can set the head onto the block with the aid of the guide studs. The head is heavy, so get help from a friend and take care not to damage the threads if you are using your head studs as guides.*

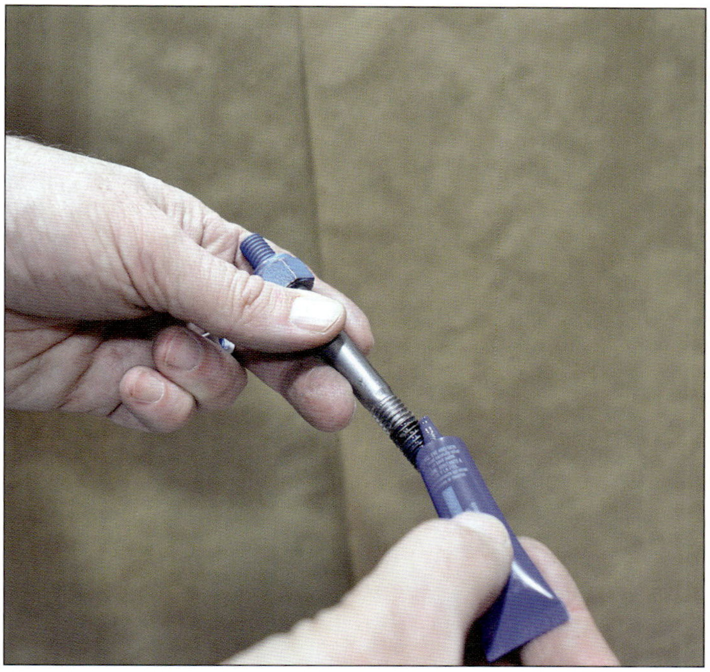

3 *The right front bolt hole goes through to the cooling passage above the water pump. If you are using bolts, make sure to apply thread sealer to prevent any coolant leakage when the engine is running. If you are using studs, the stud may thread deep enough to contact the water-pump impellor. If so, remove 3/16 inch from the bottom of the stud and recheck for no contact. Apply sealer and install the stud.*

4 *Torque the head bolts using the proper sequence in three stages: 55 ft-lbs, 65 ft-lbs, and 70 to 75 ft-lbs. Stud nuts are tightened in three stages to 80 ft-lbs.*

CYLINDER HEAD BOLT TORQUE PATTERN

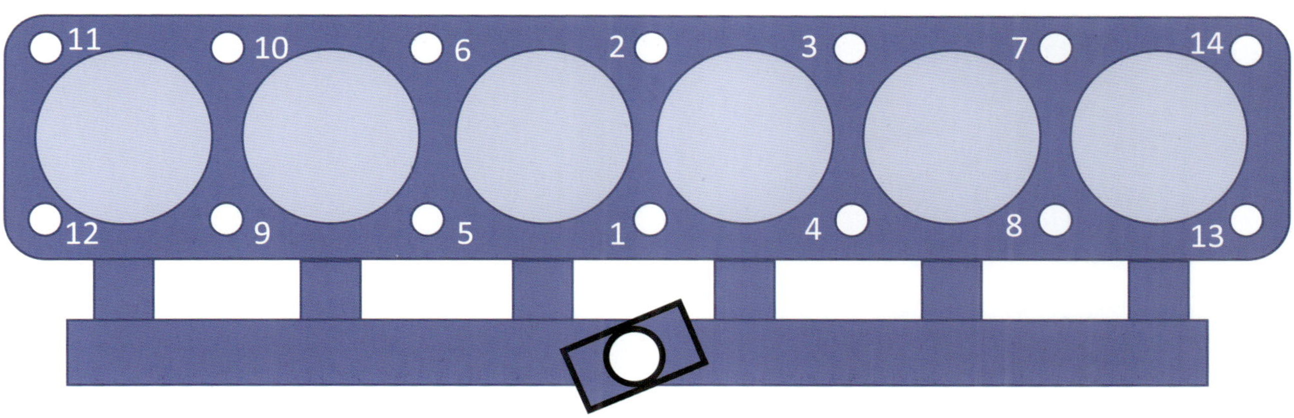

5 *Torque the head bolts or studs in the order provided in the Ford shop manual. Start at the center by the carburetor and work in a circular fashion to the ends. This sequence is designed to minimize the amount of stress on the cylinder head during torqueing and must be followed to prevent warping the head.*

If you are reassembling the engine using head studs instead of bolts, install two of the studs to use as guides when lowering the head onto the block. Put them in the left front and right rear locations. If you are assembling the engine with head bolts, it is advisable to use two long bolts with the heads cut off and the rough edges removed as guides. With the guides in place, install the new head gasket and make sure to follow any instructions from the manufacturer, such "front," "this side up," etc.

Now, carefully set the head in place on the block. It is heavy, so take extra care not to drop it onto the block and damage the gasket surfaces. With the head in place, install two bolts finger tight to keep the head located. The right front cylinder-head bolt hole is a through hole to the cooling passages below. Use the appropriate thread sealer on this bolt to make sure that you do not have a coolant leak when the engine is run—this is important!

If you use studs, apply sealer as with the head bolts, but take special care to not thread the stud so deep that it contacts the impellor of the water pump. If your head-stud kit does not have one stud that is shorter than the others for this purpose, cut 1/4 inch from the end that threads into the head; it's usually the end with coarse threads. Clean up the threads and install to test fit for interference.

If you are assembling with head bolts, now that you have two head bolts installed finger tight, you can remove the guide studs. Now install the remaining bolts or studs and prepare to torque them. The torque sequence is very important to keep from warping the head before the engine is run. The head bolts are torqued in three steps to the final value. Step one: torque to 55 ft-lbs in the specified sequence. Step two: torque to 65 ft-lbs in the specified sequence. Step three: torque to 70 to 75 ft-lbs (the final torque value) in

Pushrod Installation

1 *Lubricate both ends of the pushrods with assembly lube and install them through the holes in the cylinder head. Adjustable rocker arms have a cup on the rocker-arm end to fit the adjuster bolt. Make sure that you put them in with the right side up.*

2 *Apply assembly lube to both the valve stem tips and the pad on the rocker arm that contacts the valve.*

3 *Position the rocker-arm assembly on the head with the rocker arms properly aligned. Install the five bolts and begin to tighten them evenly in steps of two turns each. Because the camshaft will have the lifters and pushrods at varying heights, some bolts will seem harder to turn against the pressure of the valve spring. Torque them to 30 to 35 ft-lbs.*

the specified sequence.

Apply assembly lube to both ends of the pushrods and install them in the passage to the top of the lifters. If you are reusing the lifters and rocker arms, install the push rods in the positions from which they came. Apply assembly lube to the valve-stem tips and the rocker-arm pads (contact point with the valve stem). Make sure that the oil holes in the shaft are facing down and position the rocker-arm assembly on the cylinder head. Install the rocker-arm assembly bolts and tighten them evenly (two turns at a time) to

Valve Cover Installation

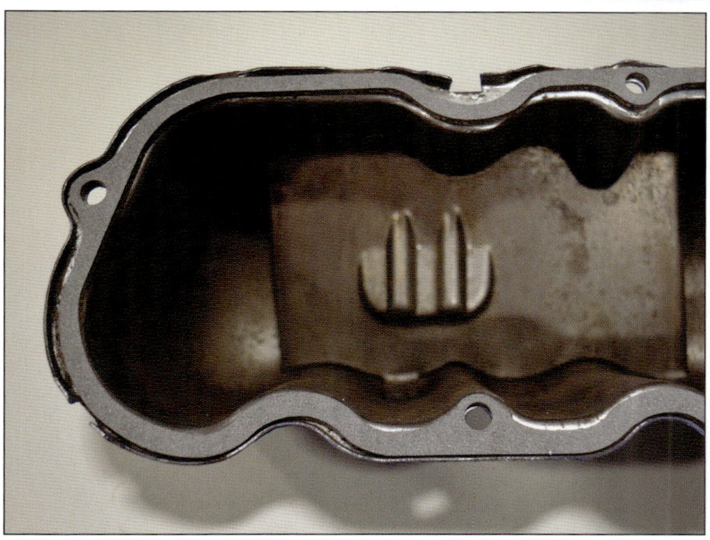

1 *The valve cover can be installed before the engine is in the car, especially if you are taking pictures for the sake of memories. However, you will find it more convenient to wait until the engine is in the vehicle. Apply gasket sealer to the gasket and place it on the valve cover. Be sure to align the gasket with the seven bolt holes.*

2 *With the gasket held in place by the sealer, set the valve cover carefully onto the cylinder head so that you do not move the gasket. Tighten the bolts to just 3 to 5 ft-lbs. After two minutes, tighten the bolts again to 3 to 5 ft-lbs. This gives the gasket time to compress and fit the gasket surfaces.*

the final torque value of 30 to 35 ft-lbs.

You may choose to install the valve cover after the engine is installed in the vehicle. The chain used to attach the engine to the hoist can come into contact with the valve cover when the engine is lifted, which can scratch the paint or even dent the metal valve cover. In either case, these steps apply.

Make sure that the valve cover gasket surface is clean and free of residual gasket material. Apply a thin coat of gasket sealer to the valve-cover side of the gasket and position it on the valve cover. Carefully position the valve cover on the cylinder head, making sure that the gasket aligns with the gasket surface of the cylinder head. Install the bolts and tighten to 3 to 5 ft-lbs. Do not overtighten them! One of the most common sources for valve cover gasket leaks is overtightening the bolts. The Ford service manual recommends retightening the bolts after 2 minutes. This gives the gasket material time to conform to the gasket surfaces before the final torque setting, still 3 to 5 ft-lbs.

Exhaust Manifold Installation

1 *It is a common practice to use an exhaust manifold gasket, even though Ford did not originally install one. Sealer is not necessary. You might find it a little tricky to install while trying to position the manifold. Try putting two bolts through the manifold and setting the gasket on the bolts.*

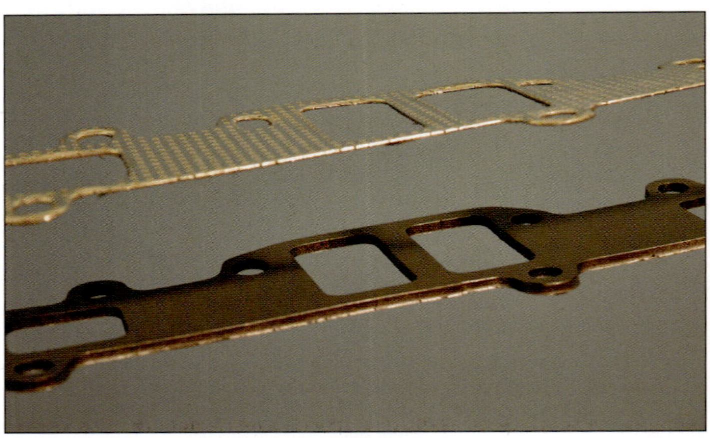

2 *There are gaskets made that can be used to compensate for gasket surfaces that are less than perfect. These extra-thick gaskets help minimize exhaust leaks. If the head and manifold had the gasket surfaces ground flat, they should not be necessary.*

3 *Exhaust bolts are subjected to extreme conditions. Replace them when you reinstall the manifold. Replacement bolt sets are available, and some come with locking washers.*

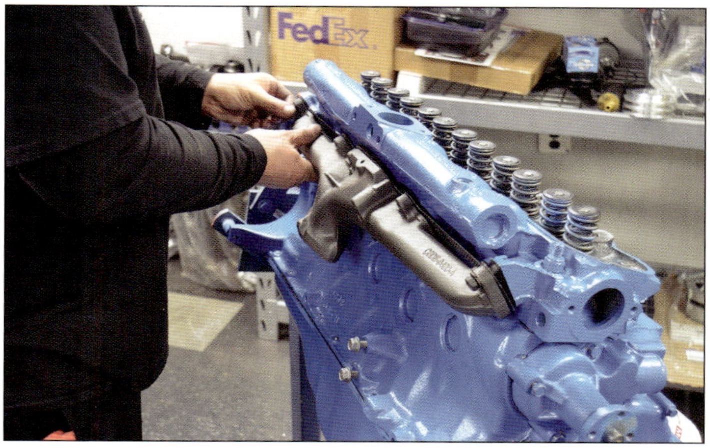

4 *Install the rest of the bolts to attach the exhaust manifold to the head. Torque the bolts to 13 to 18 ft-lbs. It is best to install the manifold before installing the engine in the vehicle.*

TECH TIP

Prime the Oil Pump

It's best to prime the oil pump and install the distributor after the engine has been installed in the vehicle. The potential for an oily mess is high if it is done on the stand.

Now that the head is in place and the valve cover is on, prime the oiling system and install the distributor. Partially fill the oil filter with break-in oil and install it. Insert the oil pump driveshaft into the distributor bore and make sure it properly engages the oil pump. Pour four quarts of engine oil into the oil-fill hole on the top of the cylinder head and allow the oil time to drain down to the oil pan. Note that the flywheel bolt holes are through holes, and if the bolts are not in place, oil may leak everywhere. Use a drill with an extension and a 1/4- or 5/16-inch deep socket (depending on the year of the engine) to rotate the driveshaft in a clockwise direction. Do not turn the driveshaft fast. You want the oil to move through the system at a low speed. ■

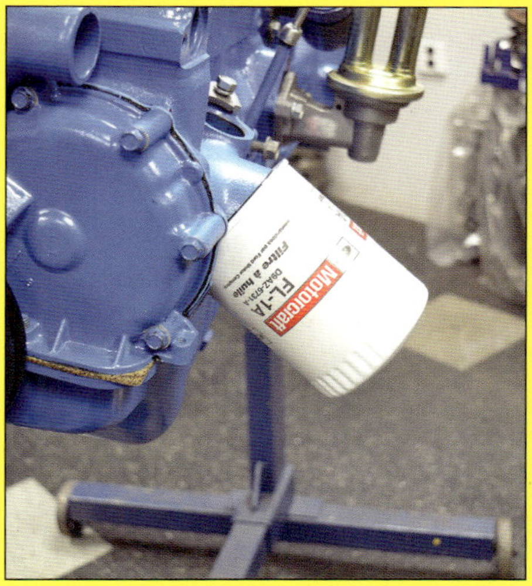

The engine-oil pump can be primed with the engine on the stand or after it is in the vehicle. Although, it must be done before the distributor is bolted in. Start by installing the oil filter if you have not already done so. Remember to prefill the filter.

Put the oil-pump driveshaft into the distributor bore and make sure that it engages the hex opening in the pump. It might be helpful to use a magnetic pickup tool. Replacements are available if the shaft is excessively worn.

Slowly turn the shaft clockwise with a cordless drill. Turning it slowly will help to make sure oil gets into as many areas of the engine as possible. If the valve cover is still off of the engine, you will be able to see oil coming from the rocker-arm assembly when the process is complete.

Originally, Ford did not use exhaust manifold gaskets. Gasket sets sold today include an exhaust manifold gasket. It is possible that the manifold or the cylinder-head gasket surfaces have become less than flat over time. Your machinist should grind both of these surfaces to ensure a good seal for the exhaust gasket. If not, or if you are not completely rebuilding your engine, extra-thick exhaust gaskets can help create a seal when the surfaces are not completely flat.

If the original bolts did not break when you removed them, you no doubt noticed that they are rusty and may have lost some of the material due to rust. A new set of bolts, preferably with some type of locking washer, is highly recommended. This is especially true if you are upgrading to a header. Position the gasket and install the manifold to the head. This can be a little tricky, so insert two bolts through the manifold bolt holes and hang the gasket on them. Then, carefully hold the manifold in position and finger tighten the two bolts. Install the rest of the bolts and

Distributor Installation

1 *Before installing the distributor, make sure that the number-1 piston is at TDC on the compression stroke. With your finger over the number-1 spark plug hole, have an assistant rotate the crankshaft by hand. You will feel the pressure as the piston comes up on the compression stroke. The timing mark on the harmonic balancer should also approach zero. The rocker-arm assembly must be installed so the valves are in the correct configuration for the compression stroke (both closed).*

2 *To know when the piston is at the top of its travel (TDC), use a wooden pencil in the spark plug hole. Turn the crankshaft by hand until the pencil stops moving upward. While it's not exact, it is close enough to put the distributor in.*

3 *Refer to your disassembly notes and photos to get the approximate location of the vacuum advance canister. Insert it into the bore with the distributor aligned to that position. You will notice that the rotor turns slightly. This is because the distributor is driven by a gear on the camshaft and the distributor gear aligns with the camshaft.*

4 *Note how much and in what direction the distributor turned during installation. Remove the distributor and reinstall it, this time accounting for how the gear will turn the rotor. The distributor is now in close enough that you should be able to start the engine.*

5 *The rotor in the distributor needs to align with the number-1 post on the distributor cap. Position the cap on the distributor. Install the hold-down clamp with the bolt and temporarily tighten it so the distributor doesn't accidentally move before starting the engine.*

tighten to 13 to 18 ft-lbs.

Installing the distributor is a notoriously tricky step that if done incorrectly will make the engine run poorly or keep the engine from starting. Follow a few important steps and you will get it right.

First, make sure the number-1 cylinder is at TDC on the compression stroke. An easy way to do this is to put your finger over the number-1 spark plug hole and turn the crankshaft. When the piston comes up on the compression stroke, you will feel the air pressure against your finger. Before the pressure stops, quit rotating the crankshaft.

Now, insert a full-length pencil in the spark plug hole. Make sure that it touches the top of the piston before you let go. Slowly turn the crankshaft again. You should see the pencil being pushed out of the hole. As soon as the upward motion of the pencil stops, stop turning the crankshaft. The piston is at TDC on the compression stroke (or at least very close).

When you removed the distributor, you should have noted the position of the vacuum advance with a photo. Once it is reinstalled, this will determine where the number-1 post on the distributor is located (based on the marking on the distributor cap). It may take a few tries to insert the distributor and have the rotor point to where you want number-1 to be. The rotor will rotate as the distributor gear meshes with the camshaft gear. Estimate how much it will move and compensate for the movement as you install the distributor.

Install the distributor hold-down and tighten the bolt. When it is time to set the ignition timing, loosen the bolt just enough to allow you to turn the distributor. After final timing is set, tighten the bolt again.

Keep in mind that you may want to install the distributor after the engine is installed in the vehicle to avoid potential damage while the engine is lowered into the engine compartment.

Carburetor

The carburetor can be reinstalled now or after the engine is back in the vehicle. Depending on the method that you use to install the hoist chain, the carburetor may be in the way and could be damaged when the engine is lifted. Whether you install the carburetor with the engine on a stand or

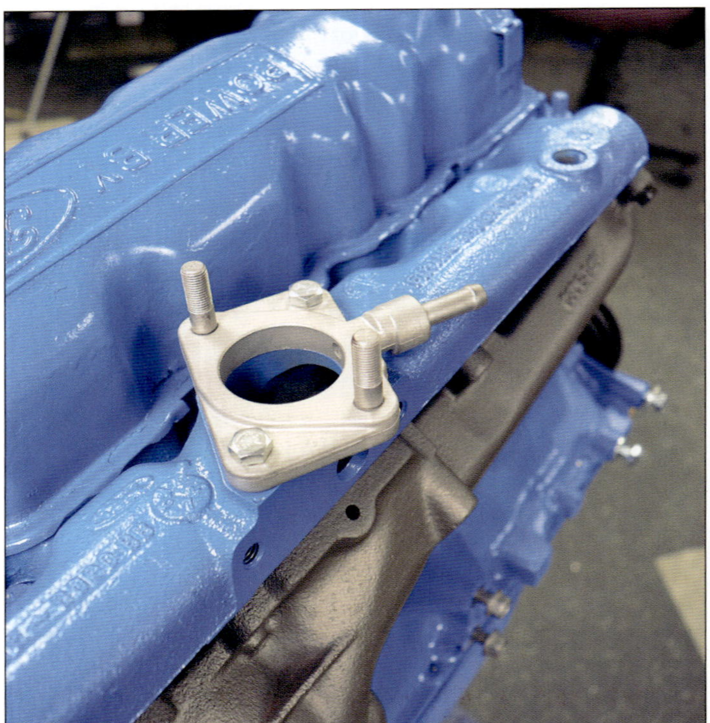

The small-six engines all have an adapter that bolts to the cylinder head and properly orients the carburetor to the engine. Install the adapter with a gasket using two bolts. Tighten the bolts evenly and do not overtighten.

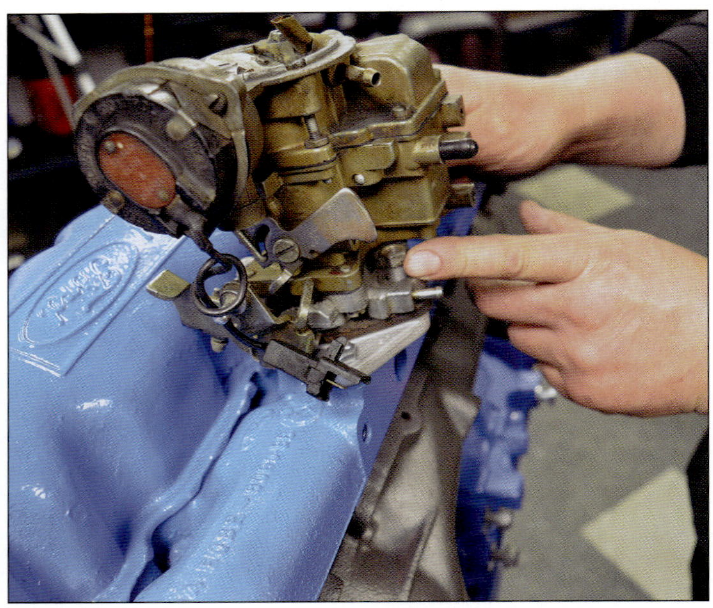

Install new carburetor-mounting studs in the adapter. Install the carburetor gasket. You may choose to attach the carburetor at this time, although it is safer to wait until the engine is in the car so that the carburetor is not damaged during the engine installation. With the gasket installed, place the carburetor on the adapter with the throttle lever on the carburetor facing the rear of the engine. Tighten the nuts evenly and do not overtighten them.

Do not forget to install the engine rear-cover plate. The plates are different for automatic and manual transmissions. If you are swapping transmissions, do not forget to get the right plate.

For an automatic transmission, bolt the flexplate to the crankshaft flange. Torque the bolts to 75 to 85 ft-lbs. For a manual transmission, install a new pilot bushing, the flywheel, and new clutch and pressure plate following the manufacturer's instructions. Tighten the flywheel bolts to 75 to 85 ft-lbs. Install the bellhousing.

after it is in the car, the steps are the same. If the engine is equipped with a spacer/adapter between the carburetor and the head, install it first with a gasket and tighten the bolts. Install the carburetor mounting studs if they are not already in place on the adapter. Then, set the carburetor on the spacer with another gasket. Attach the two nuts to the carburetor studs and tighten them evenly. Do not overtighten them because it may result in damage to the carburetor base.

Prepare to Reinstall Engine

At this point, you are basically ready to install the engine back into the vehicle. Secure the engine to the engine hoist and remove it from the engine stand. If you have a manual transmission, install the engine rear-cover plate. Install a new clutch pilot bushing and bolt the flywheel, clutch, and pressure plate to the crankshaft. Tighten the bellhousing to engine block bolts to 23 to 33 ft-lbs. If you have an automatic transmission, position the engine rear-cover plate and bolt the flexplate to the crankshaft. Torque the flywheel bolts to 75 to

REINSTALLATION AND BREAK-IN

Your engine is reassembled and ready to be installed in the vehicle. Use as much care, if not more, when reinstalling the engine as you did when you removed it. The engine has probably been painted, and you may have spent time refurbishing the engine compartment. Now is not the time to get in a hurry or take chances of scratching or denting something.

Safety should always be your main concern. The following steps will be given as if the external components are already attached to the engine before the engine is installed. In the case of the distributor and carburetor, you may choose to install them after the engine is in the vehicle to avoid potential damage.

As with removal of the engine, reinstallation is easier if the hood is removed from the vehicle. This provides more room to get the engine or the engine-and-transmission assembly positioned for dropping into the engine compartment.

With the engine on the hoist, move the hoist into position and take care not to let the engine hit the radiator core support or any side of the engine compartment. Enlist a helper and lower the engine into the approximate location where it will be bolted in. Carefully guide the engine to the transmission.

For an automatic transmission, align the studs on the torque converter with the holes in the flexplate. Start the transmission bolts by hand to ensure that the transmission is in place and prevent cross-threading the bolts. Tighten the bolts to 23 to 33 ft-lbs to secure the transmission to the engine. Now, lower the engine into place on the motor mounts and attach the hardware to secure the engine to the mount brackets. Attach the torque-converter nuts and torque to 20 to 30 ft-lbs and install the inspection cover. Bolt the starter motor to the transmission and torque the bolts to 12 to 15 ft-lbs.

With a manual transmission, the bellhousing may be attached to the transmission, or it may have been removed with the engine. If it is still attached to the transmission, guide the transmission input shaft into the clutch and ensure that it is firmly seated. Bolt the bellhousing to the engine and torque the bolts to 23 to 33 ft-lbs. Bolt the starter motor to the transmission and torque the bolts to 15 to 20 ft-lbs.

Engine Installation

1 ***Remove the hood and prepare the engine bay for the reinstallation. Move everything out of the way because after you start to install the engine, it is very tempting and dangerous to put your hands in to move something out of the way.***

2 *Raise the engine on the hoist high enough to clear the radiator support. Make sure that the engine rear-cover plate is in place on an automatic-equipped vehicle. Lower the engine while moving it toward the transmission.*

3 *The engine should have dowel pins to help locate it to the automatic transmission.*

4 *For an automatic transmission, rotate the torque converter until one of the studs aligns with the holes in the flexplate. Push the engine into its final position on the transmission.*

5 *It may be easier to install the lower transmission bolts from under the vehicle. Install the top bolts from the top of the engine. Torque the bolts to 20 to 30 ft-lbs.*

6 *Lower the engine onto the motor-mount brackets. The mounts should already be installed to the engine. Attach the mounting hardware.*

7 *For an automatic transmission, install the four torque-converter stud nuts through the starter opening or from underneath the vehicle. Rotate the crankshaft by hand until one stud is visible. Start the nut by hand and tighten it to 20 to 30 ft-lbs. Rotate the crank to each of the other three nuts and tighten them in turn.*

8 *Bolt the starter to the transmission. If you are swapping the transmission, make sure that you get the right starter for the new transmission. Early cars use a two-bolt starter for a manual transmission and a three-bolt starter for an automatic.*

Fuel Line and Carburetor Installation

1 *Install the tank-to-fuel pump line to the pump at this time. Use a line wrench to tighten the fitting without damage. New pre-bent, steel fuel lines are available for some vehicles and should be used if they are available. Attach the line from the pump to the carburetor. Avoid using long lengths of rubber hose. Any hose you use must be intended for fuel, but it does not have to be for high pressure on a carbureted engine.*

2 *Connect the original linkage to the carburetor. This is typically a snap-on fitting and does not require tools. Install the throttle return spring.*

3 *If the carburetor uses a hot-air tube to the choke assembly, install it next. Kits are readily available that provide fittings, tubing, and insulation. Without this tube, a hot-air choke will not function, and drivability will suffer.*

4 *Install the vacuum line from the carburetor to the distributor. Pre-bent replacements are available in many cases, and it is recommended to use a new part. The line will flex and bend enough while rotating the distributor that timing adjustments will be possible.*

Attach the fuel line from the chassis to the fuel pump. Attach the fuel line from the fuel pump to the carburetor. Connect the throttle linkage to the throttle lever and attach the throttle return spring. Connect the hot-air tube from the exhaust manifold to the automatic-choke assembly or connect the choke cable to the manual choke assembly. Connect the vacuum line from the carburetor to the distributor vacuum advance port.

Coolant Hose Installation

1 *Install the radiator and take care not to damage the cooling fins. Aluminum radiators are available in both custom-built and factory styles.*

2 *Install the lower radiator hose. Carefully position the hose clamp screw so that you can tighten it without interference from other parts. Do not install the clamp too close to the end of the hose. Use the right clamp so that you do not have excessive length with the clamp tightened.*

3 *Install the upper radiator hose. Position the clamps for easy access and aesthetic purposes. The clamp is sufficiently tight when the hose rubber just begins to squeeze into the slots on the clamp.*

4 *If the vehicle is equipped with an automatic transmission, install the transmission-cooler lines. Be very careful when starting the fittings onto the radiator. Brass fittings are very easy to cross-thread. Do not exert too much pressure to start the fitting on the threads.*

5 *Install the bottom hose from the heater core to the heater hose fitting on the right front corner of the cylinder head and tighten the clamp.*

6 *Install the hose from the water pump to the top fitting of the heater core and tighten the hose clamp at the pump. If you are planning to replace the hoses (and you should), the hoses attach to the heater core inside the vehicle on some cars. You may wait to tighten the clamp at the water pump until the cooling system has been filled. It is probably safer to tighten it now so that you do not forget it.*

Install the lower radiator hose from the radiator to the water pump and tighten the clamp. Next, install the upper hose from the thermostat housing to the radiator. Use caution and do not overtighten the clamps on rubber hoses. The clamps are too tight if hose material begins to squeeze through the slots in the clamp. If the vehicle has an automatic transmission, connect the transmission-cooler lines to the transmission cooler on the radiator. The male fittings on the lines thread into brass fittings on the radiator. One reason that the fittings are brass is because it is pretty easy to cross-thread the lines to the fittings. Having brass fittings makes it less likely to damage the fittings on the cooler lines or at the radiator. Either of these situations likely require replacing the parts or a costly repair.

Connect the heater hoses. Refer to the photos that you took during disassembly to ensure that the routing is correct. Position the clamps at least 1/8 inch from the end of the hose and tighten the clamps. If the engine uses a carburetor adapter with a coolant passage, be sure to connect the hoses properly to each side of the adapter.

Exhaust System

Install a new exhaust gasket on the exhaust pipe. From underneath the vehicle, lift the exhaust system into place at the exhaust manifold and ensure that the gasket is properly seated on the manifold. Slide the flange up the pipe and attach it to the exhaust-manifold studs with two fasteners but do not tighten them. Make sure that the pipe is not in a bind by slightly moving the exhaust pipe side to side. Then, tighten the nuts evenly to 25 to 35 ft-lbs. Tighten the fasteners evenly to avoid causing deformation to the exhaust gasket.

Install a new gasket to the exhaust pipe. Most vehicles use a thick, round gasket referred to as a **donut** *for obvious reasons. The thick, soft gasket easily conforms to uneven joints at the exhaust manifold.*

If you have already installed the heater hose to the water pump, remove it at this time to purge air from the cooling system as you fill it. Fill the radiator with coolant mixed 50/50 with water until the coolant comes out of the hose fitting on the water pump. Reinstall the heater hose and clamp.

Filling the Cooling System

Before adding coolant to the cooling system, make sure that the drain is closed on the radiator, the block plug is installed in the engine block, and all hose clamps (with the following exception) have been correctly tightened. If everything is properly installed, remove the heater hose from the water pump to allow air to escape while you begin filling the system with coolant. When coolant begins to come out at the water pump, reinstall the hose and correctly tighten the clamp.

Continue filling the radiator to within 1 inch of the top of the filler neck. If time allows, fill the coolant several hours before engine start-up. This gives the engine time to purge more air naturally. In any case, the level will drop after the engine begins to run the first time. Be prepared to top it off.

Unless you performed a transmission swap or had the automatic transmission rebuilt, you will probably only need to top off the transmission fluid level. The final transmission fill will be done after the transmission has warmed up and been put in the different gear ranges.

Continue adding coolant until the level is approximately 1 inch below the filler neck. When the engine is started and begins to warm up, the coolant level will likely drop due to more trapped air escaping. Be prepared to top off the coolant level when this happens. If possible, fill the coolant several hours before you start the engine the first time. Leave the cap off and give the system a chance to purge some of the air that is invariably trapped in the cooling passages.

Engine and Transmission Oil

For an automatic transmission, top off the transmission fluid. How much you need depends on how much you did to the transmission. If you only removed the torque converter and reinstalled it, you likely did not lose much fluid. On the other hand, if the transmission was rebuilt at the same time as the engine rebuild, you will obviously have to add more. Do not overfill the transmission. After the engine has been warmed up and the transmission is at normal operating temperature and has been put in gear, recheck the fluid level and top it off as needed.

It is a good idea to wait to add the engine oil close to the engine start-up time so that you get the most oil at the top and in the passages as you can. If you did not fill the engine with oil while it was out of the vehicle, remove the oil fill cap and add the specified amount of oil.

During reassembly, it was mentioned that you can install the valve cover with the engine in or out of the

If it has not already been done, fill the engine with oil at this time. If the valve cover is not on yet, pour the oil onto the top of the cylinder head along its length. This is just one more small attempt to get oil to as many places as possible before initial start-up.

If the valve cover is installed, use the fill tube on the valve cover. Be careful not to spill oil on your nice, clean engine.

Break-in oil should be used for the initial start-up, so you should not have to change the oil between start-up and the break-in driving process. Break-in oils are specially formulated with extra zinc to help protect moving parts until they have time to develop beneficial wear.

Install the engine ground from the body to the block. This ground is very important to the proper function of all electrical devices on the vehicle. If there is any doubt at all about the condition of the ground strap, replace it. Make sure that there is a good metal-to-metal connection at the firewall and the engine.

vehicle. If the valve cover is still off, pour the engine oil onto the top of the head along the whole length of the head. Be careful not to pour it too fast because it can run over the side of the head. This will not only make a mess but it also makes it difficult to know how much oil you have put into the engine. This method will help to distribute the oil to as many passages as possible before you start the engine. Now is a good time to prime the oil pump if you have not already done so.

Electrical

Connect the engine wiring harness now. At a minimum, connect the oil pressure and water temperature sending units, ignition coil, and starter. Make sure the connections are good. A poor connection now might mean the difference between the engine starting and lots of wasted time trying to figure out why it won't start.

Connect the body-to-engine ground strap. This strap provides the ground for most electrical components on the vehicle so make sure it connects to bare metal and that the fasteners are properly tightened.

The alternator/generator wiring can now be connected. Make sure to do this before the battery is connected to avoid damage and

Alternator wiring looks tricky. It is important to have each wire where it belongs. Refer to your notes or look up the connections and install the wire harness to the alternator.

Since the ground strap is installed, attach the positive cable first from the starter solenoid to the battery. If the ground cable is not attached to the battery, there is no chance of accidental arcing. Attach the ground cable to the battery last. This should be the last electrical connection made to protect the rest of the vehicle from accidental shorts to ground.

potential injury if the cables are accidentally shorted to ground during installation. The electricity flowing through a wire or cable directly to ground generates tremendous heat and will cause serious burns to skin. Even if you avoid injury, the wiring will likely be ruined, and it will have to be replaced.

Connect the battery positive cable to the starter solenoid and tighten the nut.

Finally, connect the ground cable from the engine to the battery. For the reasons already provided, it is important to connect the ground cable to the battery last. Just to reemphasize, *last* means that this should be the final connection made before the engine.

We did not discuss choke adjustments, but you should refer to the Ford service manual for the procedure. Before initial start-up, make sure that the choke closes properly when you depress the throttle pedal.

Starting

Sometimes, the hardest part about doing a job is not all the work required to do it but rather getting up the nerve to see if all your hard work paid off! Let's face it, you haven't failed until you try it, and it does not work.

However, that's a negative view. It is more likely that you are very anxious to hear the engine start. Once you are sure all of your bolts and clamps are tight, start the engine. If you do not have experience with this, it is a very good idea to have someone with you who has done this before.

Fuel

During the time the engine was out of the vehicle, fuel may have leaked or evaporated out of the open fuel line from the fuel tank. We know the fuel pump and the fuel line to the carburetor are empty. The carburetor itself will also most likely be empty of fuel. All of this means that when you start cranking the engine for the first time, there will not be fuel available.

Initial Start-Up

The engine has to crank for quite some time to draw the fuel from the tank to the pump, and then to pump it to the carburetor. This can cause the battery to become weak, so it is common practice to put a battery charger on the car during the initial start-up.

Exercise caution when cranking for extended periods. Do not crank the engine for more than 10 seconds at a time to help prevent the starter from overheating. Wait 20 to 30 seconds before cranking again. After two cranking cycles, fuel should be present at the carburetor. Pump the gas pedal two or three times and make sure the choke has closed. Crank the engine again, and it should try to start. If fuel is present and the initial timing is set close to the base timing, the engine should start and run.

If the engine does not attempt to start, you may need to advance the timing a little. With the hold-down bolt loosened slightly, rotate the distributor counterclockwise a few degrees. If the engine will not start and there is a backfire through the carburetor while cranking, recheck to ensure that the distributor is not installed 180 degrees off. This can happen if you install the distributor and point the rotor to the number-1 spark plug wire tower while cylinder number-1 is at TDC on the exhaust stroke instead of the compression stroke.

Do not be embarrassed if this happens. If you watch enough car-rebuilding shows on television, eventually you will see a professional do it.

Timing

With a timing light connected and the vacuum-advance line disconnected and plugged, check to see if the base timing is at or near specification. The engine idle speed will also need to be somewhere close to specification. There is a balancing act between ignition timing and idle speed. The idle speed needs to be close so that the timing can be

The engine should start now but may need a timing adjustment. Have the timing light hooked up before the engine is started. Be very careful with the routing of the timing-light cables so that they do not come into contact with the fan. Disconnect and plug the vacuum line at the distributor before starting the car. Loosen the distributor hold-down bolt slightly so that you can turn the distributor to make adjustments.

If the engine is idling too fast on its own, lower the idle speed using the screw on the carburetor base. The location of the screw will vary based on the type of carburetor.

adjusted and the idle speed can be set to specification. Easy, right?

Idle Speed

As stated above, when the ignition timing is right, the idle speed can be set. For early engines with a manual transmission, the target idle speed is 575 to 600 rpm. With a Thermactor system, it is 625 to 650 rpm. Automatic transmission–equipped vehicles idle a little lower (500 to 525 rpm). With a Thermactor system, it is 550 to 575 rpm. Thermactor is the early California emissions system.

Break-in Procedure

1 *During the initial engine start, the coolant level may drop. When it does, top it off to within 1 inch of the top of the fill neck. After initial start-up, wait for the engine to cool enough to safely remove the radiator cap and top it off again (if needed) before driving the vehicle.*

2 *If you are using adjustable rocker arms, remove the valve cover and check the adjustment after the first 150 miles or so of driving while the engine is hot. Carefully spin the pushrod between two fingers. It should spin with slight resistance. It is necessary to rotate the engine to check each one without valve-spring tension.*

Detailed idle mixture and idle speed setting procedures can be found in the appropriate Ford service manual.

There are several phases to the break-in process: initial start-up (sometimes referred to as camshaft break-in), for the first 200 miles or so, and then up to about 500 miles.

To begin the process, use a quality oil designed to be used for the break-in period with engines running a flat-tappet camshaft. These are motor oils specially formulated to cling to the surfaces of the engine that experience wear during initial start-up. Look for additives such as ZDDP or zinc camshaft additive. It is generally not recommended to use synthetic oils for the break-in period.

Partially fill the oil filter before it is installed to minimize how much the engine has to crank before oil starts to be distributed through the engine. The oil filter sits at an angle on the small six, so you will not be able to fill the filter completely. Always use quality filters because any money you save is quickly wasted if there is a filter-related failure.

This is also a good time, if you have not already done so, to prime the system by spinning the oil pump with a spare pump driveshaft and an electric drill. Spin the shaft clockwise at a relatively low speed. Watch the rocker arms for evidence that oil has reached the top of the engine. You can use the break-in oil for the entire break-in period. Change it at the end and refill it with a quality motor oil. Replace the oil filter at this time. Some builders like to cut open the used oil filter to inspect for abnormal amounts of shavings or debris.

There are a number of resources that offer methods for breaking-in an engine. Feel free to research the plethora of recommendations. Most techniques start the same: start the engine and run at a high idle (1,800 to 2,400 rpm) for 15 to 30 minutes. During this time, vary the engine speed occasionally to change how the oil splashes while the engine turns. You can also use this period to adjust the timing.

Some resources will suggest repeating this step one or two more times. The purpose of this initial break-in is to begin to establish the wear pattern of the camshaft and other moving parts.

During initial start-up, look for leaks from the cooling system, fuel system, and engine oil. Monitor the coolant level in the radiator and top it off as needed. Even with careful filling, air pockets are likely, and as the engine heats up, the air will be forced out and coolant can be added.

Fill the coolant system several hours before you plan to start the engine for the first time. Leave the cap off during this period, and some air will naturally get purged from the system. When starting, do not install the radiator cap at first. Removing the cap from a hot radiator is dangerous and can result in serious burns. As the air purges and you are able to top off the coolant, install the cap. Stop the break-in process if there is a fuel leak and fix the leak. Minor coolant or oil leaks can be repaired after the initial break-in.

After the initial break-in, drive the vehicle 150 to 200 miles at various speeds. Avoid driving the vehicle at a steady speed for prolonged periods. You want to establish a good wear pattern on all moving parts during this step. Keeping the engine speed constant for too long will cause wear-in patterns that lead to premature wear.

At the end of this phase, remove the valve cover and check the rocker arms to ensure that they are still properly adjusted (adjustable arms only.) This is done by turning the pushrod between your fingers. Be very careful. This needs to be done while the engine is hot, so take care not to burn your fingers. It is very likely that at least some rocker arms will need to be adjusted. If the arms have a locknut, loosen it and turn the adjusting bolt until the pushrod will just turn between your fingers.

The final step is to drive the car normally with no hard acceleration for the remainder of the first 500 miles. Do not exceed 4,500 rpm during this time. Avoid long periods of engine idling. You are still trying to develop wear patterns that will extend the longevity of the engine.

At this point, the break-in period is complete, and you can drive normally. It is highly recommended to change the engine oil and filter now with quality parts. Break-in oil is no longer needed.

Performance Upgrades

When an owner decides to keep the 6-cylinder engine, the next decision is whether to keep it stock or upgrade for better drivability and performance. If a part needs to be replaced, sometimes it might not cost any more to upgrade than it would to replace with new, stock parts.

As it turns out with the Ford small six, upgraded parts generally cost more than stock replacements, and sometimes they cost substantially more. However, a lot of the stock parts are either very performance restrictive or only available as remanufactured units.

Remanufactured parts (especially carburetors and distributors) are typically inexpensive alternatives to new replacement parts—that's if the replacements are available as remanufactured units at all. The major concern that most rebuilders have with remanufactured parts is the chance that the body of the part, which almost always is a reconditioned original, can have deficiencies in the original design, or more typically, warpage or other dimensional issues that are difficult to detect and repair during the remanufacturing process. Many issues show up once the part has been installed on the car and has been in use for some time.

The carburetor top (where it screws to the main housing) is the easiest part to envision this on. A warped top can cause easily detected issues, such as vacuum or fuel leaks, or more subtle issues, such as making the float difficult to properly adjust for proper performance.

Fortunately, there are parts available to replace many of the original parts that will improve the starting and drivability of the car while vastly improving the performance.

V-8 engines have often been described as an air pump, and the inline 6-cylinder engine can also be thought of in this way. Whether that is an accurate description is debatable, but it offers a good visual for how air enters, gets mixed with fuel, burns to create the force to move the pistons, and is finally expelled through the exhaust. The engine configuration does not change the cycles that an automobile engine goes through to produce power, so any upgrades that you can perform on a V-8 can also be done on an inline six.

The goals of performance upgrades are to improve the efficiency of air intake and the subsequent mixing with fuel, increase the intensity and stability of the spark used to ignite the fuel mixture, compress the mixture and contain the

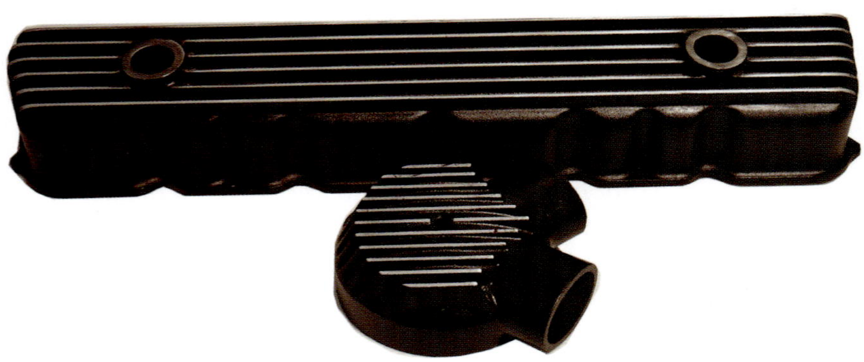

Whatever level of upgrades you choose, plan the project well and pay attention to details. Some owners take custom parts and customize them even more. Painted accents give the engine a professional look when they are done well.

The best reason to upgrade parts on your engine, and the easiest way to make the decision, is if an original part is malfunctioning. Other than worn-out internal engine parts, the most common sources of drivability problems are the carburetor and distributor. An issue on older engines with the Autolite 1100 1-barrel carburetor is that the housing can warp, leading to fuel or vacuum leaks.

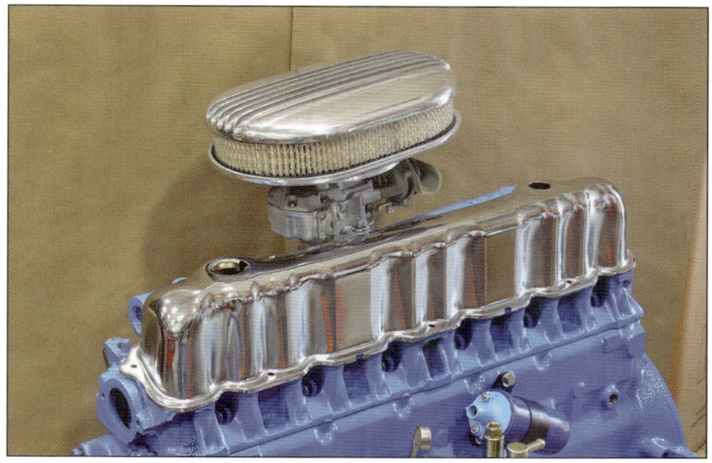

For some classic car owners, customizing the look of their car is as easy as a clean engine compartment with a few dress-up parts. Chrome valve covers add a timeless look, and air-cleaner adapters are available to fit aftermarket air cleaners on the Autolite 1V.

Car shows are a popular pastime for classic car owners, and it can be pretty underwhelming to open the hood and see a stock, dirty engine. The truth is, if the dirty engine is a 6-cylinder, you will probably just leave the hood closed. Don't worry, this is a before *picture.*

Here is the after *picture of the same engine. This is an engine that anyone would be proud to show off.*

The Four-Stroke Cycle

Throughout this book, there are reference to the different cycles, or strokes, of the engine. Before we go any further, let's go over what the different strokes are called and what they do.

Otto Cycle

Nikolaus Otto first described the four-stroke engine cycle in 1876. It is therefore also known as the Otto cycle. In the Otto cycle, the crankshaft makes two full revolutions for each complete cycle in a single cylinder bore.

Intake Stroke

The first stroke in the cycle is called the intake stroke. During the intake stroke, the exhaust valve is closed, and the intake valve is open. The crankshaft turns, and the piston moves down. As the piston moves down, it creates a vacuum that draws the air/fuel mixture into the cylinder, thus, the name *intake stroke.* The cylinder and combustion chamber are now filled with the air/fuel intake charge.

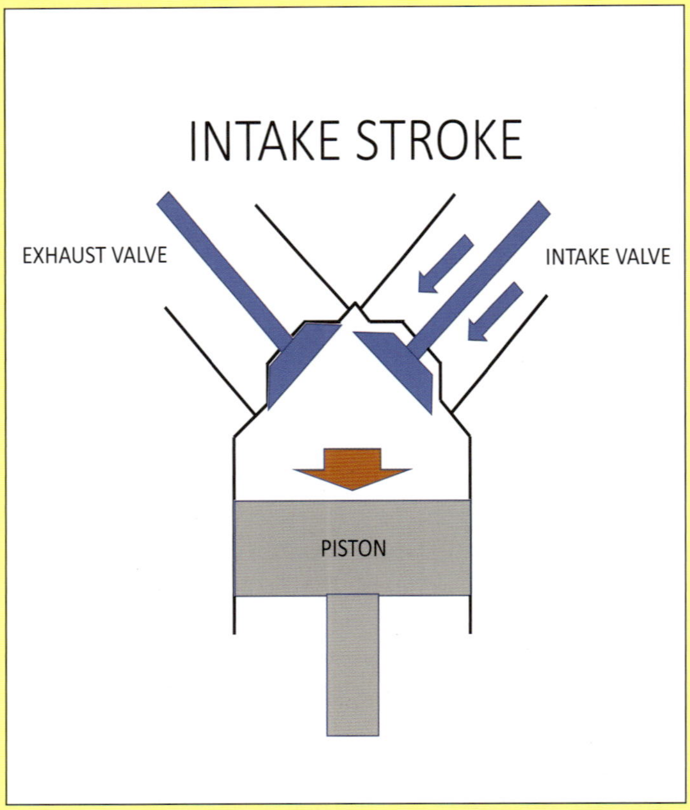

When the intake stroke occurs, the exhaust valve is closed and the intake valve is open. The open intake valve allows the air/fuel mixture in the intake manifold to be drawn into the combustion chamber as the piston travels down in the cylinder bore.

Compression Stroke

The second stroke is called the compression stroke. The crankshaft completes the first revolution as the piston travels back up the cylinder bore. Both the intake and exhaust valves are closed during the compression stroke. The piston compresses the air/fuel mixture into the very small area of the combustion chamber. After the compression stroke (but before the next stroke), the spark plug ignites the air/fuel mixture. This triggers the next stroke.

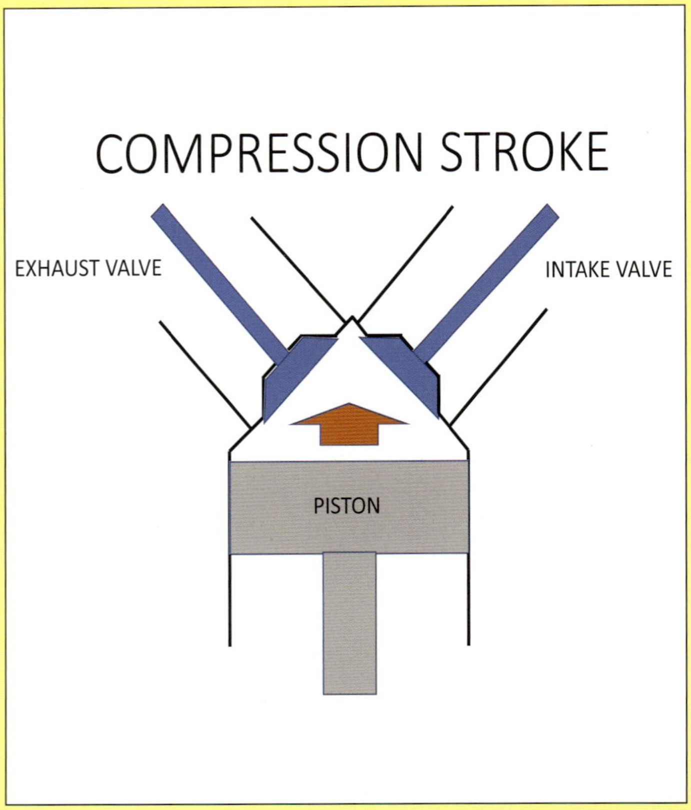

The compression stroke happens when the piston travels back up the cylinder and squeezes the intake air charge into the combustion chamber. For this to happen, both the intake and exhaust valves must be closed. Slightly before the piston reaches the top of its travel, the spark plug creates the spark that ignites the fuel mixture. This brief time between the spark and the piston reaching TDC is the ignition timing advance.

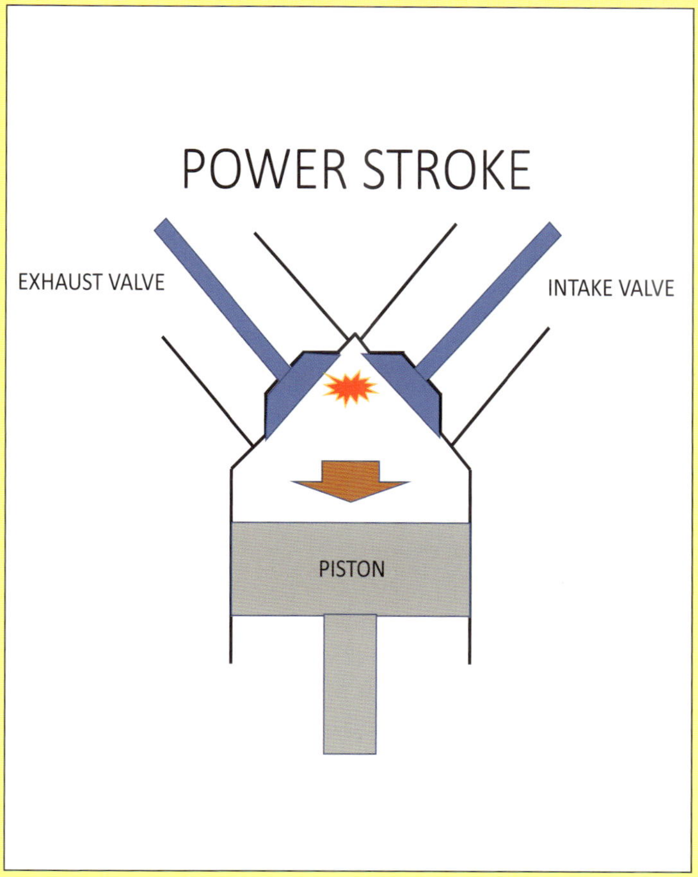

The power stroke happens with both valves closed. The spark ignites the intake charge, and the resulting expansion of the gases forces the piston down the cylinder and provides the power that moves the vehicle. A common misconception is that the intake charge explodes in the combustion chamber. This is not the case in a properly performing engine. The burning intake charge heats up and causes it to expand.

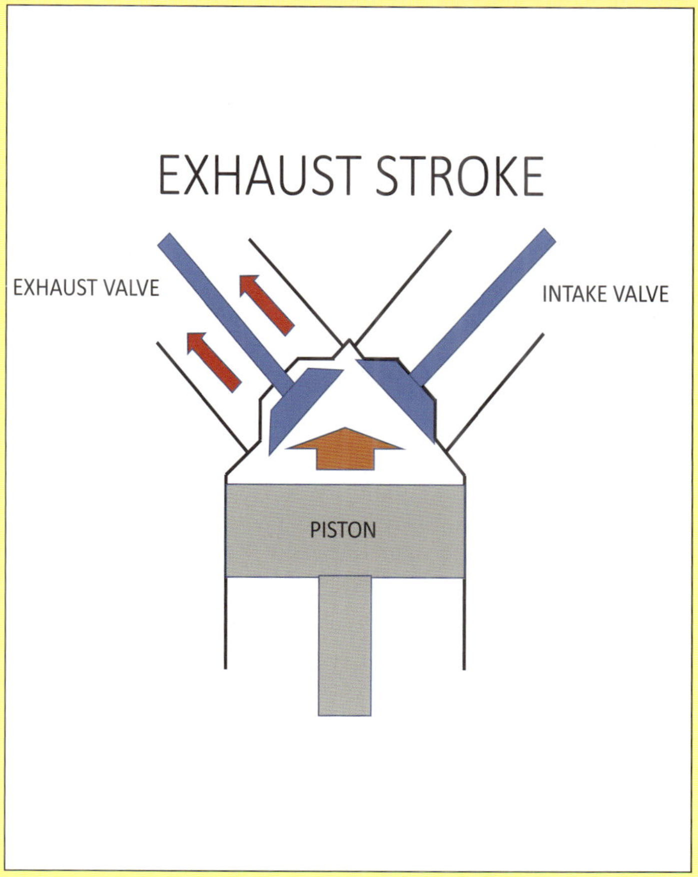

The final stroke in the four-stroke cycle is the exhaust stroke. The intake valve is closed and the exhaust valve is open so that the spent combustion gases can be forced out of the cylinder as the piston travels back up the cylinder.

Power Stroke

With the valves still closed and the air/fuel mixture ignited by the spark plug, the piston is forced down the cylinder bore by the rapidly expanding fuel mixture, turning the crankshaft as it starts the second revolution. This stroke is known as the power stroke, which provides the force that allows the engine to create power.

Exhaust Stroke

The final stroke occurs as the crankshaft completes its second revolution. The intake valve remains closed and the exhaust valve opens. As the piston travels up the cylinder bore, it forces the spent gases out through the exhaust valve. This is known as the exhaust stroke.

The cylinder in question has now completed a four-stroke cycle. In the Ford small-six engine, there are five other cylinders that are at various stages of the cycle at all times. Each cylinder helps provide power during its power stroke. The compression stroke for each cylinder is provided by another cylinder that is on its power stroke.

There are many nuances (such as valve timing, spark timing, and valve overlap) that allow this cycle to provide pretty smooth power up to as much as 6,000 rpm on these engines. At a more-reasonable 4,000 rpm, this means that each cylinder completes 2,000 four-stroke cycles per minute, or 33 times per second under acceleration. ■

expansion of the flame after ignition, and expel the burnt exhaust gases as efficiently as possible.

At the risk of overusing the word *efficiency*, the most important concept here is efficiency. You have probably heard bench racers (or real racers) discuss the pitfalls of "too much carb" or the reality that "bigger is not always better." These are common cautions, especially with smaller-displacement engines, because there is an upper limit to values such as carburetor size, camshaft duration, and even exhaust diameter that when exceeded produce negative results due to the inefficiencies that result. Think of it like the Goldilocks parable: it can be too big, too little, or just right. You want it just right.

Let's start at the top of the engine, actually at the air cleaner, and go all the way through the engine and out the tailpipe.

It may be best to think of upgrading systems rather than just replacing parts. For example, on the early small sixes, the carburetor and distributor were tied together by the spark control valve (SCV) on the carburetor and the vacuum-only advance feature of the distributor. If you do not consider the interaction between the fuel and ignition systems, you might replace a part that is not compatible with a related system. This is the fun part, though, so read carefully and plan out the upgrades that you desire.

Air Intake

The nice thing about upgrades to the air-intake system is that you normally receive the added bonus of a visual upgrade as well. As attractive as a stamped-steel, painted enclosure with a snorkel on it is, most people want to upgrade the air cleaner because it is such a visible part of the engine.

Open-element, chrome air cleaners not only look good but they also increase the amount of air that the engine can take in. They do this by eliminating the literal bottle-neck created in many factory air cleaners by the small-diameter snorkel. Most engines do not need the amount of air that can be drawn in through one of these filters, but unlike some other engine systems, the engine will only use the air it needs.

The drawback to open-element filters is that they sit on top of the engine where the air is usually hot. We all learned in science class that hot air is not as dense as cool air. This means that there are not as many oxygen molecules in the same volume (amount) of air. Of all the elements in air, the only one that the engine needs to burn fuel is oxygen. Less dense air means less oxygen to the engine.

For decades, racers addressed this fact of science by attaching hoses to the air-cleaner housing and drawing air from somewhere besides the hot engine compartment. This setup is known as a remote-air intake system or sometimes a cold-air intake. It is important to keep in mind that to be a cold-air intake, the relatively cool air must come from outside the engine compartment. A remote-air

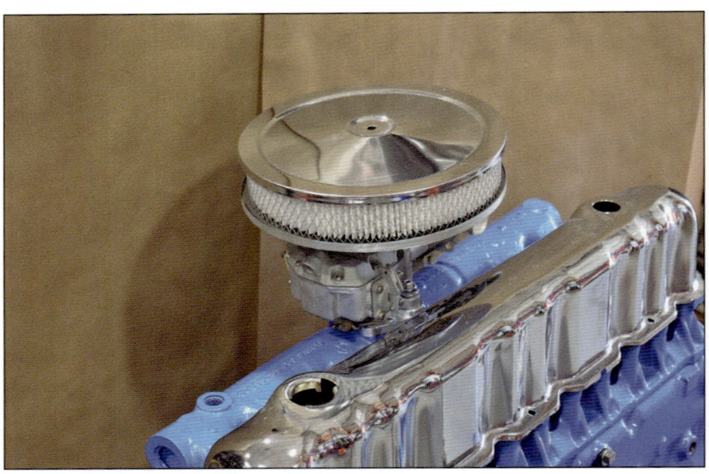

The open-element air filter is a classic design that improves airflow to the carburetor. The increased surface area allows more airflow than the design of most OEM air cleaners. Whether or not it is a stock engine with a 1-barrel carburetor that needs more air is beside the point. They just look good.

If you have an Autolite 1100 carburetor, Vintage Inlines sells air-cleaner adapters that allow you to install most aftermarket air cleaners with a 5⅛-inch base. The adapter was designed to not interfere with the choke linkage.

Vintage Inlines has adapters for other carburetors used by Ford as original equipment and service replacements. The Holley 1940 is one such carburetor. The adapter for the Holley 1940 uses an additional component along with the Autolite 1100 main piece.

For some time now, remote air intakes (RAIs) have been popular. They gained popularity when import cars with 4-cylinder engines became popular with young drivers and street racers. From a practical standpoint, moving the air filter to a cooler part or outside of the engine compartment provides cooler air that improves performance.

A low-profile carburetor hat provides the connection point from the air filter to the carburetor. The carburetor hat is no taller than an original air cleaner and can be installed to point away from the exhaust side of the engine.

The basic components of an RAI include the carburetor hat, connectors, tubing, and air filter. Filters are normally open element and may be conical or cylindrical. They may have chrome ends for a more appealing look.

intake may consist of tubing that moves the air-filter element to a part of the engine compartment that is not as hot as the rest.

On an inline 6-cylinder, it is not hard to imagine that the engine compartment on the opposite side of the exhaust manifold is cooler. Cooler is a relative term, but any decrease in temperature helps.

Carburetor/Fuel Injection

The next part of the engine that we come to after the air intake is the carburetor. The carburetor has one main function: provide the correct mixture of fuel and air to the engine in all operating conditions. The gadgets and compromises involved in doing this are why carburetors look so complicated. They are also why engineers began using electronically controlled fuel injection on new cars as soon as it was feasible.

The first adjustment that the carburetor has to make when you start the engine is to provide much more fuel than is actually needed to run the engine. It needs to do this because the atomized fuel mixture tends to turn back into liquid as it contacts the cool inner surfaces of

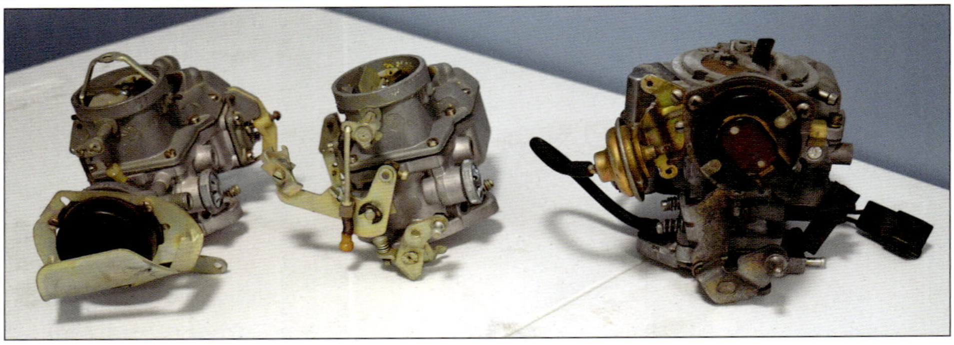

The three types of choke systems used on most American cars were manual, hot air, and electric. Manual chokes used a cable routed inside the car for the driver to actively close and open the choke. Hot-air chokes use heated air from the exhaust manifold drawn through the choke housing by a slight vacuum.

the intake manifold or the intake log. In the case of the Ford small six, it has an intake log. The carburetor has a choke valve that closes, restricting airflow, which makes the fuel mixture richer (having a higher ratio of fuel than air). In this way, the carburetor supplies enough fuel and air to the cylinders to allow combustion when the engine is cold. As the engine warms up, the choke valve opens and allows the air/fuel mixture to lean out some. Lean means there is relatively more air in the mixture.

The Autolite 1100 was the stock carburetor on Ford 6-cylinder engines from 1963–1969. Over the years, there were changes in venturi size and cubic feet per minute (CFM), but the carburetor bore remained constant at 1 7⁄16 inch. With the exception of the 1966 and 1967 California emissions engines and the 1968 and 1969 200s, all 1100s had SCVs to provide vacuum to the distributor.

The choke is a feature of all original carburetors that aided starting the engine when it was cold (not at operating temperature—it doesn't have much to do with ambient air temperature). The choke plate restricts airflow to the engine so that the air/fuel mixture is rich for starting.

For efficient combustion under normal driving conditions, the engine requires almost 15 parts of air to 1 part of fuel. This air/fuel ratio can be much richer during start-up.

The electric choke became popular toward the end of the 1960s. It operates by an electric current that heats the choke spring. For this reason, an electric choke has a circuit that provides 12 volts when the ignition switch is in the **Run** *position.*

Hot Air Choke Assembly

The first carburetors on Ford small sixes used a hot-air choke assembly. The carburetor had a vacuum passage to the choke housing. This slight vacuum pulled hot air through a tube from a location on the exhaust manifold. It is important to note that it did not pull exhaust fumes into the choke housing. Because exhaust gases are corrosive, the choke components would not last long. The tube passed through the manifold and allowed air to be heated before it reached the choke. As the engine heats up, the air gets hotter and causes the clock spring in the choke to turn and move the choke plate lever. Hot-air chokes were barely adequate when new.

Electric Choke

In the 1960s, electric chokes began to gain favor, and most carburetors had an electric choke by the end of the decade. The electric choke operates by sending current through the spring, which heats it up. As it changes temperature, the spring tightens or loosens and opens the choke plate just like the hot-air choke did. The difference is that the electric choke will be much more reliable because the operation does not depend on the presence of heated air from the hot-air tube.

Conversions

The aftermarket and carburetor manufacturers have developed a line of electric choke conversion kits for many carburetors that originally had manual, cable-operated choke assemblies. Much less common are kits to convert hot-air chokes to electric. There is at least one option for the Autolite 1100 common on Mustangs, Falcons, and other 6-cylinder Fords built in the 1960s. Vintage Inlines sells a billet aluminum, electric choke conversion for owners who wish to keep their original-style carburetor. While there is no performance improvement when converting to an electric choke, drivers will notice the consistency when starting and as the engine warms up when compared to a hot-air choke.

The Autolite 1100 uses a hot-air choke. Concerns with the hot-air choke include damaged or disconnected tubes, warped choke housings, and plugged vacuum passages in the carburetor or the adapter.

The principle operation of whatever automatic choke the carburetor has is the same for all. There is a bi-metallic clock spring in the housing that retracts when it is heated. As it turns, the spring rotates a lever attached with linkage to the choke and opens the choke. When the engine is off, the springs cool, and the choke closes in preparation for the next start.

Many carburetor models with manual or hot-air chokes can be converted to electric with readily available electric-choke conversion kits. The Autolite 1100 is not one of them. Classic Inlines developed a billet electric choke housing kit to convert the hot-air choke. Vintage Inlines offers the kit that includes the two-piece housing with a new brass bushing and electric choke spring. Detailed instruction explains how to install it.

Adapters are available to bolt a 2-barrel carburetor to the stock intake manifold. This lineup from Vintage Inlines includes Weber and Holley/ Autolite 2-barrel adapters for both the small and large log manifolds. They are designed to be used without the original adapter in place.

Carburetor Upgrades

1 *The large log adapters have the correct bolt spacing and orientation to attach to the intake manifold and align the carburetor in its original configuration. The adapters include a funnel-shaped insert that provides a smooth transition from 2 barrel to 1 barrel.*

2 *The small log adapters are of a similar design and are made to bolt to the small log manifolds. The insert is installed here. Notice that the attaching bolts are not visible and do not interrupt airflow.*

3 *With the insert removed, you can see where the attaching bolts are located. Some adapters on the market do not use an insert; they simply drill through a solid one-piece adapter. It is unclear if the disruption in airflow has any significant impact on performance.*

Upgrading the carburetor to a later, larger version of a 1V carburetor improves starting, as most later-model carburetors were equipped with electric chokes, and performance is generally improved due to the larger size and/or newer technology. Going backward by installing an earlier carburetor is generally not recommended for these same reasons. A smaller carb with a hot-air choke is not an upgrade.

Carburetors from 1969 and on had a bolt spacing of 3⅛ inches and require an adapter when they are installed on a small log head. Carburetors on small log heads had a bolt spacing of 2⅝ inches. Because of this difference, an adapter is needed to put the larger-base carburetors on a small log intake. These adapters are

TECH TIP

The Lowly Load-O-Matic

A very important consideration when changing the carburetor on pre-1968 vehicles is the distributor. Through 1967, distributors were known by Ford's name: Load-O-Matic. These distributors were unique in that they used a modified vacuum signal from the carburetor. This signal was achieved by the use of a spark control valve on the carburetor. The modified signal was a combination of vacuum from both above and below the throttle plate. The vacuum strength changed when the throttle plate was opened and closed. The difference in the vacuum strength controlled the timing advance at the distributor.

The distributor did not have a centrifugal advance feature and was controlled entirely by the vacuum signal. Centrifugal advance gets its name from the timing advance plate that advances ignition timing as the plates spin faster with increased engine speed. The plate has calibrated weights and springs that spread by centrifugal force and provide the advance. Without centrifugal advance, the distributor does not have the ability to provide the type of advance curve that helps power under acceleration. For this reason, when converting to a carburetor without an SCV, it is highly recommended to change to a 1968-or-later distributor or an aftermarket distributor. ■

commercially available, and well-engineered versions keep the proper orientation of the carburetor to the intake. Proper orientation generally allows the use of the original carburetor linkage. Holley 1946 carburetors from the late 1970s require conversion to a throttle cable when installed on earlier model vehicles.

Fuel Injection

While not exactly new, bolt-on throttle body fuel injection systems are fairly new to the Ford 6-cylinder engine scene. The 2V adapters available for the small six make it possible to bolt one of the new 2V systems to the integral intake manifold either with a 2V to 1V adapter or preferably by using a conversion adapter to get the most benefit from the swap. Two manufacturers are getting the most attention at the time of this writing, but do your own research and talk to owners who have made the swap for their opinions.

Distributor

On engines in vehicles built before 1968, the distributor was a unique design that did not have a centrifugal or mechanical advance. It instead relied on a modified vacuum signal from an SCV on the carburetor. This distributor was known as the Load-O-Matic and had no redeeming performance qualities. When a carburetor is replaced with a non-SCV upgrade, the Load-O-Matic distributor will provide even worse performance than before. The answer is to upgrade the distributor as well.

For builders who want more reliability from their original distributor, there are electronic conversion kits that allow you to replace the original points. The most well-known is the Ignitor from Pertronix. It is important to remember that while the electronic conversion requires no maintenance and provides a much more stable pickup signal, it does not upgrade the voltage output of the original distributor by any noticeable amount.

To get better performance and stay on budget, there are a few Ford original equipment options that can be salvaged from the junkyard or purchased as remanufactured units from your local auto parts store. The easiest swap for a Load-O-Matic is the distributor from a 1968–1972 vehicle. These distributors use an unmodified vacuum signal and, more importantly, have a centrifugal advance feature.

Holley Sniper EFI 2300 Self-Tuning Kit

The kit includes the following:

- Bolt-on 2300 flange carburetor replacement
- Supports up to 350 hp with two 100 lb/hr injectors
- Equipped with C4/C6 Ford transmission kickdown lever and TH350, 400, and 700R4 provisions
- Accepts many common 5⅛-inch OEM or aftermarket air cleaner assemblies
- Throttle body–mounted ECU (no extra boxes to mount)
- Integrated ignition timing control
- Only four wiring connections required: battery +, battery -, switched ignition, and RPM
- Internal fuel pressure regulator eliminates the hassle of plumbing an external fuel pressure regulator (preset to 58.5 psi)
- High-resolution, full-color touchscreen for initial setup, tuning, and gauge displays
- Simple Calibration Wizard: answers a few questions about your engine and creates the base map, then starts tuning on its own. No laptop required.
- Self-tuning ECU means you don't have to be a computer-tuning wiz to have EFI
- Genuine Bosch LSU 4.9 wideband oxygen sensor provides real-time fuel map learn
- OEM-style TPS/IAC and fuel pressure regulator for years of dependable service
- Includes clamp-on oxygen sensor kit for 2¼-inch exhaust, ensuring a leak-free oxygen sensor installation, with stainless steel T-bolt clamps and a stainless-steel (weldable) oxygen sensor flange
- Sniper EFI software is free to download that allows for real-time tuning
- holley.com/products/fuel_systems/fuel_injection/sniper_efi/sniper_2300_2bbl/sniper_2300/parts/550-849

The FITech Go EFI 2-Barrel System

The system includes the following:

- High-flow aluminum throttle body in a classic carburetor gold finish
- Bolts onto H-2300 bolt pattern and R2G manifold with a TD-P#2086
- Four FiTech flow-matched injectors capable of up to 400 hp
- Single-fan control and A/C input kicks up idle
- Self-learning technology for wide-range, super-fast dial-in correction
- Voltage control fuel pump control
- Suitable for crate engines and stock rebuild
- Throttle body mounted ECU for an easy installation
- Pre-programmed with bolt-n-go technology for out-of-the-box performance with minimal input required
- Internal fuel pressure regulator eliminates the hassle of plumbing an external fuel pressure regulator (preset to 58.5 psi)
- Use of ignition timing control is optional and not required
- Accepts many common 5⅛-inch OEM or aftermarket air cleaner assemblies
- Designed for natural aspirated engines only
- Self-tuning ECU for the most user-friendly setup tuning with no computer necessary
- Wideband oxygen sensor with mounting kit that provides real-time fuel MAP learning
- Only four wiring connections required: pump, key, power, and tach
- Includes a clamp-on oxygen sensor kit that ensures leak-free oxygen sensor installation with stainless steel clamp and oxygen sensor flange
- High-resolution full-color touchscreen for initial setup, tuning, and gauge displays
- Annular wet-flow technology discharge design
- OEM-style TPS/IAC and fuel pressure regulator for years of dependable service
- fitechefi.com/product/39001-go-efi-2-barrel-400hp-system/

Duraspark

They are still triggered by points and have a condenser, so while it is an easy swap, there are better choices. Starting in 1973, Ford used an electronic distributor known as the Duraspark. The Duraspark was all electronic, which means that there were no points to wear out or adjust. This upgrade requires the correct coil, the electronic control module (normally mounted to the inner fender), and the wiring harness to connect the components.

When searching for a donor vehicle, you must make sure all of the components are there, including the spark plug wires, although you will probably replace or upgrade them. A good rule of thumb is to take as many related or attached parts as

The first electronic distributor offered by Ford was the Duraspark, which was introduced in 1973. It used a control module and an electronic pickup to provide true electronic control of the coil operation. The Duraspark still used a vacuum advance to control timing advance. The Duraspark had a small-diameter distributor cap that led to the potential of spark jumping inside the cap due to the high voltage generated by the system.

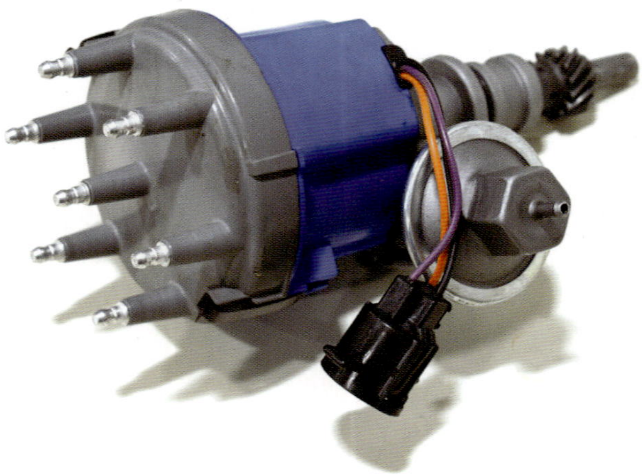

In 1975, Ford improved the Duraspark system and introduced the Duraspark II. The Duraspark II featured a redesigned module and a significantly larger distributor cap. The cap supported 8-mm spark plug wires and provided needed separation between the contacts.

They are getting harder to find, but it is still possible to get entire Duraspark II systems from donor cars in salvage yards. If you upgrade this way, make sure that you get as many parts of the system as you can. The main components are the distributor (including the cap and wires), coil, module, and wire harness that connects them. If possible, try to get other wiring connectors that feed the system to make a more professional-looking installation.

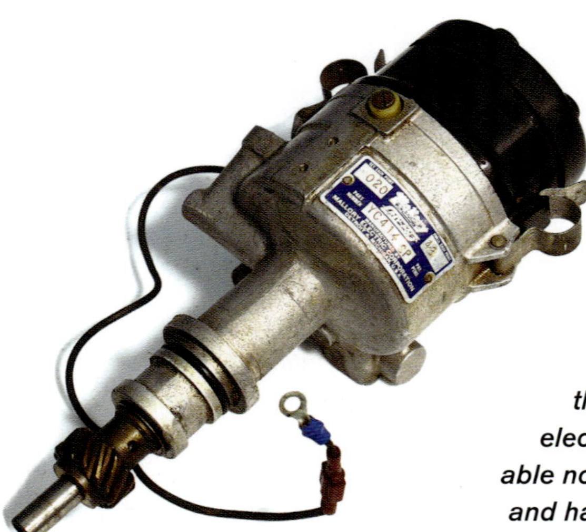

Before there was Duraspark, Mallory sold a performance distributor that was popular with racers in different venues who used these engines. They are no longer sold and are hard to find in the used market. Realistically, the electronic distributors that are available now provide superior performance and have warranties, but these are still sought-after vintage performance parts.

you can get, including attaching hardware and brackets.

Duraspark II

In 1975, Ford updated the Duraspark with the most visible difference being the large-diameter distributor cap. Due to the increased voltage of which the distributor was capable, Ford found it necessary to use a larger cap to reduce the possibility of the spark jumping inside the cap from one post to the next. This problem leads to misfires that affect performance and can be felt while driving.

The new, improved distributor was known as the Duraspark II and was the last factory upgrade to the small-six ignition system. Because they were put on more vehicles in the 1970s and early 1980s, the Duraspark II is a better and more plentiful choice than the original Duraspark.

If this sounds like a lot of work to get used parts, and it kind of is, but it is the least expensive way for builders on a budget. If there are problems, the individual components can be replaced with parts available through local auto parts stores or online parts suppliers.

Aftermarket Distributors

Over the years, there have also been aftermarket choices. In the 1960s, Mallory made a high-performance dual-point distributor, and Unilite later offered an electronic replacement. Both are very rare now, and replacement parts to rebuild a worn-out original are almost impossible to find. While both of these choices offered significant power and drivability improvements, the real improvements have come more recently with offerings that produce 50,000 volts or more. They

The high-performance Duraspark II distributor kit manufactured and sold by Performance Distributors produces well over 50,000 volts for reliable, high-energy spark that improves all aspects of driving from start-up to fuel economy. The kit includes the distributor with a full-length shaft bushing, control module, and harness to connect them. High-performance spark plug wires from the LiveWires line are also available.

The DUI from Performance Distributors installs with a simple one-wire connection to a switched 12-volt source. The only other connection (if needed) is to the tach signal. This signal works for most aftermarket tachometers on the market today.

Also from Performance Distributors is the Davis Unified Ignition (DUI) distributor. Based on the General Motors HEI distributor, Performance Distributors produces distributors for many engines, including the Ford small six. The Performance Distributors DUI is also available for the 144- and 170-ci versions and is the only electronic distributor made for these engines.

can also be tuned by a process called recurving that matches the amount of ignition advance and, when it happens, to the modifications of the engine. Recurving has always been an option, but it is most effective when using a high-performance distributor.

Performance Distributors

A company called Performance Distributors in Memphis, Tennessee, has been very helpful to the Ford small-six engine community. Over the past few years, it has been willing to develop ignition products for these engines that other companies would not. These products allow engine builders to take full advantage of other performance upgrades. Along with a performance-modified version of the Duraspark II that features a full-length bronze bushing, Performance Distributors offers high-performance control modules and coils to complete the Duraspark II package. This allows car owners who want to upgrade and still keep their cars "all Ford" to do so.

For owners who are okay with putting other parts on their cars, Performance Distributors also sells a distributor called the Davis Unified Ignition (DUI). The DUI is based on the HEI-type distributor from General Motors. The most recognizable feature of the HEI-type distributor is the cap, which contains the control module and the coil. This feature makes the DUI a desirable upgrade because you do not need to worry about wiring harnesses or where you are going to mount the control module.

The other feature that makes HEI-type distributors so popular is the one-wire hook-up. It literally requires one wire, a clean 12-volt signal in *start* and *run* mode, to power the distributor. All other functions

The DUI is especially convenient for 1964–1966 Mustang owners who want to install a reproduction Rally-Pac. Electronic tachometers can be hooked up to any electronic distributor, but the DUI makes it a simple plug-in operation.

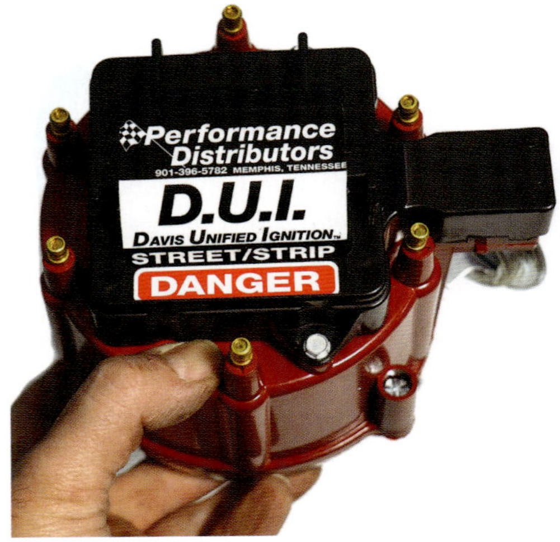

This tongue-in-cheek warning comes on the DUI distributors from Performance Distributors.

are controlled internally. There is another connection on the distributor that makes it very easy to connect an aftermarket tachometer, including the reproduction Rally-Pacs for early Mustangs.

These distributors, like the performance Duraspark II, are capable of producing over 50,000 volts. This level of spark is necessary to produce the most possible power from the small-six Ford engines. It also makes the car easier to start and helps with many drivability issues. Most experts agree that many symptoms on the 1960–1967 small sixes with the Load-O-Matic distributor that are first thought to be carburetor related can be solved by upgrading the distributor.

If you choose to upgrade the distributor, you have chosen wisely! See the tech tip to understand why you need to change the vacuum source to the distributor vacuum advance.

TECH TIP

Which Vacuum Source?

While it is acceptable to upgrade the distributor to one with vacuum and centrifugal advance on an engine with an SCV-equipped carburetor, it will be necessary to plug the SCV outlet and switch to manifold vacuum for the vacuum advance. However, this situation is not ideal because the vacuum signal is always present at the vacuum advance. There has been considerable debate as to whether this causes any problems. The general consensus is that it does not. The idle speed and timing will have to be set for best performance and idle characteristics, but that's always true.

When swapping in a 2V carburetor or a 1V with no SCV, use the ported vacuum fitting on the carburetor. Ported vacuum comes from within the carburetor body by way of two separate passages. One passage originates below the throttle plate in the closed position. This is the strongest vacuum signal. The other passage is slightly above the closed throttle plate. The passage is opened as soon as the throttle plate begins to open. In this way, the vacuum advance receives two types of manifold vacuum signals: one that indicates idle and another that indicates when demand is present. ■

Exhaust and Header

Improving the capability of the exhaust system by installing a

The stock exhaust system is clearly restrictive on cars equipped with 6-cylinder engines, but the problems start before the exhaust even gets to the exhaust manifold. The exhaust ports in the head are small and have a defined bend between the valve-bowl area and the manifold port. These issues, along with regular production casting issues, create a poor-performing head on the exhaust side.

performance muffler or a header provides many benefits, but there are also minor drawbacks to consider. The benefits include better fuel economy and improved throttle response and power. Keep in mind that any improvements in how much air and fuel the engine can take in must be accompanied by how much exhaust gas it can expel.

The problems with the stock exhaust system start in the cast-iron cylinder head. The original exhaust ports are small, have rough casting surfaces, and a restriction in the valve bowl area. These deficiencies can be improved with porting while the head is off.

The Problem with Stock Distributors

The Load-O-Matic distributor uses a modified vacuum signal to control the ignition timing advance. The modified signal is a combination of manifold and venturi vacuum created by the SCV. Manifold vacuum is the vacuum that exists below the throttle plate of the carburetor.

When the throttle is closed in low-demand situations, the manifold vacuum is high (around 19 mg). When the throttle plate is opened during acceleration, the manifold vacuum drops but is still present.

The other type of vacuum used by the SCV is venturi vacuum. Venturi vacuum is the vacuum that exists above the throttle plate at the narrowest point of the carburetor throat. Venturi vacuum indicates engine speed because the faster the engine turns, the more air is drawn in at higher speed. The high-speed air causes higher vacuum. When the throttle is closed, the vacuum is very low because the venturi in the carburetor is not completely open to the vacuum created by the running engine drawing in air.

At idle or in low-demand circumstances, the SCV senses the difference in the vacuum level between the manifold and venturi and does not allow a strong vacuum signal to the distributor's vacuum-advance feature. When the throttle opens under higher demand, the vacuum readings in the manifold and venturi are closer to each other, so the SCV interprets this as high demand and increases the vacuum signal to the distributor, causing the timing to advance. The timing advance is necessary as the engine speed increases during acceleration.

Problems begin when there is something that affects the vacuum signals to the SCV. Both vacuum sources reach the SCV by way of passages in the carburetor. If either passage develops blockage, the signal will not be correct. The SCV itself is a serviceable component and should be replaced whenever carburetor service is performed. ■

The SCV is needed to allow proper operation of the Load-O-Matic distributor. It is located on the side of the carburetor. Shown here is an Autolite 1100, but any carburetor used with the Load-O-Matic distributor will have an SCV. If you buy a remanufactured carburetor for your Load-O-Matic-equipped car, pay special attention to the presence of the SCV. Later Autolite 1100s did not have an SCV.

If you are using a carburetor with an SCV, inspect the vacuum passage from the adapter to the carburetor while the carb is off. Make sure that your carburetor baseplate gasket has the proper hole to match the passage.

Whether you use the stock exhaust manifold with performance improvements or upgrade to a single- or dual-outlet header, there are advantages to a dual-exhaust system. A properly sized system will improve the efficiency of the engine, thus providing more power and better fuel economy. At the same time, the sound of a dual-exhaust system is very exciting to most owners and gives them options for improving the looks of the exhaust as well.

Header

An improvement in all areas over a modified stock manifold is a header. Headers are available in single- or dual-outlet varieties. Most engine builds can achieve top performance with a single-outlet header with a 2- or 2¼-inch exhaust system exiting through a single performance muffler. Dual-outlet headers are generally not necessary for performance gains over a single outlet, but they do allow the owner to easily add a dual-exhaust system to the vehicle. The advantages are sound quality and appearance. When building for maximum performance, a dual-outlet header and full dual exhaust is recommended.

All headers are not created equal. As already stated, there are single- and dual-outlet designs. Another choice to be made is stainless steel or mild steel. Stainless-steel headers typically have a higher purchase price but last longer than mild steel and do not rust. In the past, you had the choice between a long-tube (full-length) header or what has become known as a shorty header. As of this writing, short-tube headers are the only option available new.

Before choosing a brand, talk to owners who have experience with the brand. Forums and clubs are the best places to get advice. Ask if anyone has encountered clearance issues with the starter, floor pan, or transmission bellhousing. Some clearance

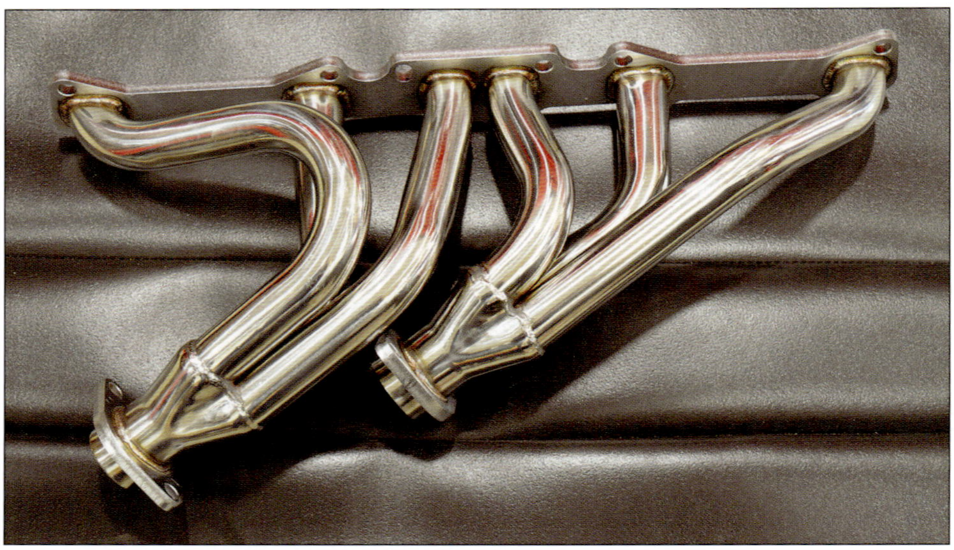

This is the dual-outlet header manufactured by DNA Motoring. The primary tubes are the individual tubes connected to each exhaust port. An important specification for headers is the primary tube diameter. The primaries on the DNA header are 1⅝ inches. The other specification that most people want to know is the collector diameter. This is where each set of three pipes exits through one tube. The DNA header collectors are 2 inches.

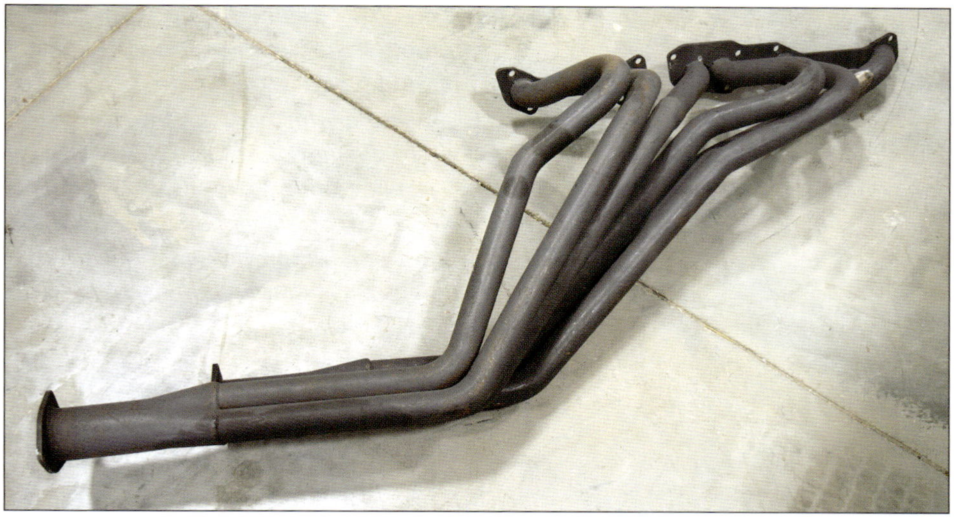

The long-tube design by Hooker Headers is a popular header that is no longer produced. Long-tube header designs are known to produce more torque than short-tube headers. Short-tube headers increase horsepower more than torque.

issues can be dealt with, but some cannot. Also consider if you are willing to deal with them.

Dual Exhaust

The next step up for the exhaust system is to install two mufflers, or what is universally known as dual exhaust. Most performance-car owners would not dream of driving a car without dual exhaust. Dual exhaust sounds better and looks better than a single exhaust tip. With some vehicles, the V-8 versions had special optional dual-exhaust systems, and these can often be replicated on a 6-cylinder car. An example is the trumpet exhausts exiting through the rear valance on a 1965–1966 Mustang GT. This look is easily achieved with reproduction parts on a 6-cylinder car with dual exhaust.

It is possible to have two exhaust tips coming from one muffler, but that improves the looks without any performance increase. The most performance potential is achieved by installing two mufflers, known as a true dual system. Many companies, such as Vintage Inlines, sell excellent street performance mufflers systems, including Waldron Exhaust.

When using a dual-outlet header, it is advisable to install an H-pipe after the header but upstream from the mufflers. An H-pipe equalizes exhaust pulses between the two sets of primary tubes and prevents a harsh-sounding exhaust note.

Any muffler shop can create a dual-exhaust system for your car. Issues to keep in mind are clearance to the body and the ground, how the system is attached, and the material used to create the system.

Ground clearance is critical because you do not want the system to scrape the road over bumps and potholes. Clearance issues to the body will not cause damage to the system but will generate annoying noises and can lead to excessive heat in the passenger compartment.

Many cars that had dual-exhaust options for V-8 cars had reinforced floor pans to mount the extra weight of the mufflers, which are usually mounted in front of the rear axle but

If the V-8 version of your car had a factory dual-exhaust option, you might be able to replicate it on your 6-cylinder. This car is in the process of being converted to the 1965 Mustang GT-style trumpet exhaust. All necessary parts are available as reproductions, and Waldron Exhaust can build the 1965–1966 Mustang system ready to install the tips.

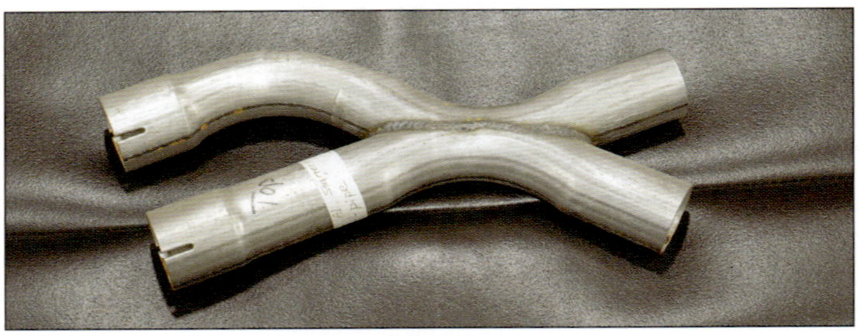

An H-pipe or X-pipe, named for their respective shapes, are recommended on dual-exhaust systems when using a dual-outlet header. X-pipes, like the one shown, balance the exhaust pulses from the dual-outlet header, increasing performance and minimizing uncomfortable in-car sounds from the exhaust.

When adding dual exhausts, it is important to properly attach the system to the bottom of the car. The muffler hangers bear the majority of the load at the rear of the car. Other hangers are necessary for the tailpipes. The systems by Waldron Exhaust include the attaching hardware.

Most exhaust systems are made of sections of pipe connected by clamps. The most common type of exhaust clamp is made of a U-bolt with a substantial cross piece to squeeze the outer pipe enough to seal it to the inner pipe. Achieve a professional appearance and gain ground clearance by properly orienting the clamps.

only on the cars that had the option. Reproduction reinforcements are made for some vehicles but certainly not all. Keep this in mind when you consider how the mufflers will be attached to the floor pan.

Finally, regarding systems built by a muffler shop, be sure to ask ahead and find out if it can build your system with stainless-steel tubing if that is your preference. Stainless-steel systems cost considerably more than aluminized steel (the only other choice you should consider for even moderate longevity), and many shops don't use it because of the differences in welding techniques and the cost to keep the material in stock.

Performance Single- and Dual-Exhaust Options

If you enjoy watching car-building shows on TV, you have undoubtedly seen commercials for bolt-on high-performance exhaust systems from well-known companies like Flowmaster and Magnaflow. Unfortunately, these companies do not make bolt-on high-performance systems for vehicles with Ford small-six engines, but there is an alternative.

Waldron Exhaust in Michigan is well-known for stock replacement exhaust systems for virtually any American car made from the early 1900s through the 1980s. Through a special agreement, Waldron makes performance single- and dual-exhaust systems for most of the Fords that originally had a small-six engine. These systems are available in aluminized or stainless steel. Vintage Inlines has an agreement with Waldron to be the exclusive retailer for this line of products. Waldron Exhaust systems for Ford small six–equipped vehicles are manufactured as a direct bolt-in system when using the header available from Vintage Inlines.

Camshaft and Valvetrain

When talking about camshaft characteristics, manufacturers typically use three terms: lift, duration, and lobe separation angle (LSA). Lift and duration are easily understood, but lobe separation, or valve overlap, is a term not normally used by the average car owner and amateur engine builder. All three are important when trying to decide which camshaft is right for your vehicle characteristics and your driving style.

Lift refers to how far the camshaft causes the valve to move, or lift, off the seat. By increasing the lobe size on the camshaft, manufacturers increase how far the camshaft causes the valve to open. Opening the valve farther allows more air and fuel to enter the combustion chamber on the intake side and more spent gases to exit on the exhaust side.

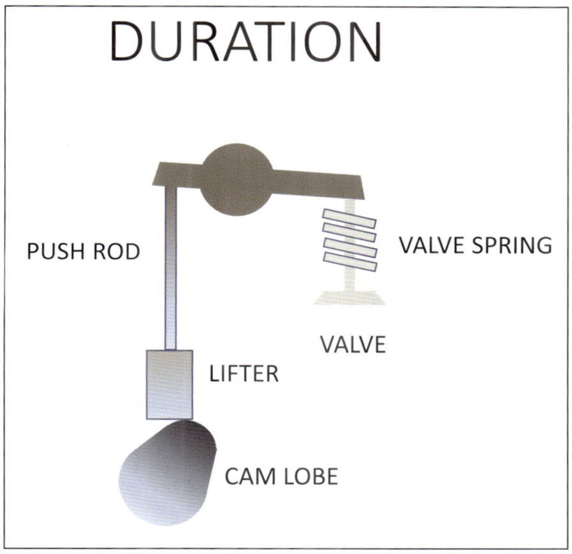

Duration is the amount of time the valve stays open due to the shape of the camshaft lobe. Duration is measured in degrees of rotation of the crankshaft. The camshaft rotates once for every two rotations of the crankshaft. Because there are four strokes, the intake valve is open in the first half of the first rotation, and the exhaust valve is open in the second half of the second rotation.

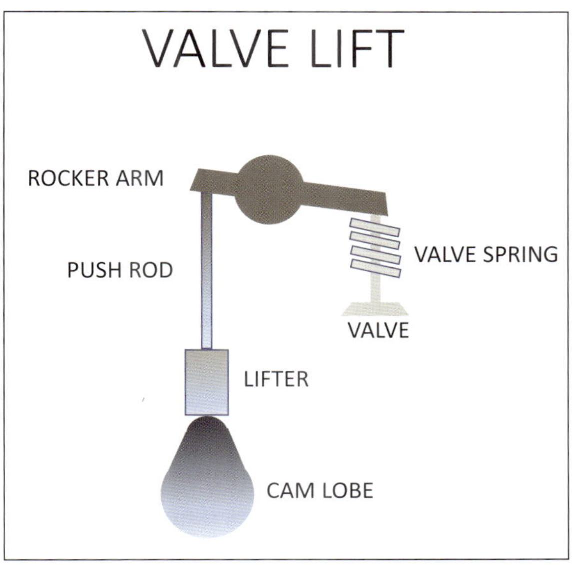

Valve lift refers to the distance the valve opens when the cam lobe moves the lifter and the motion is transferred through the rocker arm to the valve stem. Camshafts are designed to provide a certain amount of lift. The more lift, the farther the valve opens, and performance is improved.

Camshaft manufacturers control the lift and the duration with the shape of the cam lobes. More lift requires a taller lobe, while more duration requires a wider lobe.

Performance camshafts designed for the street will normally provide from 0.450- to 0.500-inch lift. The ratio of the rocker arms has a direct impact on the amount of lift. A ratio of 1.5:1, the stock ratio for Ford small-six engines, opens the valve one-and-a-half times the amount of the lift that the camshaft provides. Increasing to a 1.6:1 ratio slightly increases the lift and is a common way to increase lift, even when using a stock camshaft. Any time the amount of lift is increased, it is critical that the machine shop checks the clearance between the valves and the piston.

Duration refers to how long the valve stays open in terms of degrees of rotation of the crankshaft. In other words, a camshaft with 240 degrees of duration is open to some extent for two-thirds of the rotation of the crankshaft's 360 degrees. I say "to some extent" because the egg-shaped profile of the cam lobe gradually moves the valve from fully closed to maximum lift and back to fully closed within the 240 degrees of rotation. It is not open at full lift for the entire 240 degrees of crankshaft rotation.

Effect of Changing Lift and Duration

Now we understand that lift and duration refer to how far the valve opens and how long it stays open. Before we discuss LSA, let's talk about what effect changing lift and duration have on the performance of the engine.

Increasing the lift independent of the duration will increase performance up to the point where interference between the valve and piston occurs. Changing only the lift will also increase the performance of the engine without changing the RPM range where the power happens.

This sounds ideal except for at least one problem. Because of the shape of the lobe, which controls duration, the valve starts to behave more like a switch going from closed to open and back to closed in a very short time in terms of crankshaft rotation. The hydraulic, non-roller lifters in these engines could not keep up and maintain constant contact with the lobe. So, camshaft manufacturers change the lobe shape to change the duration, which gives the valve more time (in terms of crankshaft rotation) to go from closed to open and back.

Giving the valve more time to accomplish its travel is not the primary purpose of increasing duration. The longer the intake valve stays open, the more time there is for the intake fuel/air charge to enter the combustion chamber. There is, in effect, a constant supply of air and fuel waiting to enter the combustion chamber while the valve is open. It follows that the longer the valve is open, the more intake charge can enter. It also follows that there is a mechanical limit, due to engine design, to how much air and fuel the engine can reasonably use.

Bigger is not always better. It is important to know how much duration is needed to support the other modifications to your engine, transmission, and axle gear ratio. Trust the camshaft manufacturers.

The duration for the exhaust side works very much the same. The longer the valve is open, the more spent exhaust gases can get out. An important development in camshaft design for Ford small-six engines with the cast-iron head is dual-pattern profiles. With a dual-pattern cam, the intake and exhaust duration are different, with the exhaust always having a longer duration. The theory is that due to the design of the exhaust ports, the exhaust duration is increased to help the cylinder head expel the exhaust gases. Many manufacturers now have dual-pattern profiles for the small-six engines.

Lobe Separation Angle

Now we know how lift and duration affect power. Let's talk about the third term: LSA. LSA, lobe center, and valve overlap all refer to the same idea, if not the same specification.

For many years, overlap was the common specification to describe this characteristic. More recently, manufacturers have changed to LSA. Combining the terms may make the concept easier to understand.

LSA is the number of degrees of crankshaft rotation between the peak points of the intake and exhaust lobes. This number determines how long the intake and exhaust valves overlap while opened in the same cylinder. This is an important concept because during the overlap time, each valve helps the other do its job. Since the intake valve begins to open while the exhaust valve is still barely open, the exhaust leaving the chamber helps draw in the intake charge during the intake stroke. Likewise, the overlap during the exhaust stroke allows the intake charge to help push the exhaust gases out the exhaust valve as it closes. That's the mechanics of LSA, but what is the effect of a change in the profile?

Effect of Lobe Separation Angle on Power Band

In simple terms, the LSA has the greatest impact on where the power band or RPM range falls. A camshaft with a tight LSA (lower number) begins to make the power at a lower RPM than a camshaft with the same lift and duration but a wider LSA.

As with any engine modification, there are trade-offs. The tighter LSA provides power and throttle response at a lower RPM, but that comes at the expense of peak horsepower at higher RPM. Conversely, a wide LSA provides the most power but at a higher RPM range than some customers are comfortable with.

Another important consideration regarding LSA is the type of transmission. A tight LSA works well with a manual transmission or an automatic transmission with a modified, higher-stall-speed torque converter.

All other things being equal, an LSA of 108 degrees, a common choice, provides power at lower RPM but has a choppy idle and less vacuum for components that use vacuum to operate (such as the power brake booster) than an LSA of 110 or 112 degrees. A compromise between idle quality and RPM range is 110 degrees, and 112 degrees provides the smoothest idle but pushes the power band higher into the RPM range.

A rule of thumb for Ford small-six engines is that a change of 2 degrees in LSA results in a change of 500 rpm for the power band. For example, a camshaft with an LSA of 108 degrees and a power band from 1,600–5,200 rpm moves the power band to 2,100–5,700 rpm with an LSA of 110 degrees. This is not totally independent of lift and duration, so study carefully when making your decision.

Camshaft Selection

Fortunately, camshaft manufacturers provide tables to explain the characteristics of the different grinds they offer. In almost every case, you will choose an existing profile rather than customize the characteristics of your camshaft. However, if you need it, the manufacturers are also very helpful in determining if you need a custom grind and what it should be. Don't worry. If you do not know if you need a custom camshaft, you probably don't. Unless you are building a race engine, you will be able to find a cam that is currently offered.

Alloy Cylinder Head

The most sought-after performance part for the Ford small-six engine is the alloy, or aluminum, cylinder head currently produced and sold exclusively by Vintage Inlines. This cylinder head was originally commissioned by Classic Inlines in the mid-2000s.

Based on the 250-2V head produced by Ford of Australia in the late 1960s and early 1970s, the alloy head features cast-aluminum construction and a separate intake manifold. Intake and exhaust ports were raised, which increases the radius and straightens out the port to some extent. The combustion chambers were updated with a high-swirl design to improve quench and fuel distribution. The intake ports are slightly smaller than the stock 250-2V, which increases the velocity of the intake charge. All of these improvements provide significant gains in power.

The aluminum cylinder head originally designed by Classic Inlines and now sold by Vintage Inlines is the basis for many of the highest-performance small sixes on the road today.

Externally, the aluminum cylinder head looks very much like the Australian Ford 250-2V cylinder head from the early 1970s. Internally, there are differences in the chamber design, and the runners were redesigned to improve flow.

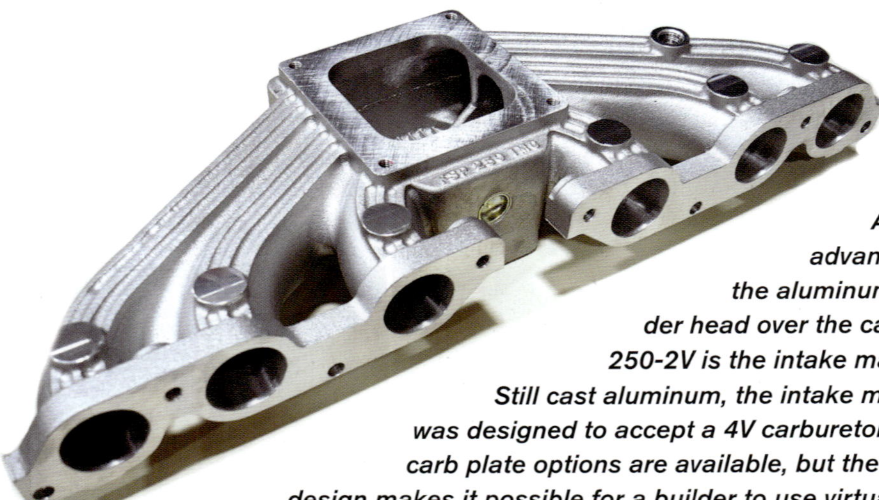

Another advantage of the aluminum cylinder head over the cast-iron 250-2V is the intake manifold. Still cast aluminum, the intake manifold was designed to accept a 4V carburetor. Other carb plate options are available, but the simple design makes it possible for a builder to use virtually any carburetor or throttle body. There are even bosses cast in to facilitate individual fuel injectors.

The cylinder-head package includes a 4-barrel intake manifold with runners designed to further increase velocity. The intake manifold requires a carburetor adapter plate to mount the carburetor. Vintage Inlines currently offers adapters to mount a Weber or Holley 2-barrel, or a Holley 4-barrel. The adapter design is simple, so a machine shop can fabricate an adapter for any carburetor with a block of aluminum and a vertical mill.

Staged Performance Upgrades

Take what you have learned so far and make a plan out of it. Your budget, time, and ambition will determine how many upgrades you can make at one time. Some builders will just want improved starting, drivability, and reliability. For these owners, upgrading some of the bolt-on parts of the engine is the way to go. We are going to call these upgrades Level 1.

Level 2 is when the real fun starts, and the budget has to go up. Level 2 will include some of the upgrades from Level 1. We will explain which upgrade from Level 1 may not quite make the grade for Level 2 and require an additional upgrade.

Level 3 is for owners who want the reliability of Levels 1 and 2 but with a little more power. If your engine is ready for a rebuild due to age or minor damage, this is a good time to perform Level 3 modifications. Level 3 includes the upgrades in Levels 1 and 2, but we will not repeat them unless there is a better alternative at Level 3.

Level 1: Bolt-on Parts

For Level 1, we recommend upgrading the distributor, exhaust system, and carburetor. These are the basic systems, and as previously discussed, the carburetor and distributor should be upgraded in tandem, especially on the older engines. Let's face it, most people who are not going back to stock will want to have a more-aggressive sound from their new engine.

Distributor

The distributor can be upgraded by installing an electronic trigger mechanism to replace the points. Remember that this upgrade alone will not increase the spark output of the ignition system. Therefore, it is recommended to replace the distributor with a full electronic unit, such as the Ford Duraspark II or one of the aftermarket HEI-style replacements. Any of these can be used with the stock carburetor, even one with an SCV.

Exhaust

Level 1 is also a good time to replace and upgrade the stock exhaust system. At a minimum, consider gasket matching the ports on the stock exhaust manifold and removing as much casting flash as you can reach with a die grinder. (See chapter 8 for modifying stock parts.)

A better choice for the exhaust manifold is to replace it with a header. Either a single outlet or dual outlet will be a huge improvement over the stock manifold. The choice between single and dual is really about your preference and budget for the rest of the exhaust system. If you like the look and sound of a dual-exhaust system, your choice is clear.

Speaking of the exhaust systems, finding a complete system for a Ford 6-cylinder is tricky, but as of this writing, there are systems available from Vintage Inlines. An alternative is to have your local muffler shop fabricate one for you.

Carburetor

At Level 1, a carburetor upgrade to a 2-barrel (2V) is the last and most important step. It is last because you can make the first two changes on any model year without worrying about the Load-O-Matic distributor on the early cars. If you swap out a carburetor with an SCV though, you must also swap the distributor. The carburetor is the most important upgrade because it allows the engine to take full advantage of any other modifications you perform.

For Level 1, the upgrade will probably come in the form of a Weber or Holley 2V carburetor using a commercially available 2V to 1V adapter. Choose the carburetor carefully. If you are not doing the Level 2 modifications at this time, you may want to use a smaller carburetor on your otherwise-stock engine.

Right after the distributor, the 1V carburetor found on all Ford small sixes from 1960–1982 is the weak link. An upgrade to a 2V carburetor, such as the Holley 350 or a Weber progressive 2V, will bring the carburetor technology ahead by a couple of decades. The swap is made possible by using a 2V to 1V adapter. Several companies make these adapters. Find the one that you think positions the carburetor the best and has the least impact on fuel mixture flow.

Level 2: Stock Cylinder Head

The upgrades to the cylinder head in Level 2 require you to remove the cylinder head. For owners and builders familiar with these engines, it is common knowledge that the stock cast-iron cylinder head (even large log versions) is the biggest hindrance to better performance. The Level 2 upgrades concentrate on the cylinder head. The engine will perform quite a bit better with these modifications, and they are well worth doing. If you are keeping the cast-iron head and choose not to make these modifications, you are not allowed to complain about the performance of your engine!

Carburetor Conversion

The first thing to improve is the carburetion. Even if you swapped a 2V carburetor earlier as part of a Level 1 upgrade, there is still room for improvement in Level 2. This is the time to convert to a 2V. Have the head machined to accept a

An improvement over the 2V-to-1V swap is what is known as the carburetor conversion. This adapter requires removing the cylinder head to mill the carb mounting boss flat and open up the carb bore to the full 2V size. Now you can take full advantage of a 2V carburetor.

While the cylinder head is off for the carburetor conversion, have the machine shop upgrade the valve size and type. Intake valves up to 1.75 inches in diameter can fit in most heads without much unshrouding. To fit 1.50-inch exhaust valves with hardened seats into small log heads, your machinist will need to select a seat that is only slightly larger than the valve face to avoid milling into the coolant passage.

The cast-iron head certainly has limitations, but any porting operations can provide a level of improvement. The bowl area (above the valves) and the ports have a lot of room for improvement. Check for casting flash and remove it from the intake and exhaust runners.

The exhaust port divider has always been controversial. It is our opinion that with a stock manifold, the performance gains must be minimal. With a header, however, it seems logical that for the exhaust gas to efficiently exit the head, it will help to have the port divider direct it to one exhaust tube or the other. It is hard to believe that there are no published dyno tests.

direct-to-the-intake adapter plate and open up the carburetor bore to match the carburetor. (See chapter 8 for a description of the conversion process.)

Valve Job

This is also the time to have a performance valve job performed. Since you are doing the valve job anyway, if the intake valves in your cylinder head are not already 1.75 inches, make the upgrade now. You can also upgrade the exhaust valves to 1.5 inches. SI Valves makes upgraded performance valves for these engines that have higher performance features than ordinary stock replacement valves.

Porting

The stock cast-iron head responds very well to basic porting operations. Removing casting flash and other obstructions to flow, tapering valve guides and other sharp features, and general bowl area cleanup are all procedures that an experienced machinist/porter will be able to do. (For more information about these procedures, refer to chapter 8.)

Exhaust Port Divider

If you have upgraded to a header (and at this point there is no good reason not to), consider installing

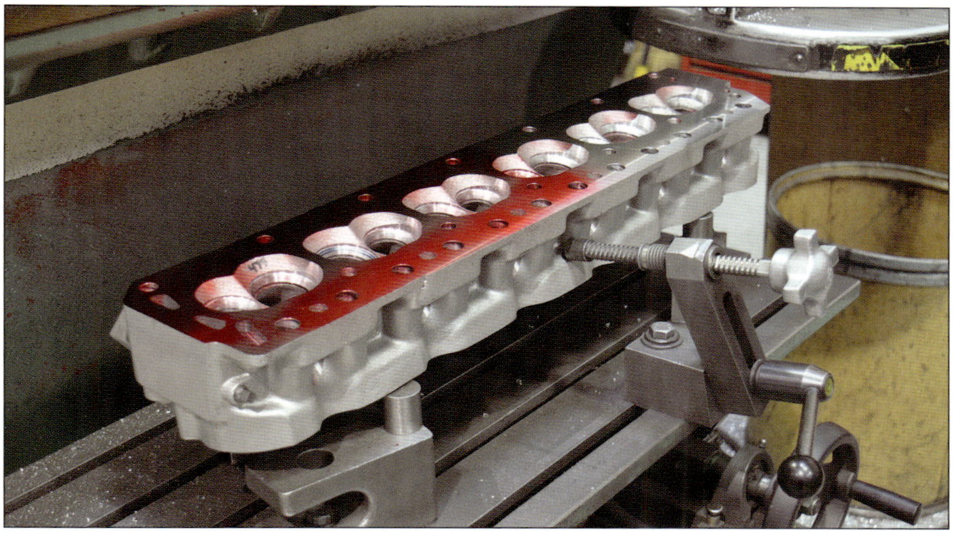

Milling the head is done to clean up the gasket surface to the perfect finish to allow the best sealing from the gasket. It is also used to change the size of the combustion chamber. Milling makes the chamber volume smaller and therefore increases static compression.

the exhaust port divider. With the port divider installed, your porter will be able to port match the head to the header.

Milling

One of the ways to increase or restore the compression ratio in the engine is to mill the head. If you wish or need to adjust the compression ratio, remember that a more effective way to increase the ratio is to zero-deck the block. You may need to do both, but plan this carefully.

Pushrods

If you mill the head and block, you may find that a stock, nonadjustable rocker-arm assembly will no longer give the correct geometry. Replacing the pushrods with correct-length replacements will correct the condition. Alternatively, you can replace the original with a stock, adjustable assembly from an early engine or upgrade to one of the higher ratio setups.

Level 3: Short-Block and Camshaft

In Level 3, you will address some durability items, sometimes referred to as *insurance*. This is also the time to select a new camshaft. If you have made the upgrades in Levels 1 and 2, the camshaft is how you take full advantage of the money you spent.

Balancing

Balancing the engine does not necessarily increase the performance, but it does make the engine last longer and, in the process, requires the machinist to put extraordinary effort into the machining and reassembly of all the rotating and reciprocating components in the engine. Do not assume this is done on every rebuild.

Piston Selection

Piston selection depends on the performance level you hope to achieve. For high performance, especially turbocharged engines, forged pistons can be custom ordered. For most builds, cast pistons are much more affordable and will work just fine.

Piston selection is also a consideration when establishing the compression ratio. A flat-top piston works best when you are able to establish the compression ratio by milling the head and/or the block. If you need to lower the compression ratio (in the case of a turbocharged engine), you may require dished pistons that create more combustion chamber volume.

Finally, if you are trying to attain a high compression ratio, you may be able to have custom domed pistons made. In the 1960s, this was not uncommon for engines used in various forms of racing. Domed pistons will require quite a bit of extra work by your machinist to safely determine the size and shape of the dome.

Main Bearing Studs

While not an upgrade that improves the power level, main bearing studs (to replace the factory bolts) will provide an extra level of insurance to keep the engine running longer if you decide to make performance upgrades.

Camshaft

As we have already established, the camshaft is the upgrade that will have the largest impact on the performance from the engine. It is critical to get the right camshaft for how you intend to use the vehicle. If you go too big, the car will be less fun to drive on a regular basis. If you go too small, you may not achieve the performance goals that you set at the beginning of the build.

Refer to camshaft manufacturers websites for guidance on camshaft selection. If at all possible, have the new camshaft degreed. The difference in performance is noticeable if the camshaft is not properly timed with the crankshaft.

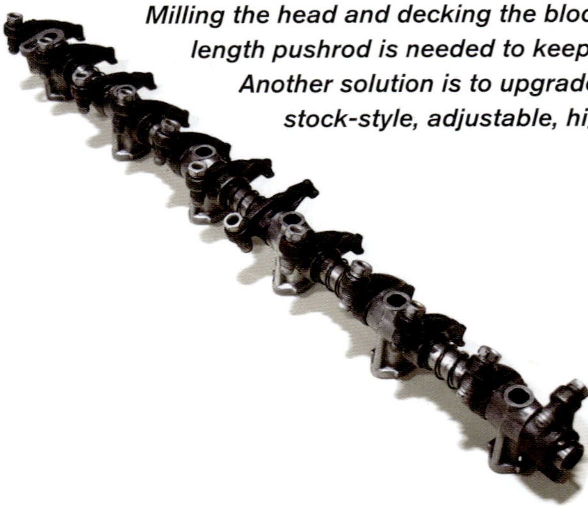

Milling the head and decking the block can remove enough material that a different-length pushrod is needed to keep the right preload on the hydraulic lifters. Another solution is to upgrade to adjustable rocker arms. There are also stock-style, adjustable, high-ratio rocker-arm assemblies available.

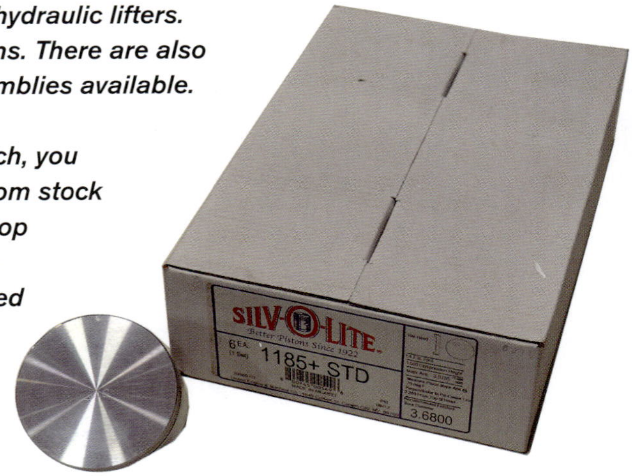

With a little research, you can find pistons from stock replacement, flat-top cast, all the way to custom-sized forged pistons. These are Silv-O-Lite cast-aluminum pistons.

Main bearing studs will not make you go faster, but they will allow you to go faster. Consider them insurance if you are building an engine with dramatically more power than stock.

You need to have the right camshaft, and it must be properly installed. Proper installation of a performance camshaft requires degreeing the cam. This process ensures that the camshaft timing is correct by starting with the intake lobe at its precise peak. Special equipment required for this process includes the degree wheel and a dial indicator.

Performance Modifications to Original Parts

In many cases, one reason to keep the 6-cylinder engine is to stay within budget. With this in mind, some of the stock engine components can be modified to yield better performance. Stock parts are not too difficult to find, so 144 and 170 owners can step up to a 200 block with relative ease. Some modifications are also very inexpensive if you are able to do the work yourself. As a word of caution, if you decide to grab a die grinder and start porting, go slowly. Like a haircut, you can always take off more, but you cannot put it back.

Cylinder Block

For best performance, it is not advisable to use the 144- and 170-ci engines. All physical dimensions of the 200-ci engine are the same with the added benefit of having seven main bearings for durability and smoother operation along with the extra cubic inches.

There are not many modifications available for these engine blocks, nor are they needed. The original crankshaft and rods are very strong and (unless they have been damaged in the past) should be more than adequate for most performance builds. Forged rods would be a nice upgrade for very high performance, turbocharged

For the best performance, it is better to replace 144 and 170 blocks with the larger-displacement 200 block. Besides the additional size, 200-ci engines from 1965 onward have seven main bearings, which improves durability and helps provide smooth power. The 144- and 170-ci engines can be quickly identified by the three core plugs on the right side of the block.

Seven-main-bearing blocks are preferred for performance builds and can be identified by the five core plugs on the right side of the block. The 250-ci engines are visually similar to 200-ci engines but are nearly 2 inches taller to accommodate the longer stroke and 3/4 inch wider at the oil pan. The 250 bell-housing bolt pattern is the same as on a small-block V-8.

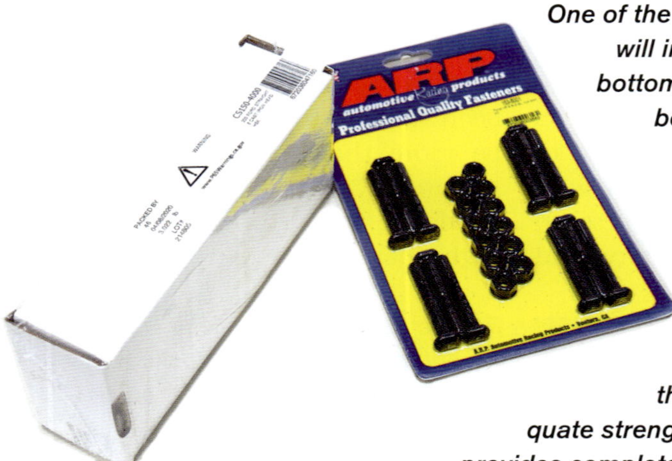

One of the few aftermarket parts that will increase the strength of the bottom end of the engine are rod bolts and main bearing stud kits from ARP. These rod bolts are designed so that each bolt can withstand the reciprocating weight of the piston and rod at maximum load. This ensures that there is more than adequate strength for the application. ARP provides complete instructions with each kit.

engines, but they are not available as of this time. For almost every build, though, they would be an expensive act of overkill. The upgrades that are available start with high-performance main bearing stud kits and rod bolts by ARP available from Vintage Inlines.

Machine Shop Work

One of the most important things to do when building an engine for improved performance is to have the machining done at a reputable shop. It is not worth the money saved to go to a shop that cannot perform all of the operations that you want to have done. While not strictly a performance upgrade, balancing the crankshaft and the piston/rod assemblies will certainly pay dividends when building performance into these engines.

Always use quality parts from trusted manufacturers. If you have not heard of the manufacturer, look them up and ask around. Some companies that make quality parts for performance builds are not well-known outside the high-performance industry, so research is important. If you are having your machine work done at a good shop, you should be able to trust their recommendations for gaskets and bearings.

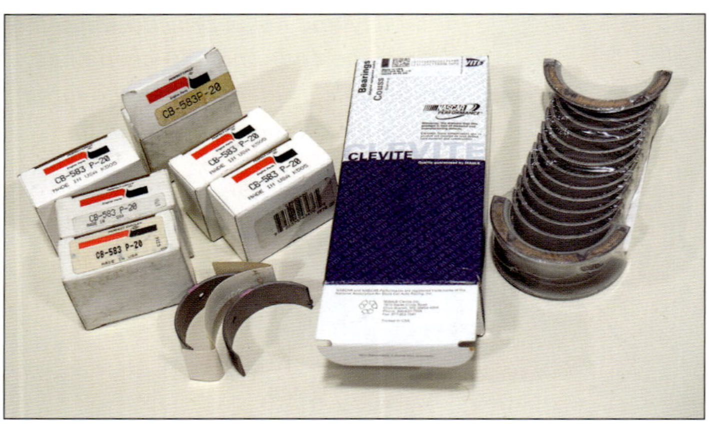

Quality main and rod bearings require materials that stay in place, have low friction to the mating journal, can embed debris, and conform to the shape of the journal and the caps that hold them in place. They must also withstand the tremendous loads of the power strokes and do it under extreme temperature while retaining all of these characteristics.

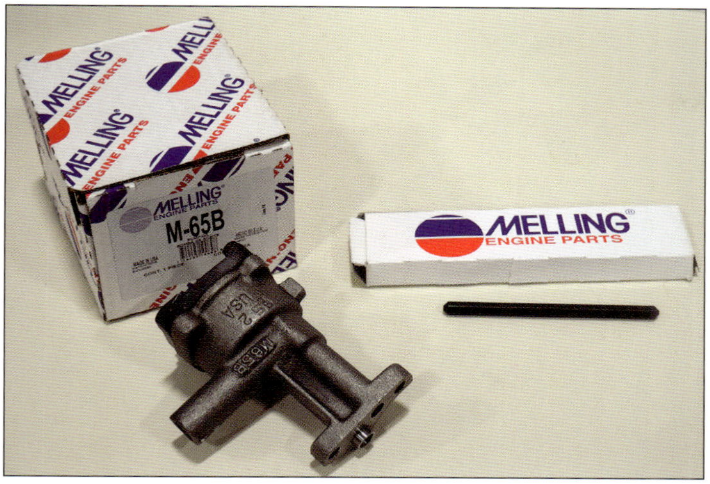

High-volume oil pumps are not needed in the Ford small-six engines. Always replace the oil pump with a quality, stock replacement pump. Be sure to check the oil pump driveshaft for any damage and replace if necessary.

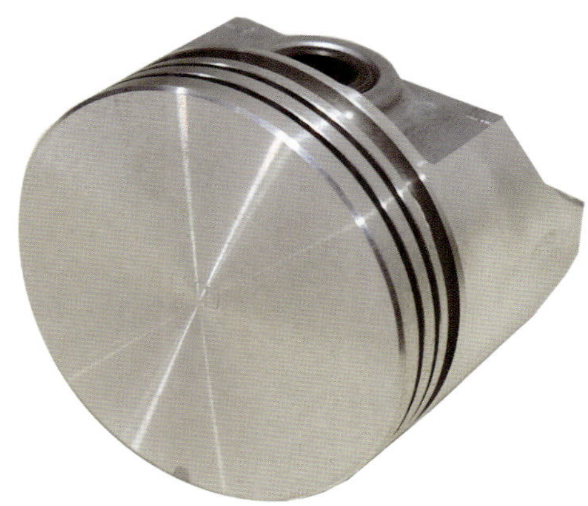

For performance builds with higher compression requirements, Silv-O-Lite offers flat-top pistons that contribute to higher compression by eliminating the stock dish in the top of the piston. They feature all of the advantages of the other pistons in the Silv-O-Lite line.

Pistons

The engine block part that has some options is the piston. The stock pistons on 200- and 250-ci engines are the same in all dimensions. The dish in these pistons measures 6.5 cubic centimeters (cc). The exception is the 1966 and 1967 California emissions cars; they had a 13-cc dish to lower compression. The dish size must be considered when calculating the static compression ratio.

Aftermarket stock replacement pistons are available in the original cast aluminum with the stock dish sizes, or in a flat-top configuration. The flat-top piston is often used when building a 200 and installing a later-model-year cylinder head. The combustion chamber size on the later heads averages about 63

Silv-O-Lite pistons by United Engine & Machine make excellent replacements for stock pistons with the correct dish based on the year. These cast-aluminum pistons are machined to a unique finish with exacting skirt tolerances. Heat treating provides tighter tolerances, more strength, and longer life at an affordable price. These pistons are available from Vintage Inlines and other retailers.

Companies such as AutoTec manufacture quality forged pistons for high-output, naturally aspirated engines and turbocharged applications. AutoTec's forged pistons are made from 4032 high-silicone aluminum alloy and are extremely durable, have great wear resistance, a low expansion rate, and have very low friction. They are very affordable for a forged piston.

cc, while the earlier, small log heads had a combustion chamber volume around 58 cc. The flat-top piston reclaims the difference in chamber size so that the compression ratio is not affected.

For owners building high-compression, naturally aspirated engines or turbocharged engines, several companies, like AutoTec, custom make forged aluminum pistons. AutoTec's website says that its pistons are designed for up to 600 hp in small-block V-8s. This is likely more than anyone will build into a small six, but if you do, Race-Tec also makes custom forged pistons for the small six.

Deck height is the amount of cylinder wall still visible (with the cylinder head removed) when the piston is at the top of its travel. A performance deck height is around 0.040 inch and includes the compressed head gasket thickness. Most modern composite head gaskets have a compressed thickness of at least 0.045 inch, so a 0.0-inch deck height should be the goal.

Combustion Chamber Volume

There are other techniques to increase the compression ratio even more to improve efficiency and power. One way is to deck the block. This process involves machining the top surface of the block where the cylinder-head bolts on. It is important to make accurate measurements to avoid removing so much material that you create piston-to-valve contact (interference). On 144- and 170-ci engines with stock parts and an original-style head gasket, 0.025 inch of deck clearance is recommended. For 200 and 250 engines with stock parts, 0.012-inch clearance is recommended.

However, due to the compressed thickness of modern head gaskets (between 0.045 and 0.055 inch) compared to the original steel shim head gaskets, it is usually acceptable to zero-deck the block. This means to machine the deck down to the highest point of the pistons' upward travel. As with any machining operation, take careful measurements and carefully plan how much surface to remove by milling.

Cylinder Head

The original cast-iron integral intake cylinder head is the part of the engine that can use the most help. From small valves to small 1-barrel carburetors, nearly every part of the head can be improved. The ultimate upgrade is the aluminum cylinder head designed by Classic Inlines and now sold by Vintage Inlines.

Exhaust Manifold

One source of poor performance is the stock cast-iron exhaust manifold. It is possible to keep a cast-iron manifold and modify it to help performance to some degree. The later manifolds on vehicles from the 1970s offer an improvement over earlier versions due in part to design changes that made them more robust and resistant to cracking under heavy use. The real improvement is just in the size of the exhaust port openings. Manifolds on vehicles built in the 1980s are not desirable due to the unique outlet configuration designed to bolt on a catalytic converter.

After selecting the manifold you will use, inspect it carefully for any cracks or broken areas. Damaged manifolds are not worth trying to save. Reproductions are available and are based on the later design.

Whichever manifold you choose to use, check the flatness of the exhaust port flanges using a straight edge. Your machinist can correct slight unevenness on a belt sander, but do not remove too much material as this will weaken the mounting flanges. Have this operation done after you have finished the other work so that you do not accidentally damage the freshly machined surface.

Measuring Static Compression Ratio

Static compression ratio is the calculation of the compression ratio assuming that the valves are closed through the entire compression stroke. Dynamic compression takes into consideration the reality that the valves have overlap and the intake valve is partially open for a portion of the compression stroke. When people talk about compression ratios, they are nearly always referring to the static ratio.

The compression ratio is the ratio of the total volume of the cylinder with the piston at bottom dead center (all the way down) compared to the volume with the piston at TDC (at the top of its travel). Both volumes consider the compressed head gasket thickness, deck height volume, and combustion chamber volume. If the pistons used have a dish, this volume must be considered as well.

The key measurements to know when using an online calculator are:

- Cylinder bore diameter (measured)
- Crankshaft stroke length (measured)
- Head gasket bore diameter (available from manufacturer)
- Head gasket compressed thickness (available from manufacturer)
- Combustion chamber volume (measured and averaged)
- Piston dome volume (if applicable, available from manufacturer)
- Piston-to-deck clearance volume (measured)

Online calculators will provide the compression ratio. So, with trial and error, you can determine the combustion chamber volume, deck clearance, and piston dish needed to achieve the compression ratio you need.

The formula is:

$$\frac{a + b + c + d + e}{b + c + d + e} = \text{Compression Ratio}$$

a: cylinder volume
b: deck height volume
c: compressed head gasket volume
d: combustion chamber volume
e: piston dish volume ■

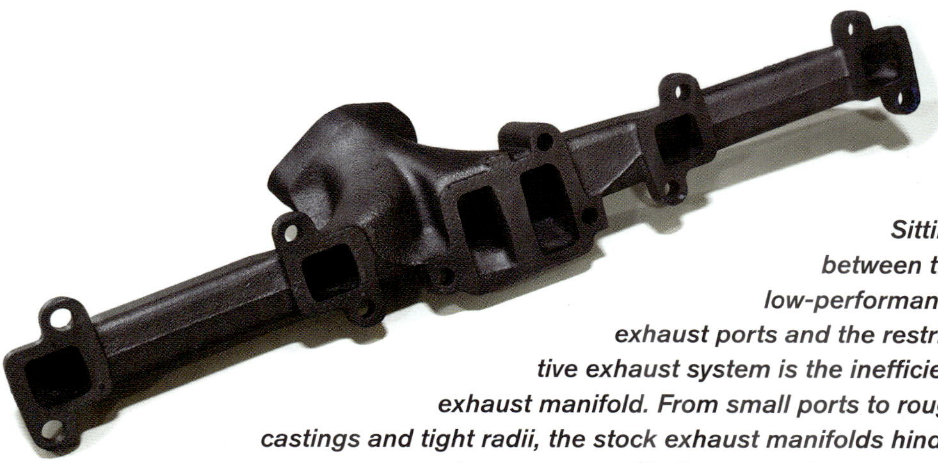

Sitting between the low-performance exhaust ports and the restrictive exhaust system is the inefficient exhaust manifold. From small ports to rough castings and tight radii, the stock exhaust manifolds hinder performance even if other upgrades are made.

One area that can yield gains from the stock exhaust manifold is the size of the ports. Use a gasket to mark the openings of cylinders number-1 and -2, and -5 and -6. Use a grinder to enlarge the openings to slightly more than the size of the gasket opening. Blend the port as far into the manifold as you can reach.

Begin the modifications by gasket matching the ports on the manifold. This is just what it sounds like. Place the exhaust gasket on the manifold and mark the openings. There are many techniques to mark the openings, but everyone should have a Sharpie marker in the garage. After marking all of the ports, begin to open them up with a die grinder and a quality burr for cast iron. Make the openings slightly larger than the gasket opening. This creates a reversion dam effect. In simple terms, it prevents the hot exhaust gases from encountering an obstruction as they exit the head and enter the exhaust manifold.

Check for and remove any casting flash from the production process that may cause disruption to exhaust flow. Do this visually and by feeling inside the passages. Grind off

Here is an exhaust manifold that has had one of the ports gasket matched. It is easy to see how matching the ports will help improve efficiency.

any flash that you can reach. Do the same in the outlet area.

Using a reworked stock manifold with a 2-inch exhaust pipe, performance muffler, and a 2¼-inch tailpipe (for improved sound) will provide better sound, a slight benefit in power, and should be considered the bare-minimum exhaust upgrade for any level of performance improvements. It is not adequate for engines with larger carburetors or a performance camshaft.

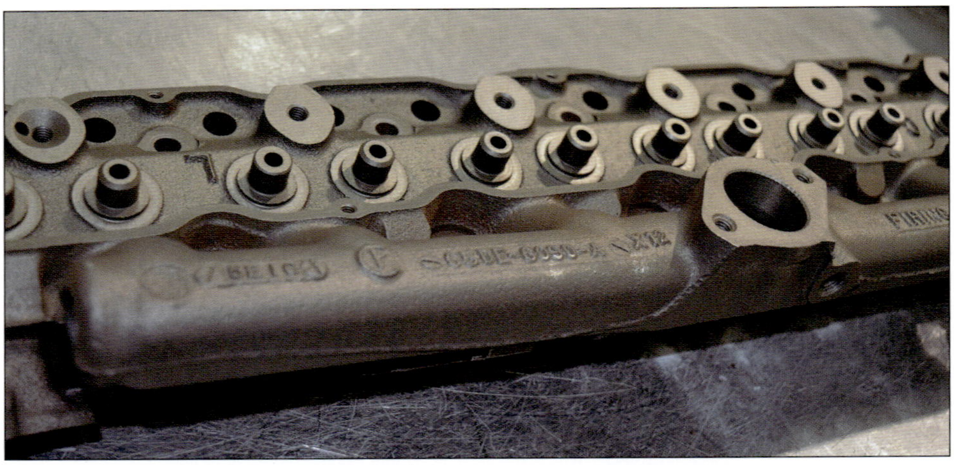

The stock cast-iron cylinder heads produced through 1968 are known to enthusiasts as the small log heads. With an intake log visibly smaller than later years, and a 1½-inch carburetor bore, the performance potential of the small log heads is limited compared to later heads.

Cast-Iron Cylinder Head

Upgrading the cylinder head starts with selecting the right cylinder head to work with.

Beginning in 1969 with the C9DE-6090-M casting number, Ford installed what enthusiasts call the "large log" cylinder head. They are called this because the intake log volume increased from 1,100 cc to 1,240 cc. With the increased log volume came a larger carburetor bore. The combustion chamber size was increased to 62 cc, which had the effect of lowering the compression ratio and was a nod toward improved emissions.

In 1977, these heads received another upgrade when Ford increased

In 1969, Ford made significant changes to the cylinder head with a larger intake log volume and a 1.75-inch carburetor bore. These new heads are known as large log heads. The casting number for the first of the large log heads is C9DE-6090-M and any head with a casting number later than this is a good starting point. Intake valve diameter increased to 1.75-inch in 1977, but the larger valves can be installed in earlier large log heads.

Most of the large log heads have what is referred to as a flat top (shown). There is a 1½-inch flat surface on the top of the intake log. The flat surface is desirable when milling to add a 2-barrel carburetor or an Offenhauser 3x1-barrel carburetor adapter. Later heads may have a hex-shaped intake log. These heads have a slightly larger intake volume, but carburetor conversion is made difficult by the narrow 1/2-inch-wide top surface.

The casting number for the cylinder head is located on the top of the intake log behind the carburetor. Remember to look for casting numbers of C9DE-6090-M or later.

the manifold volume again, to 1,345 cc. Perhaps more importantly, Ford increased the intake-valve diameter to 1.75 inches, up from 1.649 inches. The exhaust valves remained at 1.38 inches.

A final upgrade before the end of the decade saw the intake volume go to 1,420 cc with no change to the valve sizes.

Another change toward the end of the 1970s was the addition of the hex-head cylinder heads. Previously and concurrently, the other large log heads had a 1½-inch-wide flat-top surface. Not much is known about the addition of the hex heads, but flat-topped heads appeared in the same years as hex heads. If you plan to mill the surface for a 2-barrel carburetor conversion, the flat-topped head is more desirable.

With the numerous casting variations to choose from, the most desirable is a mid- to late 1970s large log with the flat top and 1¾-inch valves. These were plentiful in cars like the Granada and Fairmont but are becoming hard to find in salvage yards.

Carburetor Swaps and Adapters

Bolting on a 2-barrel carburetor is the first improvement to the cylinder head and can be made with the head on the car as discussed in the section on carburetor swaps. More involved than the carburetor swap is what has been termed the 2-barrel conversion.

The conversion requires removing the head. With the head off the engine, the machine shop mills the carburetor mounting surface down and mounts the conversion adapter by drilling and tapping four holes. The advantage to the conversion is that the carburetor bore can be opened up to the full 2-barrel-sized shape.

Adapters are made to install Weber 2V downdraft carburetors and Holley/Autolite 2V models. A certain amount of hot rodding must be done to complete the installation when converting to a 2V carburetor that was never installed by the factory.

Besides the fuel lines, vacuum lines, and choke wiring, installations

A very effective modification for the stock cast-iron cylinder head is to modify the intake for a 2-barrel carburetor by milling off the carburetor mounting boss and installing a conversion adapter for either a Weber or Holley 2-barrel.

After milling, the adapter can be used as a template to drill the machined surface and tap the holes for mounting bolts.

Before mounting the adapter, open up the carburetor bore to the size of the 2-barrel carburetor you will be installing. Here, the adapter has been bolted on and you can see the enlarged carburetor bore. It is ready for a larger, newer design carburetor.

Aftermarket bell-crank kits exist, such as this one for Weber carburetors. It is less expensive to install a bell crank, and you may be able to use all of the original linkage. You must make sure that there is no binding at all through the full travel of the pedal.

When upgrading to a 2-barrel carburetor, most builders find it necessary to convert to a throttle cable due to the orientation of the throttle shaft being off by 90 degrees from the original. Direct-replacement aftermarket pedals are available for some cars, but if the original pedal is not equipped for a cable, it is possible to mount a pedal from a different car to the early firewall. Lokar makes pedals for early Mustangs that make the conversion easy and look very good.

on vehicles not originally equipped with a throttle cable will need a new pedal and cable fitted. This is because the original-style throttle rods will not connect to the new carburetor. Aftermarket pedals designed to convert to a throttle cable exist for some vehicles, but it is possible to fit a salvage yard pedal by fabricating a bracket to attach to the firewall.

For the truly creative, it might be possible to adapt an existing bell-crank mechanism for proper operation or fabricate your own and avoid the conversion to a throttle cable.

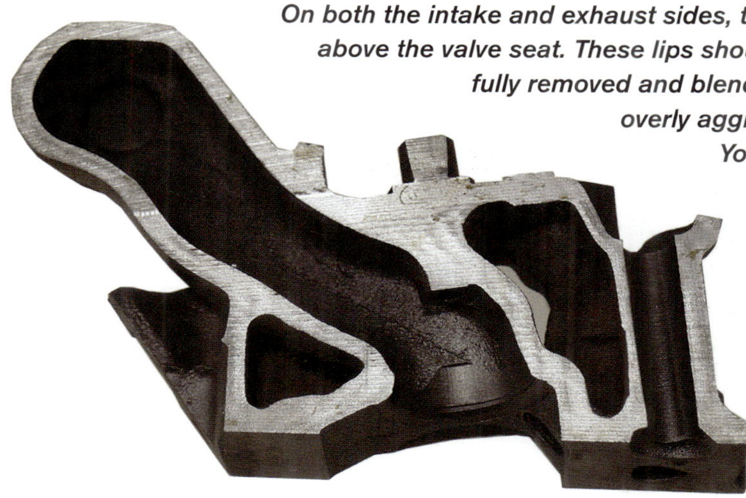

On both the intake and exhaust sides, there is a lip above the valve seat. These lips should be carefully removed and blended. Do not be overly aggressive here. You just need to remove the lip that projects into the bowl area.

Cylinder Head Porting

Porting is a familiar term to anyone who has read a performance car magazine. It may not be clear to everyone what porting actually is, though. The ports in the cylinder head are the passages that the air/fuel mixture follows from the intake log to the combustion chamber and where the spent exhaust gases flow from the combustion chamber out to the exhaust manifold.

The term porting comes from the process of modifying these ports by grinding away metal in a precise manner to improve flow into and out of the combustion chamber to a level never possible with mass production. Casting imperfections, rough surfaces, and obstructions to airflow were just too expensive to correct on mass-produced cars and honestly would not have been worth the effort on 6-cylinder cars. However, when the other deficiencies of these engines are corrected (weak distributor, small carburetor, and restrictive exhaust), the gains from porting are multiplied to the point where they are certainly worth the effort.

Porting should begin in the valve bowl area. The bowl is the area above the valve when the head is in its upright position. With the head upside down on the bench, the bowl is under the valve when the valve is removed. The goal in the bowl area is to reduce and taper the valve guide bosses and smooth any sharp areas, especially where there is a radius.

Intake Ports

Because the intake manifold is cast as part of the head, the amount of porting that can be done in the intake port is extremely limited. Using your finger, reach into the port as far as possible to check for casting flash. If any is found, make every effort to remove it. Polishing is

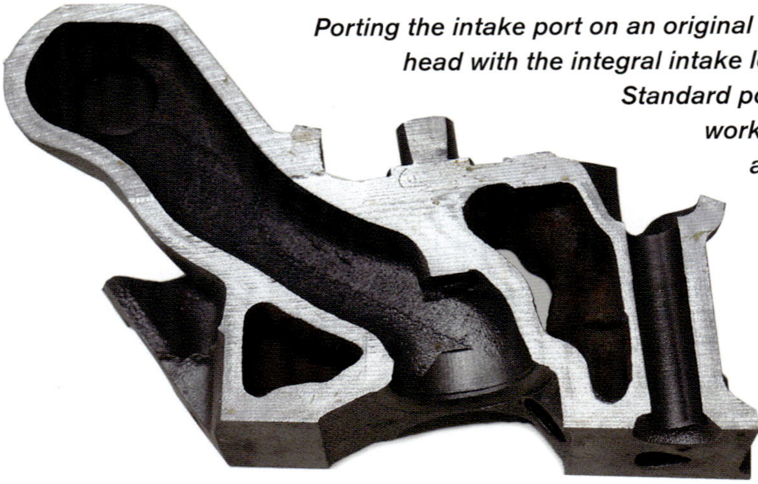

Porting the intake port on an original cast-iron cylinder head with the integral intake log is challenging. Standard porting procedures work in the valve bowl area. The problem is that with no access from the manifold end of the port, it is difficult to fully work the surfaces of the port.

not necessary on the intake ports as some amount of turbulence helps to keep the fuel/air charge atomized as it enters the combustion chamber.

Exhaust Ports

Porting the exhaust ports is easier because you can get to both the valve end and the manifold end of the passage. The exhaust ports have a severe restriction as the bowl transitions to the exhaust port. Reducing and smoothing the valve guide boss and reshaping the radius of the port

This is what the intake port looks like before any work has been done. Porting the head means the restrictions and obstructions are reshaped or removed. Polishing means to grind the ports with progressively finer abrasives to polish the surface, sometimes to a near-mirror finish. Other than the exhaust ports, highly polished surfaces are not necessary for these heads.

You cannot port all the way down the intake port, so use your finger to check for casting flash. If you find flash, make every effort to remove it. Flash is disruptive to airflow and hinders performance.

This exhaust port is similar to exhaust ports on other engine types. There is access from both ends so it is easier to achieve the highly polished surface on the roof of the port that helps expel the hot exhaust gases. There is a lot of work that can be done on the exhaust ports.

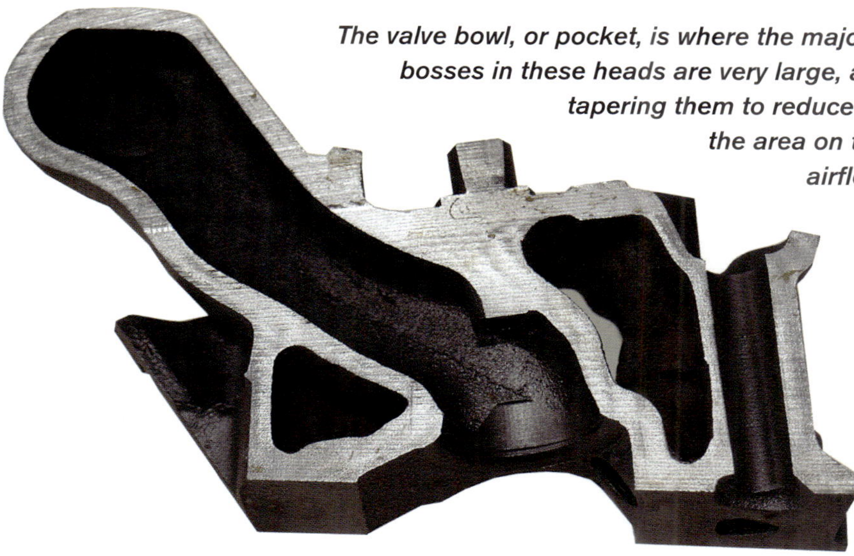

The valve bowl, or pocket, is where the majority of the work will be done. The valve guide bosses in these heads are very large, and performance will benefit from blending and tapering them to reduce obstructions. It is not necessary to highly polish the area on the intake port because some disruption in the airflow helps keep the air/fuel mixture atomized.

The exhaust gases leave the combustion chamber at very high speed and contact the roof of the exhaust port. For this reason, it is recommended to enlarge the exhaust port and completely remove imperfections that cause any obstruction to airflow. Polish the surface as much as you can.

Gasket matching the exhaust ports may be one of the most satisfying things you can do to the head. Using the exhaust gasket, mark the shape onto the head. Grind the port opening to match the shape of the gasket. Blend the enlarged port well into the head for best results.

Cylinders number-3 and -4 present a unique problem. For reasons not well understood by the average car owner, Ford combined the exhaust ports for these two cylinders into what is known as a Siamesed port. Polishing the port roof is still necessary, but gasket matching does not help as much as on the other cylinders.

A solution to the Siamesed port problem is the port divider that was invented in the 1960s and sold by Jack Clifford. The port divider is installed by grinding it to have a fairly tight fit into the Siamesed port, and then tack welding it in place. Proper installation is a must to prevent the divider from coming loose, which can cause a lot of noise and potentially damage the head.

The installed port divider can now be worked much the same as the other exhaust ports. If you are installing a header, use the header gasket to gasket match the reshaped exhaust ports. Polish the port roof as well. This one needs a little more work.

floor will help eliminate the restriction. Since the hot exhaust gases exit the combustion chamber and contact the roof of the exhaust port on the way to the header, it is also important to raise the roof of the port to increase the volume.

Using an exhaust gasket, mark the openings and grind the port to increase the size and match the shape of the gasket. Finally, a very smooth, almost mirror finish helps reduce resistance to flow. The smoother finish also helps slow the buildup of carbon.

Of special note on the exhaust ports of cylinders number-3 and -4 is the Siamesed port shared by the two exhaust ports. When installing a header, the port shapes do not match. There has been controversy for many years over the effectiveness of a part designed by Jack Clifford in the 1960s. The part is known as the port divider. It is designed to be installed in the Siamesed -3 and -4 port and separate the two ports. In doing so, the machinist can then shape the exhaust ports to match the exhaust gasket and smooth the roof of the modified ports.

Original, stock-size intake valves can be replaced with later 1.75-inch valves for an increase in performance. Stainless-steel Port Flow valves from SI Valves are a further upgrade over stock. From right to left are the stock 1.649-inch intake valve from a 200 head, a 1.75-inch stock replacement valve from a 1977-and-later head, and a 1.75-inch Port Flow valve from SI Industries.

Exhaust valves remained at 1.38 inch from the 1965 200 head throughout production. A nice upgrade here is the 1.5-inch Port Flow stainless-steel valves from SI Valves. On the left is the stock 1.38-inch valve, and the 1.5-inch Port Flow is on the right.

Pay special attention to potential valve shrouding when installing larger valves. Shrouding occurs when the valve is too close to the combustion chamber wall. This restricts flow through the open valve. Shown here is a 144 head that was modified for hydroplane racing in the 1960s. Notice the size of the valves and the work done to reduce shrouding at the chamber wall.

Valves and Combustion Chamber

The next upgrade to consider is installing 1.75-inch intake and 1.50-inch exhaust valves (with hardened seats on the exhaust side, if not already equipped). Even if the head you have already has the larger intake valves, a good three-angle valve job will improve performance to some degree.

Upgrade Valve Size

When installing larger valves, your machine shop can determine

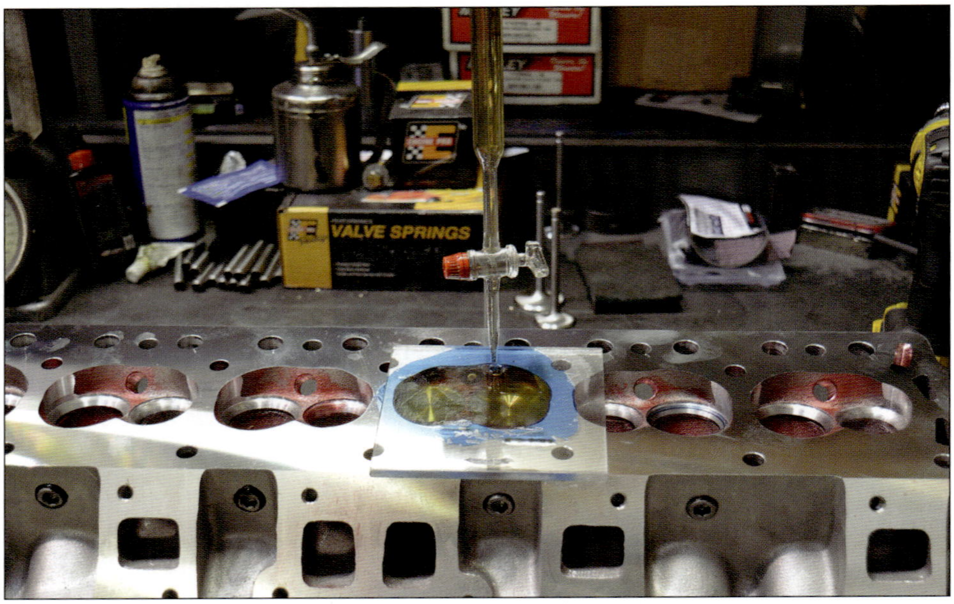

To determine the size of the combustion chambers for compression ratio calculations, you have to cc the chambers. It gets its name from determining the cubic centimeters (cc's) of the combustion chamber. Use the size of the smallest chamber and mill the head for the desired chamber volume.

The stock valvetrain was designed to provide years of dependable service. High performance was never a consideration. Upgrades to the springs, retainers, valves, and rocker arms can bring out a little more performance than stock without sacrificing durability in an otherwise-stock cylinder head.

As with everything else, technology has improved valve lifters, especially the hydraulic type. The improvements in aftermarket parts are evolutionary, not revolutionary, but they will help the engine run better than the original stock style.

if valve shrouding has occurred. Shrouding occurs when the valve is large enough that there is not sufficient clearance in some direction, usually to the closest wall of the combustion chamber. This lack of clearance affects the flow of the air/fuel charge into (or the spent exhaust gases out of) the combustion chamber. Shrouding can be fixed by carefully grinding the combustion chamber to restore the necessary clearance. Grinding the wall to remedy shrouding will remove material from the combustion chamber, thus increasing the combustion chamber volume. For this reason, it is best to install the valves and correct any shrouding before performing the last step, which is milling the head.

Milling the Head

The most common way to increase the compression ratio is to decrease the size of the combustion chamber by milling the bottom of the cylinder head. Milling the head is most commonly done to ensure that the gasket surface is as flat and smooth as possible for good sealing, but it can also be done further to improve performance.

Milling the head involves removing material from the entire bottom surface to decrease the volume of the combustion chamber. Before performing the milling operation, have your machine shop *cc* the chambers. This term refers to measuring the volume of the combustion chambers using an oil such as automatic transmission fluid. The process involves removing enough of the bottom surface of the head to get the volume of the smallest chamber to the size you desire. You can make all of the chambers smaller by milling the head, so work with the size of the smallest chamber.

Valvetrain

The valvetrain is the collection of components that transfers the lift from the camshaft into the movement of the valves in the combustion chamber. As previously discussed, camshaft specifications are what determines how much the valves open and how long they stay open. Since the valves are not directly connected to the camshaft, the rest of the parts in the valvetrain make that connection. The valvetrain consists of the camshaft and valves, and (in order of appearance) the lifters, pushrods, rocker arms, valve springs, spring retainers, and spring keepers.

Lifters

Lifters are the parts that ride on the lobes of the camshaft. As the camshaft rotates, the flat bottom of the lifter stays in contact with the surface of the camshaft lobe. When the ramp of the lobe comes around, the lifter is the first component to start the transfer of lift to the valve.

Solid Lifters

Lifters have been designed in several forms through the years. Originally, the small-six engines were equipped with what are known as solid lifters. As the name implies, the lifter itself was a solid piece that directly transferred the height of the cam lobe to the rest of the valvetrain. This was generally considered a positive feature when talking about high-performance engines. There were several drawbacks to solid lifters that could be easily overlooked in a performance engine but were more of an annoyance on daily driven stock engines. These include noise and regular required maintenance.

The noise is easy to imagine. The valve spring does a reasonably good job of keeping the parts of the valvetrain in contact with each other in most circumstances. The exceptions to this are during cold start-up and higher-RPM operation.

Because the valvetrain components expand when they are hot, it is important to accurately set the valve lash. Valve lash is the term used to describe how tight the components of the valvetrain are in relation to each other. Too little valve lash leads to premature wear on the lifter and camshaft lobes, while too much lash leads to noise at least and valvetrain damage at worst. Setting the valve lash to the correct specification is very important. The correct setting, though, requires being a little too loose when the engine is cold, which creates slight noise until the engine warms up.

The other annoying part of solid lifters is the need for constant maintenance. Valve lash is set during the engine building process, and it's necessary to check the lash periodically

A solid lifter is just that: solid. There is no movement to absorb changes to length caused by temperature changes and wear. This will lead to some noise and degradation in performance as the gap in the parts expands. This is known as valve lash. The 144- and 170-ci engines had solid lifters from the factory.

Checking and adjusting valve lash is not difficult, but it is time consuming and a little messy. Refer to the appropriate year of the Ford service manual for the full procedure to adjust valve lash.

and adjust as needed. Performance is dramatically affected if the valves are not continually adjusted.

The adjustment process requires removing the valve cover, which is a dirty job. Still, many owners perform their own maintenance either happily or grudgingly. The owners who did the work grudgingly prior to 1962 were probably overjoyed when Ford announced the introduction of hydraulic lifters for the 1963 model year.

Hydraulic Lifters

Hydraulic lifters were designed to eliminate the unwanted noise and constant maintenance associated with solid lifters. They perform this job well by creating an internal shock absorber of oil from the engine's oiling system. In contrast to solid lifters, hydraulic lifters are made up of several pieces. The pieces allow the oil pressure in the lifter to expand the lifter to keep zero lash in the system at all times regardless of temperature or the level of wear on the other components.

Hydraulic lifters sound like just the miracle that valvetrains need to be trouble free. This is true for most applications. The exception is high-performance engines. At high RPM, the oil pressure within the lifter struggles to keep the lifter pumped up. This slight change causes various conditions. One is a drop in performance due to the full amount of the camshaft lift not being transferred to the pushrod. This happens because the lifter is no longer able to stay in contact with the camshaft lobe, especially after the cam lobe has reached its peak and the valve begins to close. This loss of contact can cause noises, intake backfires, and physical damage to valvetrain parts. For these reasons, solid lifters are always considered the choice for high-performance high-revving engines, even after hydraulic lifters became widely available.

For the small-six engines and most other engines, the manufacturer designs the block to either have solid or hydraulic lifters. As already stated, hydraulic lifters use engine oil pressure to stay pumped up. A series of passages in the engine block and the lifter bores provide the oil, which is under pressure, to accomplish this. Earlier small sixes did not have these passages, so they are forever fated to use solid lifters.

Owners of later engines that were designed for hydraulic lifters have the option of hydraulic lifters for normal and mild performance applications or solid lifters for high-revving high-performance use. The design and quality of modern hydraulic lifters make them suitable for all but the most extreme small-six builds.

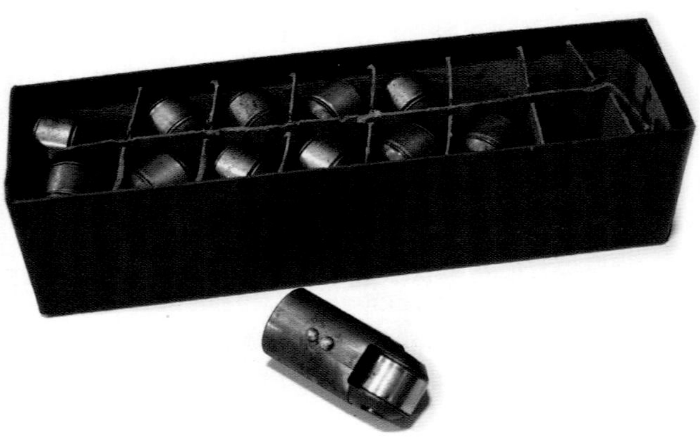

Early racers knew the advantage of roller lifters. The engine block had to be extensively modified to use these lifters as roller lifters are not made to rotate in the bore. The modifications caused increased wear to the lifters, so they were not good choices for everyday driving.

Roller Lifters

At this point, you may be asking, "What about roller-tipped lifters?" Roller lifters, and the improved camshaft lobe designs that come with them, have been around longer than the Ford small-six engine that we all know and love.

In fact, racers in the early 1960s modified their small sixes to accept roller-tipped lifters that allowed them to take advantage of more-aggressive camshaft grinds. To accomplish this, they cut grooves in the lifter bores using a process called broaching. Think of it as taking a file and repeatedly rubbing the side of the lifter bore until you have worn a squared-off groove in it. Then, the builder used an appropriately sized aftermarket roller lifter designed with buttons on one side to ride in the groove in the lifter bore. All of this is necessary with roller-tipped lifters to keep the lifter from rotating in the bore.

Other engine designs are able to use a bridge or a connection between adjacent lifters to prevent rotation. This is a much more economical solution to the problem, but there is unfortunately not enough room in the area of the lifter bores in the small six to accommodate the bridges. Because of the difficulty and expense involved, roller cams and lifters are not commercially available for the small six at this time.

Pushrods

In contrast to lifters, there is not much to say about pushrods. They continue the process of transferring camshaft lift to the valve. The pushrods are steel shafts, normally hollow but occasionally solid, that sit verti-

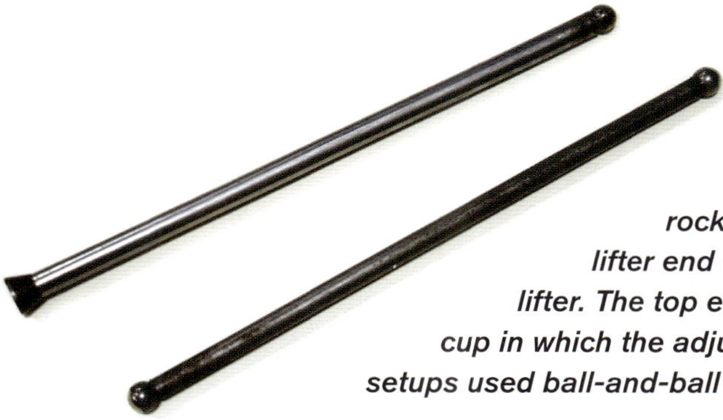

Pushrods for stock engines came in two types. The ball-and-cup design for early adjustable rocker arms had a ball on the lifter end that rode in the top of the lifter. The top end, at the rocker arm, had a cup in which the adjuster bolt rode. Nonadjustable setups used ball-and-ball pushrods.

Roller rocker arms by Yella Terra have roller bearings and roller tips to reduce friction. The mounting technique blocks the oiling passage in the head, so hollow pushrods must be used.

cally in the small-six engine between the lifter and the rocker arm. The two types of pushrods used in stock small-six engines are referred to as the *ball and cup* and the *ball and ball*.

The ball-and-cup style is called this because a steel ball that seats into the top of the lifter is manufactured into the bottom end. On the other end is a steel cup into which the adjuster bolt for the adjustable rocker arm seats. Adjustable rocker arms were originally found on solid-lifter engines. The adjustable rockers are required to allow for the frequent rocker-arm adjustments discussed earlier.

Ball-and-ball pushrods are used on hydraulic lifter–equipped engines. The ball on the bottom end performs the same function as on a ball-and-cup pushrod. The ball on the top end seats into the nonadjustable rocker arm used with hydraulic lifters.

Rocker Arms

If all we had were stock-style rocker arms, this would be the end of the pushrod story. However, Yella Terra, an Australian company, makes an adjustable, full-roller rocker-arm conversion kit that requires a different-style pushrod. In addition to the pushrods, this conversion requires an oiling-type lifter. The oil pressure that feeds the hydraulic lifter is passed through the lifter to the pushrod. The difference is that these pushrods have to be drilled, which means they have a hole in each end. The hollow pushrod allows the oil from the lifter to travel up and lubricate the roller bearings of the Yella Terra rocker arms. The Yella Terra rocker-arm conversion seems to be the only aftermarket roller rocker-arm upgrade for the small-six engines at this time.

Roller Rocker Arm Advantages

There are some advantages to using full-roller rocker arms. One is the increased power from decreasing valvetrain friction. The two worst friction hot spots in the valvetrain are where the rocker fulcrum rides on the shaft and where the tip of the rocker contacts the valve stem. The power used to overcome this friction, however small the amount, is energy that is not converted to rotational force of the crankshaft. This means less power to the rear wheels. This is not a tremendous loss, but every bit of power that you can save is power that does not have to be made. A roller bearing at the fulcrum point dramatically reduces the friction associated with the bushings found on stock rocker arms.

In addition, by placing a roller bearing on the tip of the rocker arm where it contacts the valve stem, the tip of the rocker arm is able to roll across the valve stem tip as it moves up and down instead of sliding back and forth across the valve stem.

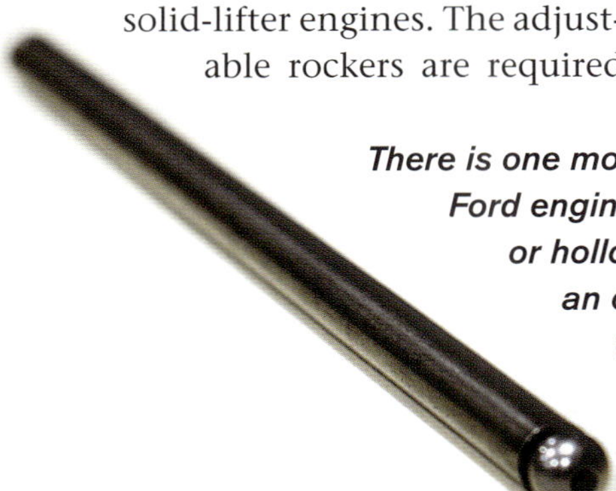

There is one more type of pushrod that has been used in Ford engines but not the small six. These are drilled or hollow ball-and-ball. This type of pushrod has an oil passage right through it to allow oil to travel from the lifter, up the pushrod, and to the rocker arm for lubrication. This style is used with an aftermarket roller rocker arm that eliminates the oil passage to the rocker arms.

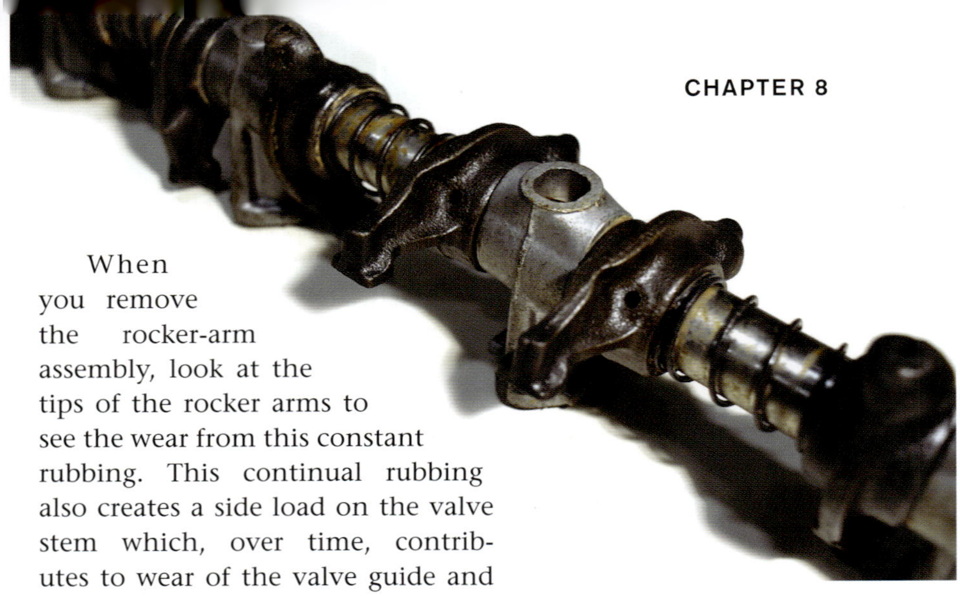

We have referred several times to the rocker-arm assembly. The rocker shaft is supported by aluminum pedestals. The shaft rides in bushings in the pedestals. The rocker arms rotate on the shaft on bushings as well. An oil passage from the cylinder head provides oil under pressure that makes its way through the shaft to each rocker arm to lubricate the shaft bushing and the rocker-arm tip.

When you remove the rocker-arm assembly, look at the tips of the rocker arms to see the wear from this constant rubbing. This continual rubbing also creates a side load on the valve stem which, over time, contributes to wear of the valve guide and leads to oil consumption and carbon buildup on the valve. This leads to loss of power and shortens the time between engine rebuilds.

Decreased friction is not the only benefit to roller rocker arms. Advantages in terms of performance exist as well. Roller rocker arms provide a precise ratio from valve to valve, and the blueprinted assemblies ensure accurate, repeatable motion of the valves. If a manufacturer is going to the effort and expense of developing a roller rocker-arm conversion, it only makes sense that they will address another feature that can enable the engine to produce more power. This is the rocker-arm ratio.

The Yella Terra roller rocker arms available for Ford small-six engines are designed with a 1.65:1 ratio. This means that they provide 10 percent more lift than the stock rocker-arm assembly. This effectively changes the cam specifications without having to change the camshaft.

Stock Rocker Arms

Stock rocker arms on the Ford small-six engines, both adjustable and nonadjustable, are known as a rocker rail. In this design, a chromed steel tube acts as the fulcrum for the rocker arms. The tube is suspended on top of the cylinder head by a set of pedestals. The rocker arms themselves are installed on the tube with springs between them to keep the proper spacing. The rocker arms are not fitted with bearings. Instead, they use bushings to prevent premature wear from normal use. The stock rocker-arm assembly is lubricated by the engine oiling system.

An oil passage at the left rear of the cylinder head matches a passage in the engine block. The oil passage in the cylinder head goes to the base of the rear pedestal. The shaft is hollow and has holes drilled along the length. The holes line up with the other pedestals and the rocker arms and lubricate the rocker arms as they rock back and forth with the movement of the pushrods.

During a rebuild, it is a good idea to chamfer, or smooth out, the oil-passage opening in the block that oils the cylinder head. This is especially true if the block has been decked because the edges will be significantly sharper after decking.

The stock rocker-arm ratio is 1.5:1 nominally. This means that the arm takes the lift from the camshaft and increases it by 50 percent. This ratio remains the same regardless of the camshaft profile.

Rocker Arms Unlimited of Redding, California, provides a 1.6:1-ratio rocker-arm assembly in the stock adjustable configuration. This setup is popular because it allows the owner to achieve a slight increase in performance without having to replace the camshaft.

Chamfering the opening of the oil passage on the block that provides oil to the cylinder head will help improve flow. It is required to restore the size and shape if the block has been decked.

Solid-lifter camshafts require the use of an adjustable rocker-arm assembly. The only difference from a nonadjustable assembly is the adjuster bolt on the end of the rocker arm. The adjustable arms can be used with hydraulic lifters in the event that there has been significant milling of the head and/or block.

Adjustable Rocker Arms

Many builders choose to change to an adjustable rocker-arm setup on engines that originally had a non-adjustable assembly. This can be a necessary swap if there have been significant changes to the geometry of the valvetrain due to cylinder-head milling or decking the block. It is acceptable to use adjustable rocker arms with hydraulic lifters, although the opposite is not true. You must use an adjustable assembly when using solid lifters.

Valve Springs

Valve springs have two main functions: (1) keep tension on the other components in the valvetrain and (2) keep the valves closed when they are supposed to be closed.

This sounds simple enough, and in practice it is. However, the engineering and calculations that go into proper spring selection are very complex. Fortunately, valve springs have been in use since the beginning of valves, so all of the guesswork has been removed.

Let's take a look at some of the features of valve springs and discuss which valve springs to use with your engine build.

First, the features of valve springs:

- Free height: The height of the spring in its uninstalled state. In other words, put it on a flat surface and see how tall it is.
- Solid height: The opposite of free height. Solid height is the height with the spring fully compressed (with every coil touching the coils above and below it).
- Installed height: The height of the spring when it is in place on the cylinder head and the valve and retainer are installed. Installed height is not actually a feature of the spring because the installed height can be affected by valve stem height, etc.
- Coil bind: The difference between the installed height and the solid height. As a guideline, maximum valve lift should not exceed the coil bind measurement minus 10 percent.
- Open height: Overall height of the spring when the valve is in the open position.
- Seat pressure: The valve spring pressure (in pounds per square inch) when the valve is closed.
- Open pressure: The valve spring pressure when the valve is in the full-open position.

Different types of valve springs are used depending on the camshaft and the RPM at which the engine will operate. If the valves are not stiff enough, they will allow the valvetrain components to lose contact with each other at high engine speed. This is known as valve float. Camshaft manufacturers can recommend the type and strength of the spring you need.

- Spring rate: The amount of pressure required to compress the spring 1 inch.
- Spring rating: A rating that combines the closed and open pressures (for example: 80/160).

All of these pressures work together to provide the right amount of tension on the components to prevent valve float while not imposing too much resistance on the valve-opening process. If the right compromise is found, the engine can reach the full potential of the other components selected.

The stock valve springs with a stock cam will work until about 4,500 rpm. This means that for any performance increase, stock springs will not do the job. See the chart below to get an idea of which type of spring will work for your build.

Valve Spring Usage Guide

Spring	*Application*
Stock	Stock springs should only be used on stock motors, which are intended for show only or occasional street use and will never go over 4,500 rpm.
289 V-8 Spring	Stock 289 SBF springs are a great upgrade for stock motors used as daily drivers but rarely rev over 5,000 rpm.
302 V-8 Spring	Stock 302 SBF springs are an excellent choice for stock or mild performance motors with 264/274 camshafts. They are used for daily drivers or weekend cruisers that occasionally rev to 5,500 rpm (6,000 rpm maximum).
Single Spring with Damper	These springs (with dampers) are an excellent choice for stock or mild performance motors with 264/274 camshafts. They are similar to the 302 springs above. However, they include a damper to reduce damaging valvetrain harmonics. The rev range Is 5,000 to 5,500 rpm (6,000 rpm maximum).
Dual Springs	These dual springs are intended for performance motors with cams in the 260 to 280 range that frequently see higher RPM ranges up to 6,500. Dual springs increase open pressure to prevent valve float at higher RPM yet maintain an acceptable seat pressure, reduced friction, and cam wear. Credit: fordsix .com/archive/www.classicinlines.com/Springs.html.

Valve Spring Retainers and Locks

The original valve-spring retainers on the Ford small-six engines were a two-piece design. While they worked well, they were heavy and slightly difficult to install. Since the early days of hot rodding the 144 and 170 engines, builders have replaced the stock retainers with lightweight, one-piece designs of various materials. There are still one-piece retainers available today, although the number of sources has dramatically decreased. Vintage Inlines sells one-piece retainers for stock-size springs and performance dual springs. Valve retainer locks, or keepers, are also still available if replacements are needed.

Get out There and Drive!

If you have followed along and have a fully rebuilt engine in your car, you are ready to put down the book and get out there and drive! It will be even more fun if you have decided to install some of the performance parts that are now on the market. Your car will start better, accelerate harder, and probably get better gas mileage due to improved efficiency.

Some people do not like to go to car shows. If you have not had your car in a show before, give it a try. The best part is when someone walks by and does a double take because they just do not expect to see a 6-cylinder.

You made the decision to keep the 6-cylinder in your car and by now, you must be glad you did!

Stock valve spring retainers are heavy, two-piece jobs that are very robust but complicated and tricky to install. One-piece retainers have been around for a long time and are commercially available again thanks to Clay Smith Cams, who offers them in sizes for both stock and aftermarket springs.